DAS REBOOT

Also by Raphael Honigstein

Englischer Fussball:
A German View of Our Beautiful Game

DAS REBOOT

How German Soccer Reinvented Itself and Conquered the World

RAPHAEL HONIGSTEIN

NATION
BOOKS
New York

Published in Great Britain by Yellow Jersey Press, an imprint of Vintage, part of the Penguin Random House group.

Published in the United States by Nation Books, A Member of the Perseus Books Group
116 East 16th Street, 8th Floor
New York, NY 10003

Books published by Nation Books are available at special discounts for bulk purchases in the Unitbed States by corporations, institutions, and other organizations. For more information, please contact the Special Markets Department at the Perseus Books Group, 2300 Chestnut Street, Suite 200, Philadelphia, PA 19103, or call (800) 810-4145, ext. 5000, or e-mail special.markets@perseusbooks.com.

Typeset in India by Thomson Digital Pvt Ltd, Noida, Delhi

A CIP catalog record for this book is available from the Library of Congress.
LCCN: 2015947738
ISBN: 978-1-56858-530-7 (paperback)
ISBN: 978-1-56858-531-4 (e-book)

First US Edition

10 9 8 7 6 5 4 3

*To Opa Leo who loved football, and
to Opa Heinrich who didn't.*

CONTENTS

This is a story about control
—Janet Jackson

ANGST 2014

The crushing bleakness of the day was sliced through by a metallic roar. Two Mercedes sports cars, driven by Formula 1 ace Nico Rosberg and Pascal Wehrlein, the teenage Deutsche Tourenwagen Masters driver, chased each other down an alpine pass. Rosberg braked sharply at a clearing ahead of a tight right–left turn, then accelerated on the straight descent towards the centre of the village of St Martin, in South Tyrol. As he passed an open wooden barn on his right, he slowed abruptly. Behind him Wehrlein squeezed his car to the left to avoid a crash and shot up the driveway of a guest house on the same side. There was no time to brake for the steward and the German spectator.

Benedikt Höwedes, Wehrlein's passenger, jumped out to administer first aid to the victims of the horrific accident. The steward, who later explained that he had tried to drag back the middle-aged holidaymaker from the closed-off rally course, suffered moderate injuries and was driven to a local hospital. The second man's life-threatening head injuries meant that he had to be airlifted to receive more specialist treatment in Bolzano. 'I think these images will stay with me for a while,' said Höwedes. The Schalke 04 defender and his club-mate Julian Draxler, who was sitting next to Rosberg, were unhurt, but needed the help of the national team psychologist Hans-Dieter Hermann in the aftermath.

The disastrous PR stunt with Mercedes-Benz, the German national team's main sponsor, midway through the training camp in northern Italy, marked the nadir of a pre-2014 World Cup preparation that couldn't have gone worse. A couple of days earlier, news of a most unfortunate off-target attempt by Kevin Großkreutz had broken. The Borussia Dortmund midfielder had urinated drunkenly in the middle of a Berlin hotel lobby and clashed with an employee and guest in the wake of his side's 2-0 defeat against Bayern Munich in the DFB Cup final. Großkreutz's lapse threatened the clean, positive image of the German team that general manager Oliver Bierhoff and coach Joachim Löw had worked very hard to cultivate. 'Oliver Bierhoff and I have had a serious talk with Kevin,' said Löw. 'International players are role models off the pitch as well as on it.'

Löw, however, it was soon revealed, had himself fallen rather short of such exalted standards. The *Bundestrainer* had to confess to having lost his driving licence after being caught speeding and using his mobile phone while driving. 'I've learned my lesson and will change my behaviour on the road,' said Löw. Bierhoff, appearing at a press conference ahead of the Mercedes event, tried to downplay Löw's offence with humour: 'These things happen, we'll make sure he'll only get cars with a speed limiter in future.' The light-hearted tone appeared particularly ill conceived when Wehrlein's car slammed into the two bystanders later that afternoon. The *Frankfurter Allgemeine Zeitung (FAZ)* deplored the German team for 'straying from reality' in their isolated Alpine set-up and for 'losing its self-control'.

The near-fatal accident outside the Holzerhof guest house was only the latest and most dramatic example of corners being cut two weeks before the start of the tournament. Löw had made it a central tenet of his 2014 World Cup plan over the preceding two years that only players in peak physical condition would be selected for Brazil, where the national manager expected to grapple with 'supernatural forces'. But the 'no compromise' line was quietly shelved as key players Manuel Neuer, Philipp Lahm, Bastian Schweinsteiger (all Bayern Munich) and Sami Khedira (Real Madrid) turned up in northern Italy in varying states of unfitness. Doubts over the physical shape of veteran striker Miroslav Klose after a season with little football at Lazio added to the pervading sense of uncertainty. Instead of being able to rely on his team's spine, Löw was staring at a team sheet full of question marks.

Neuer, the outstanding goalkeeper, had hurt his shoulder in the DFB Cup final and missed the first days of the training camp, along with the consistently excellent and versatile Lahm, who was nursing a complicated ankle injury. 'There were days when I couldn't run in straight lines,' recalls the captain, sitting in his agent's office in Munich's fashionable meatpacking district. 'The team were already in Italy, yet I was still with the doctors in Munich. They were saying that they couldn't really tell me anything because the scans looked so strange. Everything was swollen.'

Khedira, the box-to-box dynamo, had looked woefully short of match sharpness in the Champions League final against Atlético Madrid after spending six months on the sidelines following cruciate ligament surgery. His central midfield partner, Schweinsteiger, the 'emotional leader', as Löw called him, had a long-standing problem with tendonitis.

Löw kept insisting that all his chief lieutenants would be back on their feet in time for the Portugal match on 16 June, but many reporters found his optimism deeply unsettling. They recalled how Löw had refused to bench a patently out of sorts Schweinsteiger in the Euro 2012 semi-final defeat against Italy in Warsaw. The *Bundestrainer*'s loyalty had been admirable in principle but an awful miscalculation in practice. The midfielder's problems in the quarter-final win against Greece in Gdansk had been apparent to everyone. Half of the questions posed to his team-mates in the mixed zone that night had inquired after the fragile state of Schweinsteiger's ankle. But Löw had wanted to believe that everything would turn out okay. It didn't. His blind faith in one of his big names was seen as one of the main reasons why Germany had failed to advance to the final of a competition they had been expected to win.

Löw's reputation had taken a severe beating in Poland. BBC pundit and former player Martin Keown told British viewers that Germany's collapse was down to 'arrogance', but, if anything, Löw hadn't been nearly arrogant enough with his selection and tactics. He had specifically adapted his formation to counter the threat of playmaker Andrea Pirlo, the bearded maestro who had driven England to distraction with his passing skills in the Kiev quarter-final.

Adjusting to the opposition is not necessarily a bad idea. But it becomes one when it undermines your own strengths or leads to a loss of your own footballing identity. Löw's team were strongest in the wide areas. In Warsaw, they had made life easy for Cesare Prandelli's side by playing narrowly.

The confusion that reigned in midfield after Mario Balotelli's two goals for the *Azzurri* was symptomatic of the muddled thinking on the bench. Perhaps Löw had overcomplicated matters or perhaps he had been too scared of the Italians – the upshot was the same for his talented but fragile team as it had been in the World Cup semi-final defeat against Spain in 2010, when Germany had felt the need to play an ultra-deep counter-attacking game that resulted in almost no attacks at all. 'We were so tired from chasing the ball that we had no energy to do something when we did have it,' Miroslav Klose had said after that chastening 1-0 defeat.

Teams often come to resemble their coach's characteristics after a while, and in late May 2014 there was a widespread belief that both the urbane Löw, a man who valued harmony and shunned open conflict, and his (overwhelmingly) likeable bunch of prodigies were just that little bit short on ruthlessness and grit. For four major tournaments in a row, they had been found wanting when it came to the crunch.

That Warsaw capitulation overshadowed Löw for the whole of the World Cup qualifying campaign. It was a game that had brought the first sporadic but noticeable calls for his resignation after six years on the *Nationalmannschaft* bench.

Germany won nine out of their ten qualifying games, barely breaking sweat. The tenth, though, a bizarre 4-4 draw with Sweden in October 2012 in Berlin, confirmed the worst suspicions. The team had played beautiful, rarefied football to take a 4-0 lead, then inexplicably conceded four goals in the last half-hour to drop two points. It was a freakish game but the message was a familiar one. When the going got tough, Löw's artistically inclined collective crumbled.

The *Bundestrainer* had tried hard to shed the 'Mr Nice Guy' image with some rousing 'now or never' speeches in the spring. But the more familiar, lukewarm, 'let's wait and see' rhetoric emanating from South Tyrol and the somewhat rudderless preparation saw the ranks of his detractors begin to swell again.

The mood back home was a strange, unforgiving mix of entitlement and grave concern. Germans would regard anything short of a heroic final defeat by hosts, and favourites, Brazil as an inexcusable failure by Löw to do justice to this golden generation. And yet they weren't at all convinced that this team and their coach had what it took to bring an end to eighteen years of hurt since the last trophy, the 1996 European Championship. Surprisingly, one well-placed expert seemed to agree. 'It's almost impossible for a European team to win in Brazil, the South Americans are basically one step ahead,' Bierhoff had said in March.

'I know we can do better,' Löw stated after the unconvincing 2-2 draw with Cameroon in the penultimate friendly before leaving for Brazil, 'sounding like a doctor trying to reassure his patient', as *Süddeutsche Zeitung* noted. Khedira, the man at the heart of the team, had been unable to set the pace. The other prominent convalescents hadn't even made it on to the Mönchengladbach pitch. And for holding midfielder Lars Bender, a man who'd come into contention for a starting place against Portugal, who boasted the Balon d'Or winner Cristiano Ronaldo, the World Cup was already over. The Leverkusen player, one of the best performers at the Euros, had suffered a torn hamstring in St Martin that would keep him out of the competition.

The loss of Marco Reus, who twisted his ankle badly in the 6-1 victory against Armenia, came as a bigger shock. The Dortmund attacking midfielder had been considered Germany's most important player in the final third: 'We will miss him in Brazil, no doubt,' said Bierhoff. For all the dozen or so creative players at Löw's disposal, there was no one with the same pace and directness. Reus, who his team-mates fondly called Woodyinho because of his passing resemblance to the cartoon character Woody Woodpecker, was so irreplaceable that the manager didn't even bother calling up another attacking midfielder as an alternative. He took an extra defender, Shkodran Mustafi (then at Sampdoria), instead.

What is the German for angst? The pre-tournament anxiety recalled a similar sense of doom and gloom before the 2006 World Cup, when worries about captain Michael Ballack (calf) and left-back Lahm (elbow) had coincided with a nationwide panic about the leaky back line. Four years later, Ballack's absence in South Africa had given rise to apocalyptic prophecies again. Germany came back with third-place bronze medals after both competitions. But the same achievement wouldn't be enough this time around, and an injury malaise on a completely different scale from the two previous World Cups made a third place look rather fanciful. This wasn't about one or two individuals potentially missing out. The fault line ran right through Löw's starting eleven.

A doomsday scenario of a flight back before the semi-finals no longer appeared unthinkable. Would Löw have a future after a such an early exit, newspapers wondered. 'I don't think [he] would continue, the pressure on him would be too great,' said Ballack, who hadn't been able to reclaim his place after the South Africa tournament.

The sudden rise of Gladbach's Christoph Kramer from twenty-two-year-old rookie to bonafide Portugal game contender underlined the extent of Löw's predicament. Kramer had never played a competitive game for Germany, nor featured in a Europa League game, let alone in the Champions League.

But making do without half of the regulars was only half of Löw's problem. The secret of Germany's generally good showings in competitions under him had been his detailed tournament preparations. Incessant tactical drills had them playing with the cohesion of a club team, a rare quality in international football where many of Löw's peers still believed that simply lining up the country's best eleven players was all that was needed. Without the team's core personnel on the training pitch, however, practising shapes and playing moves would be all but impossible.

Worse still, the very suitability of Löw's strategy was in doubt, too. German FA chief scout Urs Siegenthaler, Löw's closest confidant since Jürgen Klinsmann had brought in both men to overhaul Germany's playing style in 2004, had publicly warned that the Germany manager's favoured passing game of the last couple of years was probably not a viable blueprint in the tropical conditions of South America. 'Possession means movement and effort,' the 'superbrain' (*tz*), told reporters, 'possession in the sense of dominating [the game] is not right for Brazil. European teams cannot play the same way they play at home.'

In a text message to Löw from the Confederations Cup twelve months before the start of the World Cup, Siegenthaler had gone further, as *Süddeutsche* later revealed. 'We are called upon to move with the times and put the idea aside,' the Swiss tactician told his superior.

Would Germany play with no idea? And who would be on the pitch? You could almost see the angry and mournful post-mortems condemning the team's failure to add a fourth World Cup winners' star to their badge: 'Those grey, oppressive days in Val Passiria foreshadowed impending misdadventure . . .'

'It makes me laugh a bit, hearing that,' says Oliver Bierhoff. He's not laughing, but a small smile of contentment adds to the pleasure of the *Fleischpflanzerl*, the Bavarian version of a hamburger, that he is eating. We're sitting in a less than quiet corner of a country restaurant full of families. Friday lunchtime in Aufkirchen, Lake Starnberg, thirty kilometres south of Munich. School's out. Just up the road is the birthplace of Oskar Maria Graf, the twentieth-century Bavarian author who chronicled the political and social changes that swept through this region from the time of German unification in 1870 to the rise of Nazism sixty years later in his book *Das Leben meiner Mutter* (The Life of my Mother). (Bierhoff has read it. 'You have to, if you live around here,' he says.) Graf took part in the failed Communist revolution of 1919 that spawned its own, still widely popular shandy, a mix of wheat beer and lemonade called Russn (Russian); it was named for the Red Army revolutionaries who were holed up in a beer cellar and diluted their drink to keep their heads clear for the impending, futile gun battle. Later, in exile in New York, Graf steadfastly refused to remove his Lederhosen. To be Bavarian is a state of mind, a deep sense of self-contentment and feeling comfortable in your own skin that other, less fortunate Germanic tribes often mistake for smugness.

Munich refers to itself, with a wink and a nudge, as 'Italy's most northerly city'. The nearby lakes, the setting at the foot of the Alps, a way of life that values family, good food and tolerance: it all combines to make the Bavarian capital and its environs the destination of choice for those who want a slice of *la dolce vita* within the country's borders.

Many former footballers have settled around Lake Starnberg, including Bierhoff himself, who came here after a successful career in Italy's Serie A with Udinese and AC Milan. He scored the Golden Goal that won Euro 96 for Germany at Wembley but as the son of an upper middle-class father who was a director of a big energy company, and as a player whose breakthrough had only materialised after a move abroad at the age of twenty-three, he was never quite classic folk hero material. The opposite in fact. A *Der Spiegel* article from April 2006 observed that, with his fashionable clothes and smart haircut, the well-spoken general manager of the national team was someone who 'didn't look like a footballer'. He lacked what Germans call '*Stallgeruch*', literally, the smell of the stable, Bundesliga pedigree. Four years later, *Die Zeit* sympathetically described his status as that of 'an alien object'. 'In the conservative environs of football, he's always been an outsider,' it concluded.

At the beginning of his ten-year tenure, Bierhoff's main task was to mediate between the almost revolutionary fervour of then coach Jürgen Klinsmann and the dithering guardians of the German game in the clubs and the German FA. Once Joachim Löw took over in 2006, however, Bierhoff assumed the role of 'bad guy', he says, for their frequent clashes with the *ancien régime* over organisational issues.

The negative coverage in South Tyrol homed in on him, too. This was shaping up to be a catastrophe of Bierhoff's very own making, the dispatches from Italy suggested, an unholy mess of hubris, foolishness and rampant commercialism gone horribly wrong.

'In fact, it was the perfect training camp,' Bierhoff says, 'the tragic accident aside.' Bierhoff and the two racing drivers visited the badly injured man in hospital but the team were not affected, he insists. 'Löw's driving licence, the Großkreutz affair and the accident, none of these things stemmed from the national team. There were no conflicts within the team. Looking back at Euro 2012, I thought I should have started a fire, attacked somebody, to give the media something to write about. It was too quiet for them there. In South Tyrol, they had a lot to write, and the team were meanwhile able to work in peace and with focus. Lahm and Neuer joining up later was good, too, because they were able to clear their heads. Internally, we were very calm. I'd say it was like the first days of winter: outside it was suddenly very cold, but inside the heating had come on. It was nice and warm, we were happy.

We never had the feeling that [the training camp] could endanger the whole thing.' The loss of Reus robbed the team of a lot of quality, as the BVB forward had been in top form, but there were never any doubts about Lahm and Neuer recovering in time, he adds.

Lahm was much less certain that everything was going to be all right, however. 'I don't think people really worried about me because I'm the kind of guy who always says "I'm okay" when someone asks me how I am. But I was still in a lot of pain when I got to South Tyrol. I couldn't move freely in the first training session, the swelling wouldn't go down. I said to the doctors: if it stays like that, I can't play – I will only hurt myself and the team. And Neuer's shoulder really was touch and go.' Lahm would wear a pressure bandage 'day and night for four weeks'. The team doctors had to aspirate the ankle a few times.

The captain was badly needed in a central role because neither Khedira nor Schweinsteiger looked as if they would be at their best come the start of the competition. Bierhoff: 'We worried about those two. We also worried about the full-backs. All in all, my feeling wasn't as good as before the Euros, I felt more sure about the team then. This time, I thought, many things could happen. We would survive the group stage, for sure, I knew that somehow. But afterwards . . . it's one game. And you don't know who you'll get and what kind of physical condition you'll be in. There were question marks about our ability to stay the course, considering that we had many players who didn't have the continuity, in terms of playing, that they should have had.'

The sheer amount of unknown variables involved had sapped the public's confidence in Löw and Co. coming up with a winning formula at last. 'That wasn't a bad thing, though,' says Bierhoff. 'A year ago I had put out the deliberately provocative theory that winning in Brazil was all but impossible. I didn't like the superficial way the success of Bayern and Dortmund, who had both reached the Champions League final at Wembley [in 2013], was being viewed. There was this sense that we were certified world-beaters again. But who had scored the goals for those two teams, how many foreign players did they have in important positions? Emotions were getting the better of people. So I pointed that out, on purpose, to argue against that sense of entitlement, and I was of course criticised for that, again. Then three months before the World Cup, the mood changed. Code red. People now thought we wouldn't make it past the group. I didn't mind that because it got everybody thinking about what's really important: our work and the team's performances.'

The coaching staff were apprehensive about another, much less discussed complication. Few outsiders knew just how bad the mood in the camp had been at the Euros, with the sizeable Bayern and Dortmund factions not seeing eye to eye and a number of younger players agitating for more playing time. In a repeat of the 2012 DFB Cup final, Germany's two leading clubs had faced off in Berlin again in the last game of the season, four days before joining up in South Tyrol, and the match had finished in controversial fashion, with the Bavarians scoring two goals in extra-time after Mats Hummels had had what looked like a perfectly good headed goal chalked off for Dortmund.

Six frustrated BVB (the club's full name is Ballspielverein Borussia 09 e.V. Dortmund) players met seven double winners from Bayern in Italy. Löw couldn't allow tribal rivalries and big egos to seep into the national team a second time. His concern was such that he had all but guaranteed Khedira a place in the World Cup squad, weeks before the Real Madrid midfielder could be sure to regain full fitness in time. The Stuttgart-born son of a Tunisian steel worker was somebody who could influence others with his positive attitude and bridge rifts between Bayern and Dortmund players as a neutral. Löw needed him in the dressing room.

The coach and his staff were hopeful that the magnitude of the challenge in Brazil would scale down pride and pretensions. But it took until the last night in St Martin for the national team general manager to witness the squad coming closer together. Very close together, in fact.

The players' council – Lahm, Schweinsteiger, Per Mertesacker and Klose – invited the entire DFB (German FA) delegation to 'sweat for the trophy' in the hotel's 'event sauna', a vast space holding eighty people. Bierhoff: 'The 2014 Sauna World Cup winner was there – no, I didn't know there was such a thing, either – and he performed a show with music and strobe lights, waving towels around. We were in there with sixty men. Every player, every staff member, symbolically sweating together for this World Cup. That was an amazing idea by the players. It came from them. I don't really believe that there's such a thing as one "key moment". But that night I remember thinking: something is happening here.'

TWO THOUSAND ZERO FOUR,
PARTY OVER, OOPS: OUT OF TIME

I spent the worst day in the history of (post-war) German football with a German 'comedian' in a TV studio. To borrow a phrase from Henning Wehn, one of the few German comedians who doesn't need inverted commas around his job description: it wasn't funny.

DSF, Deutsches Sport Fernsehen, had invited me to their Euro 2004 talk show in an echoey hangar, hidden in an as yet ungentrified section of Lisbon harbour, not far from the spot where Chelsea owner Roman Abramovich had moored his yacht, to talk about the ramifications for Sven-Göran Eriksson's England after their quarter-final exit against the hosts, on penalties, a few nights before. I don't know why they invited the comedian.

As we were about to go on air news broke that Ottmar Hitzfeld would not be taking over the Germany job. 'My heart said "yes" but my head won out,' the former Bayern Munich coach declared from his Swiss holiday resort. 'I'm currently not in the right physical shape to help the national team until the 2006 World Cup. My batteries are flat.' To call Hitzfeld's decision a surprise didn't begin to get close to the cataclysmic effect it had on a footballing nation that lay curled up on the floor after the second traumatic group stage fiasco in as many European championships. A bomb going off at the German FA headquarters in Frankfurt couldn't have created more devastation.

Two dour draws against the Netherlands (1-1) and Latvia (0-0), had been followed by the *coup de* (dis)*grâce* at Sporting Lisbon's Estádio José Alvalade, administered by a Czech Republic B team without any of their big-name players. Popular *Bundestrainer* Rudi Völler had resigned the morning after the degrading 2-1 defeat, explaining that the 'heavy baggage' of this horror show made it impossible for him to carry on for the next couple of years.

German football's despondency was only tempered by the expectation that Hitzfeld, the agreeable, universally respected coach would come in to avert an even bigger tragedy at the World Cup on home soil two years later. His startling refusal after a few sleepless nights of soul-searching plunged the country into deep despair. The hoped-for saviour had abandoned his country, hinting that the scant amount of talent available made righting the *Nationalmannschaft* a task beyond his powers. Völler had come close to admitting as much, too. 'The players wanted to play better,' he said clemently at his farewell press conference. 'You can't blame them.'

The men in charge were desperate to change Hitzfeld's mind. He was so obviously the ideal candidate for the job. The gentle man and gentleman from Lörrach, a small city on the Swiss border, had won six championships and the Champions League twice, with Borussia Dortmund (1997) and Bayern Munich (2001), two of only three European Cups hoisted by Bundesliga clubs since Bayern's heyday of three consecutive wins in the mid-1970s.

They called him '*der General*', and he'd once worn a *Pickelhaube*, the spiked helmet of the Prussian army, to a Dortmund trophy party (Borussia is neo-Latin for Prussia) but his wasn't an iron-fisted regime. He never said anything controversial, always backed his players in public, didn't engage in petty squabbles with rivals, drolly rolled his Rs to make 'Profi', the German abbreviation of 'professional', sound like 'Prrrrrofi'. He also had the quirky habit of turning up the collar of his voluminous trench coat on the touchline, giving him the resemblance of a Cold War spy overlooking a prisoner exchange at Checkpoint Charlie.

A qualified teacher (subjects: maths and sport), he regarded team-building as a psychological puzzle. He compared the intricacies of squad composition with putting together a Formula 1 racing engine. 'Bayern are a sensitive construction, like a Ferrari motor,' he said, 'every detail has to be right.' Hitzfeld's teams had strict hierarchies, with one or two leaders, mid-ranking employees and a few youngsters and fringe players who were expected to follow orders. His sides' strong collective ethos, defensive solidity and hard work frequently got the better of more talented outfits, including Real Madrid's *galácticos*, a bunch of megastars whose showy, individualistic and defensively deficient approach was considered anathema to the German football culture. Hitzfeld's international successes, garnered with the help of a sweeper system, were symbols of defiance: the traditional virtues – Run. Fight. Run a bit more – were not yet done with.

Thus, his refusal to heed the Fatherland's call was met with incomprehension bordering on denial. 'The whole of German football wants Hitzfeld,' exclaimed Borussia Dortmund general manager Michael Meier. 'He now has to give something back to German football.' But he had given enough. Six years in charge of the madhouse that was Bayern had left him burnt out. He needed a break. There were rumours that Manchester United had lined him up as Sir Alex Ferguson's successor in 2005.

Who could pick up the pieces, the talk show host asked. I had no idea. The minimum expected of TV experts is being able to fill the silence with big opinions and recognisable names but I was caught short, unable to come up with anyone who seemed remotely plausible to take on this job.

FA president Gerhard Mayer-Vorfelder was at a loss, too. 'I don't have a plan B in my pocket,' he told reporters on the steps of Lisbon's Le Meridien hotel. Other FA board members flew in to deliberate, there was talk of a coup against 'MV' in the offing. Franz Beckenbauer, the head of the World Cup organising committee, was so afraid of the host team spoiling the party that he mooted the employment of a foreign coach. Dutchman Guus Hiddink? Above all, the German FA were at pains to avoid another chaotic appointment procedure like the unedifying mess of 1998, when former international and World Cup winner Paul Breitner had received an offer to take on the role of *Bundestrainer* for a few hours, only for it to be withdrawn to allow the appointment of Erich Ribbeck and Uli Stielike as manager and assistant respectively. They needed a speedy, less messy resolution this time around.

Otto Rehhagel, who was leading Greece to the most unlikely of triumphs with the help of ultra-negative tactics at the Euros, had ruled himself out. Leverkusen's Christoph Daum, in exile at Turkey's Fenerbahçe, was damaged goods after testing positive for cocaine. Matthias Sammer had just signed a deal to take over VfB Stuttgart from Felix Magath, who had in turn been employed as Hitzfeld's successor in Munich. And Thomas Schaaf, a mustachioed man of few words and even fewer smiles, was firmly ensconced at Werder Bremen after winning the Bundesliga that year.

Inevitably, Lothar Matthäus expressed an interest. The Franconian was always interested in any job going. The mention of him was the cue for the comedian to bring up the former World Cup winner's taste for younger women.

The most-capped international, the legendary captain of 1990 had become the butt of puerile jokes in the course of his long, unsuccessful search for employment in his home country; a laughing stock, along with almost everyone representing German football at international level. But no one in the audience of Germany supporters stranded in Portugal after the *Nationalmannschaft*'s untimely departure cracked a smile. Lothar's demise, it dawned on them, sadly mirrored that of the nation's most cherished sporting representatives.

*

Some consolation could be found in the fact that Germany wasn't the only big country which had underperformed at the Euros. Italy and Spain had also been eliminated in the group stage, England and France in the quarter-finals. The giantkilling substantiated Rudi Völler's long-held view that there were 'no more minnows' in international football.

The effect of the Bosman ruling, a European Court of Justice case that enabled free movement of footballers within the European Union in 1995, had narrowed the qualitative gap between national teams. Smaller nations, too, could now muster starting elevens made up of players from Europe's top leagues. Lessons learned from the training regimes at elite clubs were filtering through to the rest of the Continent; technically, physically and tactically the underdogs were no longer so far behind the curve. German football, which had for decades relied on the sheer number of good players at its disposal and on their superior fitness levels, as opposed to, say, honing playing skills or new tactical systems, was now being hit doubly hard by this convergence of performance standards. Smaller nations had become just as good without the ball or perhaps even better, and the number of prospective *Nationalmannschaft* contenders, as a percentage of all Bundesliga professionals, had almost halved in the space of a decade.

In 1993–4, foreigners made up only 17 per cent of the 358 players in the top division. Bosman and the economic boom of the Bundesliga saw that figure rocket up to 49 per cent by 2003–4. Energie Cottbus had already broken an unwritten rule when they became the first Bundesliga side to field eleven foreigners in April 2001. Their three substitutes were non-Germans, too.

Growing squad sizes partially offset the net loss of job opportunities for natives in the top flight, but a fifth of German players had disappeared altogether in the course of those ten years. Naturally, many of the foreigners who'd replace them were big earners and important players, so the actual talent pool to choose from for any *Bundestrainer* was shallower still.

At champions Werder, professionals from abroad accounted for two-thirds of all pitch appearances in the 2003–4 league season. Even at Bayern, the richest club, only five German players – goalkeeper Oliver Kahn, centre-back Thomas Linke, midfielders Michael Ballack, Jens Jeremies and Bastian Schweinsteiger – played regularly that year. Völler's 'no more minnows' line hid a more alarming truth: Germany had stopped being a big football nation.

The shortage of skilled personnel wasn't an entirely new problem, either. As early as 1997, there had been so few decent German strikers in the league that national manager Berti Vogts was forced to lobby the government to naturalise South African-born Sean Dundee of Karlsruher SC, a forward without any German background whatsoever. Dundee received his passport in January 1997 but never played for the *Nationalmannschaft* after picking up an injury before his first scheduled game, a friendly against Israel, and losing his form soon after.

Vogts' successor, Erich Ribbeck, equally desperate for goalscoring talent, approached another Bundesliga import, Brazilian forward Paulo Rink (Leverkusen). Rink was able to unearth German grandparents and quickly joined the fold. Fittingly, his game was more German than Brazilian. The muscular but rather immobile striker didn't score once in thirteen internationals from 1998 to 2000.

The unprecedented recruitment of these two *Gastarbeiter* betrayed the onset of a fundamental malaise. At the same time, the influx of GDR-trained professionals who were supposed to make 'Germany unbeatable for years to come', as Franz Beckenbauer had so confidently predicted after winning the World Cup in 1990, had also all but dried up along with the state funding for the specialised sports schools which had drilled talents like Sammer from a very young age. The nation was running out of players, and casting envious glances at the multi-cultural make-up of World Cup 98 and Euro 2000 winners France. Mayer-Vorfelder bemoaned the fact that Germany had lost her colonies after the First World War and thus couldn't compete with the athletic style of her neighbour.

In the German FA's defence, they soon understood that the whole youth development set-up needed reform and a sizeable cash injection. By 2004, the first fruits of the changes at grass-roots level were becoming visible in the shape of youngsters like Schweinsteiger and Lahm. Bundesliga clubs hit by the 2002 bankruptcy of the Kirch media conglomerate, their broadcast partner, had also tentatively begun to give players from their own academies a chance. They were cheaper.

Magath's young VfB Stuttgart side of 2003–4 had become trailblazers for this new trend when they beat Manchester United in the Champions League with a squad full of homegrown kids like Timo Hildebrand, Kevin Kuranyi and Andreas Hinkel. 'The boys definitely benefitted from the Kirch collapse,' Thomas Albeck, Stuttgart's head of youth development, says. 'The club was not in a position to buy any players for eighteen months and suddenly youngsters like Hinkel, Hildebrand and Kuranyi were seen as an option. Two years later, we were in the Champions League with them. Dortmund and Hertha both struggled financially and had to play their youngsters, too. It's worked out well for them. More and more clubs woke up to the fact that they could create real value by spending money on the kids.' The Bundesliga found that fostering talents was not only good for the balance sheet but also for the brand. Fans flocked to the stadiums to see homegrown players with whom they could identify.

The national teams of Messrs Ribbeck and Völler were hardly touched by those youthful awakenings, however. You had to be an established Bundesliga player to get anywhere near a shirt with the eagle on the badge. That's how it had always been, that's how it still was. Experience was the paramount criterion. At Euro 2000, the average age of Ribbeck's team was twenty-eight and a half. Sebastian Deisler, hailed as Germany's talent of the century, for lack of any peers, was the only squad member under the age of twenty-three. The inclusion of Schweinsteiger, Lahm and 1. FC Köln teenager Lukas Podolski four years later lowered the average age to twenty-seven but Völler's side were unable to benefit significantly from the fresh impetus.

In the six years after the poor World Cup showing in France, the national team's enduringly unappealing performances had given rise to the term '*Rumpelfußball*'. The Federal Republic's best players didn't really play football any more: they rumbled, lumbered and cluttered. Ribbeck's ineptitude – corners were only practised if players felt like it – and Völler's laissez-faire style were contributing factors but the gravest problems were structural in nature. The dearth of creative world-class players had seen Germany receding further and further into their own shell, braced for the onslaught, hopeful of sneaking a headed goal from a dead-ball situation or with a shot from distance. 'Being determines consciousness,' as Hertha midfielder Thorben Marx so memorably put it. Or was it Karl? (No relation).

Völler and his team were instinctively aware of their limitations. Just like Hitzfeld's Bayern in big European ties, they devoted most of their energy to keeping a clean sheet, ceding possession and space to the opposition. Grim, obdurate midfield enforcer Jens Jeremies (Germany and Bayern) openly confessed that stagnancy was preferable to uncertain offensive play. 'If it doesn't go for you, you have to stand well,' he said after the Bavarians' flattering 0-0 Champions League draw away to Celtic in November 2003.

Standing well the *Nationalmannschaft* could still do. They strangled the flow of the game to 'hold' their opponents, stoically sitting out attacks until the other side punched themselves out and made a mistake out of sheer exhaustion. Fantasy was fought with discipline.

These were the tactics of the underdog. The fact that the German national team and Bayern, the country's best two teams, were muddling through with this kind of reactive, preventative football should have set alarm bells ringing. But in football, as in life, the most powerful lies are always the ones you tell yourselves. Joyless, motionless, goalless performances like that of Champions League holders Bayern at Old Trafford in March 2002 were hailed as a tactical masterclass and a show of the team's 'true face' (Stefan Effenberg). 'These games earn us a lot of respect in Europe, we have to make use of that,' said Oliver Kahn.

Uli Hoeness praised the drab 0-0 as 'a beautiful game, something for gourmets'. I questioned the sausage factory owner's taste buds in one of my first football articles and then got the fright of my life three days later, during an unsuspecting stroll on London's Oxford Street. Hoeness was on the phone, complaining about the sarcastic tone of the piece.

In an age when defence was considered the best line of defence, keeping the ball out of the net was unsurprisingly elevated to an act of heroism. Kahn, a constantly overmotivated alpha male between the sticks who occasionally nibbled on an opponent's earlobe, was the superstar of this era of sterility, quite literally 'the last man' standing between his team escaping with pride and the net unruffled and a humiliating shafting at the back.

While the English media often misspelt his name as 'Khan', subconsciously channelling Mongol emperors or Klingon warlords, Germans lionised the Karlsruhe-born son of former KSC keeper Rolf Kahn as the '*Torwart-Titan*', the titan of goalies. He had helped Bayern to their first European Cup win in twenty-five years in 2001 with dozens of crucial saves in the knock-out rounds and three parried penalties in the Milan final against Valencia, then dragged Germany to the World Cup final in Japan/South Korea a year later. Ironically, it was his mistake that allowed Ronaldo to score the opening goal in Brazil's 2-0 win in Yokohama, in what was, also ironically, the national team's best game of the competition.

The runners-up received a hero's welcome in Frankfurt, in recognition of having made the utmost of their limited abilities. But the shine of their silver medals blinded too many to the extent of the *Nationalmannschaft*'s regression into minimalism. Aided by an absurdly easy draw, Völler's men had nonetheless barely scraped past Saudi Arabia, Cameroon, the Republic of Ireland, Paraguay, the USA and South Korea to record their best World Cup finish since winning the trophy in 1990.

The inability to beat any big footballing nation in a tournament (without recourse to penalties) since that 1-0 win over Argentina in Rome was a more reliable indicator that Germany had slid down the pecking order. Even when friendlies and qualifiers were included, the record against the better sides appeared extremely poor. A 4-1 victory against (a still nascent) Spain in Völler's first friendly in charge (August 2000) and the 1-0 qualification win over England at the old Wembley (courtesy of Didi Hamann's free-kick and goalkeeper David Seaman's poor positioning) in October of the same year were the sole two positive results against above average opposition in four years of negativity and embarrassment: 0-1 v France (February 2001), 1-5 v England (September 2001), 0-1 v Argentina (April 2002), 1-3 v Netherlands (November 2002), 1-3 v Spain (February 2003), 0-1 v Italy (August 2003), 0-3 v France (November 2003) – Germany now expected to lose against the big boys. Getting hammered 5-1 by Romania (April 2004) and 2-0 by Hungary (June 2004) was harder to stomach but the most painful spectacle was that of Völler's team being forced to abandon their conservatism and go on the offensive by rank outsiders defending in numbers.

On TV Günter Netzer regularly bristled at 'footballing methods that [came] close to desperation'. The cultural decay was at its most pronounced in a unspeakably awful 0-0 draw away to Iceland in September 2003. 'A new low point,' Netzer nodded, in agreement with ARD presenter Gerhard Delling. Netzer, the former West Germany great, was further angered by the players' attempts to sugarcoat the performance at the Laugardsvöllur National Stadium in their post-match interviews. 'I don't understand them. Why don't they just say "We played some real crap stuff today"? There are no excuses. [Instead], they are going on about Iceland's strengths and all the things they did better here? That can't be the benchmark.'

Völler, who was listening in a studio next door, blew a gasket, live on air. 'It's a disgrace. "Low point", "a new low point", "an even lower new point" . . . I can't listen to that shit any more. That's beyond the pale. They [the two ARD pundits] should change jobs. If they want Saturday evening entertainment, they should do an entertainment show. I've been sitting here three years, having to listen to such nonsense. Okay, 0-0 is not enough. We didn't move enough, we should have done more. But this shit that they're talking. They're rubbishing everything. You know how much shit they played in Netzer's days? You couldn't watch that, it was football without running . . . I won't take that for much longer, I can tell you that. Iceland are top of the table. You are saying we have to dominate them away from home? What kind of world are you all living in? You have to get off your high horse, with your delusions about the kind of football we have to play in Germany.'

Why was he being so acrimonious, anchor man Waldemar Hartmann cautiously inquired.

'I'm not acrimonious. You are acrimonious,' Völler replied.

'Me? I'm not.'

'No, not you, Waldi. You sit here comfortably on your sofa having drunk three *weissbier*, you are very relaxed. But they [the pundits] are [acrimonious].'

'I accept that we played a lot of shit in the past,' Netzer replied after Völler's outburst, 'I say that often enough. But the regularity of bad games of Völler's team is worrying. We used to have poor games, but they were followed by ten outstanding ones. That's not the case here. We weren't overly critical either. They got off lightly over the course of the last year.'

Völler and his TV critics did agree on one thing at least: Germany's plight was mainly due to a lack of effort. 'Will we see them run their arses off [in the next game]?' Hartmann asked. This kind of comment passed for match analysis at the time. It was obvious that things were going badly wrong, but the complex reasons behind the mess couldn't be properly articulated. Scapegoats were being sought instead.

Kicker magazine noted too many 'long, aimless balls' being played from the back in Reykjavík. They mostly blamed the team's haplessness on one player, though. 'Ballack couldn't influence the game,' read the headline of their match report.

The tall, upright son of an architect was the only regular outfield player even approaching world-class status among this generation. 'Ballack and nothing else,' wrote *Frankfurter Rundschau* after Euro 2004; he'd been the one member of the squad to survive the tournament with his reputation unharmed. Ballack's excellent technique, learned at the KJS (Kinder und Jugendschule) Görlitz, a state-run sport school for budding athletes in East Germany, made him stand out a mile among the Carsten Janckers and Paulo Rinks. He was good in the air, could shoot with both feet, had an eye for a killer pass and won important duels. Bayer Leverkusen boss Reiner Calmund dubbed him 'the little Kaiser'.

Ballack's flashes of brilliance were sorely missed in the 2002 World Cup final. He was suspended. That game and the next two years demonstrated that Ballack hadn't just become the most important player in Völler's system as far as occasionally troubling the opposition goal was concerned. He had become the system itself. 'Clean sheet plus Ballack header/shot from outside the box,' read the Rudi formula. 'Anything can happen, apart from Ballack getting injured,' the national manager had said before Euro 2004.

The player's special status created its own difficulties, namely completely unrealistic expectations. 'They wanted me to win the ball at the back, dominate in the centre, pass to myself in the final third and score the goal,' Ballack lamented. He was identified as the '*Führungsspieler*', the leading player, and as such he had to win the game on his own. The less football Germany played, the more the tabloids and former players and coaches on TV chat shows cried out ¡ leader to marshal the troops. Few people realised just how patholo¡ that reaction was: a darkly emotional longing for a strong man to steer Fußball-Deutschland out of its depression and indignity on the international stage.

'*Führungsspieler* is one of those German expressions that are total nonsense,' Arsenal keeper Jens Lehmann said in May 2004. 'It probably stems from our sad history. It's a German thing. Churchill once said that he admired the Germans but not their adulation of people in power and leaders. He hit the nail on the head there. You don't need *Führungsspieler*. You need players who are good, who you can depend on. Our captain Patrick Vieira is a super midfielder but he doesn't have to lead me. Maybe I'm having a bad game and he turns it around for us. But on another day, the left-back can make the difference. Let's say you have your *Führungsspieler* in Germany, and your opponents mark him out of the game. Then everything breaks down? There has to be a different way.'

Ballack took responsibility by scoring the crucial goals. But when the national team lost, the public were quick to diagnose insufficient leadership. He was a quiet, controlled player, not one to scythe down an opposition playmaker, shout at the referee or rough up a team-mate. Netzer famously wrote in 2003 that Ballack was 'not predestined for the leadership role of days gone by' because the socialist GDR had been a country where 'the collective counted' and 'the path for geniuses was blocked'.

As a character assassination, Netzer's polemic in *Sport-Bild* was effective. As a piece of analysis, it firmly belonged to days gone by. Bundesliga football was slower than that played in the Premier League – 'It's like an overland train compared to an Intercity Express,' Lehmann said – but the game had nevertheless sped up significantly since Netzer's glorious 1970s. There was no longer time to gather your team-mates around you in the centre circle and bark orders at them. And, if anything, the lack of a collective approach to playing was a much bigger problem for German football than inadequate leadership by one or two demigods in shorts. The best teams, like Arsène Wenger's Arsenal, had learned to move as a unit. That, along with better technical coaching, was the key to faster, more fluid play. Lehmann: 'In Germany, when pace is brought into the game, you always feel that somebody will make a mistake. Here [in England], that's not the case.'

It wasn't just the national team's football that was stuck in the past. The public discourse about it was, too. Less than two years ahead of the World Cup on home soil, Germany had no coach, no team, no functioning FA board and no realistic understanding of their predicament on the pitch.

A MAN OF SMALL GOALS

The national team had scored thirty-six goals in ten games on their way to topping Group C in the 2014 World Cup qualifiers. But Oliver Bierhoff was worried. Three months before Germany faced Portugal in their group opener in Salvador, the general manager warned that the team needed to be more clinical in the opposition box. 'Efficiency in attack is key,' the former AC Milan striker told me.

Efficiency. There was a word that hadn't been mentioned by those in charge for a long time. It belonged to the classical canon of German football, along with other venerable tenets of the nation's game that had fallen out of fashion in the Klinsmann/Löw era. Their teams had worked so hard to get away from the minimalistic, reactive style of the past that the art of winning close matches with few openings seemed to have been lost along the way. A kind of playfulness had infected the *Nationalmannschaft*'s game, a tendency to overelaborate in the final third. 'They get carried away with their own beautiful football from time to time,' Bierhoff said.

Captain Philipp Lahm, ever the optimist, felt that this concern was 'actually a sign that things are going well'. He remembered 'times when we would struggle to create any goalscoring opportunities at all, even against the the so-called minnows'. You could only miss many chances if you created many chances, he insisted in a phone call from his Andreus hotel room in South Tyrol. Lahm had a point.

His superiors saw things differently. Joachim Löw had identified '*Chancenverwertung*' (the conversion of chances) as 'our biggest problem' straight after Germany's first win in qualifying Group C, a 3-0 victory against the Faroe Islands in September 2012. 'We need too many chances to score,' he said. The numbers supported that view. At the World Cup in South Africa, Germany had converted 37.2 per cent of their goalscoring opportunities, more than a third. That figure had fallen to 28.6 per cent at Euro 2012. Germany had needed thirty-five chances to score ten goals in that competition.

Bierhoff, too, admitted that an emphasis 'on fun elements' – passing, movement, combinations – in recent years had possibly detracted from the small matter of putting the ball into the net. 'They want to pass it sideways in front of goal, or score with a back-heel. We have to change that mentality.' Specifically devised training exercises in South Tyrol were supposed to encourage quicker, more decisive shooting. The players were made to score under pressure, in internal competitions, and with a shot clock running. Bierhoff: 'When you do something on a daily basis, it becomes a habit and part of your mentality. We had seen before how dangerous it was to play without that final bit of determination to score that goal at all costs. You saw it sometimes in the body language, in the expression on players' faces when they missed a chance. They thought: "I'm good, the next chance will come along."'

Chief scout Urs Siegenthaler warned that Europeans had to 'adjust to temperatures of forty-three, forty-four degrees in the sun at lunchtime' at the World Cup. 'Most importantly,' Bierhoff added, the team had to avoid 'going behind and chasing games' in the group games that were clustered in Brazil's hot north and set for afternoon kick-offs. 'In other words: we can't afford to give anything away.'

Some critics felt that Löw, rather than the players, was to blame for this feebleness in the box. Hadn't he done away with specialist strikers in the national team? In November 2012, in a friendly against the Netherlands, of all teams, a side long envied and belittled by Germans in equal measure for playing stylish and unsuccessful football, the *Bundestrainer* broke with 104 years of convention to field the first Germany team without a recognised centre-forward. Löw had been mulling over the idea for a while. 'Spain are our role models,' the coach had openly admitted after Vicente del Bosque's side had triumphed at Euro 2012 without an orthodox attacker in their line-up. When the moment came, with the then Dortmund player Mario Götze as a 'false nine' (an advanced midfielder tasked with goalscoring) at the Amsterdam Arena, it didn't exactly result in fireworks. '*Gähn-Gipfel*,' the summit of yawn, *Bild* called the 0-0 draw. But the new system took root.

Injuries to Miroslav Klose and Mario Gómez, the two Serie A-based strikers, saw Mesut Özil take up regular 'false nine' duties over the next year and a half. The then Real Madrid playmaker went on to finish the qualifying campaign as the best goalscorer, with eight goals.

Löw wasn't just copying Spain, in some quixotic quest for aesthetic perfection, he insisted, the change had been forced on him. To blunt Germany's combination football, opponents were playing much deeper than before, which in turn made smaller, creative players more likely to find a gap in the defensive walls. 'Would you rather take a Smart [car] or a van to look for a parking space in town?' Siegenthaler asked. In addition, the German FA analysts, supported by fifty student volunteers from the sports university in Cologne, had deduced that the opponents in the group stage, Portugal, Ghana and USA, were more vulnerable to pace and ingenuity than the brute force of a battering ram. 'It's not necessary to have the big, bulky striker up front any more,' Löw said. The composition of his World Cup squad reflected that view. Veteran Klose, thirty-six, was listed as the sole official 'attacker' in the twenty-three-strong group.

The *Bundestrainer* knew full well that he had opened up a new avenue for criticism if he didn't succeed that summer. As a football country Germany loved her strikers, the Uwe Seelers, Gerd Müllers and Rudi Völlers. It was hard to envisage winning anything without one. *Bild* duly lined up former target men to voice their doubts. 'If there are no goals [in Brazil], people will look at the system,' said VfL Wolfsburg's sporting director Klaus Allofs, a Euro 1980 winner. Stefan Kuntz, a member of the Euro 1996 team that lifted the trophy at the old Wembley, felt that Löw's army of midfielders didn't have the prerequisite 'instinct of a real goalscorer in the box'. Even TV pundit Mehmet Scholl, a technically gifted midfielder in his day, thought that Germany were missing 'punch' without a proper number nine. Löw's answer was to dismiss such thoughts as narrow-mindedness and being overly concerned with terminology. '"False nine", "real nine", these things have little meaning to me,' he said. 'Müller, Klose, Götze, Schürrle, Podolski, Özil – these are all strikers for me, attacking players.'

Twelve minutes into the game in the sweltering Fonte Nove Arena, Löw's strategy was vindicated. Germany did not have an out-and-out striker but they did have three attackers on the pitch, and here they were, all ganging up on Portugal's left defensive side, along with midfielder Sami Khedira, who, curiously, had taken up an even wider position, next to the touchline. Mesut Özil, Mario Götze and Thomas Müller ran towards the edge of the box within ten metres of each other, from deep positions, at full pace. Müller played a crisp one-two off Özil's heel, then instantly found Götze, who'd continued to cut inside. João Pereira pulled the Bayern midfielder down. Penalty. Yellow card. No arguments.

The spot-kick was Müller's to take. He'd only been on '*Elfmeter*' duty at Bayern since the autumn of 2012, when he converted his first penalty, in a Champions League game in Lille. Bastian Schweinsteiger called his team-mate's technique 'spectacular', but he was not being entirely serious. Müller took his penalties in the same scruffy way he wore his playing kit: socks half-rolled down, white muscle shirt limply hanging out from beneath his kit. With his five-euro haircut and legs like beanpoles, the feeling was inescapable. He didn't really look like a modern footballer at all.

Müller stepped up, took four quick steps, and then, and then . . . then he delayed the last one, to give Rui Patrício a chance to decide which way to go. But the Portuguese keeper had done his homework. He knew Müller always waited for the keeper to move first, so he didn't. Unperturbed, Müller hit the ball low into the left corner of the goal. Patrício never got anywhere near it.

It was the kind of shot that's routinely described as '*trocken*' (dry) in German newspaper match reports: plain, unpretentious, artless, even. The first German goal at the World Cup was – if you discounted the geometrically perfect sequence of movement that led to it – purely functional, successful football reduced to its essence. The ball had to go in. Müller could do that for you.

Müller had once scored 120 goals in one season (1998–9) for his hometown club TSV Pähl, a village of 2,000 people, fifty minutes drive south-west of Munich, set between two lakes, the Ammersee and Starnberger See. The son of a BMW engineer, Müller was eight at the time. A year later, Bayern Munich scout Jan Pienta spotted him at a youth tournament. Müller's mother, Klaudia, didn't want her son to move to the club from the Bavarian capital but Bayern were so keen they offered a compromise: Müller was allowed to train at Pähl for most of the week and to go up north for matches only.

His inelegant style saw him being played as a central defender at Bayern, but the hunger for goals proved much stronger than the positional discipline needed at the back. 'He couldn't help but push forward, so I put him into right midfield,' recalled Teong-Kim Lim, Bayern's U13 coach. Müller credits Lim as one of two coaches who most helped him to become a professional, and the Malaysia-born Lim, known as 'Mr Kim' to everyone at Säbener Strasse, Bayern's headquarters, still has a little yellow note on which the twelve-year-old Müller was to describe what constituted 'a team' as part of his homework. 'Togetherness', 'always fighting' and 'don't grumble if a team-mate makes a mistake' were Müller's answers, Lim told *Süddeutsche Zeitung* in 2010.

The other coach responsible for his success was Louis van Gaal. The Dutchman's predecessor at the Allianz Arena, Jürgen Klinsmann, had found little use for the teenaged Müller and allowed him to pursue his career elsewhere. 'He told me that I could go to Hoffenheim, that there was no place for me in the squad,' Müller said. FC Basel of Switzerland, where former Bayern midfielder Thorsten Fink was in charge, were also interested. Bayern's A team youth coach Hermann 'Tiger' Gerland vetoed the move. Müller had scored sixteen goals for him in the third division. He had a rare and valuable talent, too: 'He can play badly for ninety minutes but still score,' Gerland said.

Müller's game bore little relation to Dutch football's ideal of beauty and grace but van Gaal was an admirer. He promoted him to the first team, and within a month of the start of the 2009–10 season Müller was a regular, finding the net frequently in a roving role that was impossible to define. 'Müller always plays, it doesn't matter whether Franck Ribéry or Arjen Robben are fit or not,' van Gaal declared. Mario Gómez, bought for the Bundesliga record sum of €30 million from Stuttgart, was another star name the youngster had left in his wake.

'It's not easy to find somebody who plays this strangely,' Müller said of his own positional vagueness. In the highly regimented Van Gaal system, he was the one player allowed to go where his intuition took him. 'I'm not great at following orders, I follow my instinct,' he said. 'It's something that's deep inside.'

Bayern general manager Uli Hoeness dismissed the notion of a call-up by Löw as '*Schmarrn*' (nonsense) in mid-September. By March 2010, however, the *Bundestrainer* wanted to add a dose of anarchy to his finely tuned team as well. Müller played sixty-seven minutes in the 1-0 friendly defeat to Argentina at the Allianz Arena. Not everyone was impressed. Diego Maradona didn't recognise Müller as a member of

Löw's squad at the post-match conference and stood by the podium, cursing, angry, gesticulating at the usurper sitting brazenly on *his* throne. Why was a ballboy sitting there? Müller eventually made way politely for the Argentina coach, and Maradona apologised after learning of the young man's identity.

That summer, a mere year after he had played in front of few hundred spectators in Bavarian villages, he was the Golden Boot winner with five goals at the 2010 World Cup in South Africa. 'Müller is a blessing, he brings an element of wildness and unpredictability to Löw's side of academics who love to play according to plans,' wrote *Süddeutsche*. His unaffected, informal manner on the pitch extended to post-match activities.

After his two goals in the 4-1 win over England at Bloemfontein, a sweaty, smiling Müller asked the German TV reporter if he was allowed to say hello to his grandparents on camera, and then proceeded to do so, adding 'it's been long overdue'. He then appeared in front of the world's media and apologised that their microphones were 'buckling because of the bad stink'.

In Salvador, meanwhile, it was Pepe's turn to make a real mess of things. The Real Madrid defender caught Müller with a stray arm in the face. There wasn't too much contact but the Portuguese defender took exception to the German's somewhat theatrical reaction. As the forward sat on the pitch, clutching his chin, Pepe pushed his forehead down on Müller's. It wasn't quite a head-butt but probably warranted a dismissal for rank stupidity. 'Pepe is a talented provocateur, but Müller got the better of him,' wrote *Süddeutsche*.

The expulsion had come five minutes after Mats Hummels had doubled Germany's lead with a well-timed header from a Toni Kroos corner. Portugal had self-destructed. All the pre-match concern about Sami Khedira's fitness, Philipp Lahm's deployment in midfield, Manuel Neuer's shoulder and the use of four centre-backs in defence dissipated a few seconds before half-time when Müller added a third in imitable style. He stuck out a leg to block Bruno Alves' attempted clearance, then reacted quickly to dispatch a low shot on the half-volley. You could describe it as opportunist but that's technically not quite right: there was full intent there, all along. Müller didn't buy the goal – he stole it, with the deftness of a pickpocket. 'He is one of those guys with a nose,' Löw said after the final whistle.

Back home in Bavaria people would call someone like him a '*Hund*'. It translates as 'dog' but carries connotations of street smartness, mental alertness and the knack of being in the right place at the right time. A man who knows all the tricks in the book and some of those that aren't; the perfect poacher, irrespective of his starting point on the pitch. Unlike regular, old-fashioned number nines, Müller didn't consider the opposition box his realm but as the enemy's treasure room, to be raided and ransacked quietly at irregular intervals.

Müller had learned to stay off the opposition radar early on in his career, out of necessity. 'There are others who are better in the air, better with their right, better with their left,' he admitted, self-effacingly. 'If you can't count on your physical attributes, you have to switch on your brain and make certain runs to avoid getting tackled.' He had transformed his weakness ('muscles don't grow on me') into a virtue, to become more proficient from the neck up.

When I meet him on a sunny September day at Säbener Strasse, within earshot of dozens of schoolkids eager to spot a '*Weltmeister*' (world champion), I ask if appearing less skilful than he actually was, with the occasional miscontrol and grungy attire, was part of a deliberate ploy to blind-side opponents. He comes close to saying yes. 'I know that I'm constantly in a grey zone: a footballer who doesn't always look like a very good footballer. I understand that many find it hard to get me. They say: "Impossible, how did he do that?" But, at some point, they maybe start thinking: "Oh, he's quite good after all." The coaches know [what I can do], so it's not a problem.

Football is like nature. You have to adapt and find your niche, in terms of the type of player you can become. I always knew I'd have no chance against a 1.90m, 90kg defender in a duel, so the key is to avoid those situations altogether. You have to pick your space and time.'

That level of self-analysis is rare, even by the standards of the current, well-educated crop of German internationals. But, then, Müller knew precisely who and what he was at the age of twenty-one. 'I'm a *"Raumdeuter"* [interpreter of space],' he said in an interview with *Süddeutsche* in January 2011. 'That would make a good headline, wouldn't it?'

Space interpreter. It's great job description of a player who eludes categories and explores areas that few care to consider, for example the gap between the back four and the goal line when there's a throw-in. To almost everybody else, it's a barren stretch of land, not worth cultivating.

Most of his team-mates at club and international levels are better with the ball. They glide and float whereas he plods and scuffles. Quite a few are better without the ball, too. In previous editions of the *Nationalmannschaft*, managers would have found it hard to see what it was he brought to the table. Müller's speciality, the discovering of space in overpopulated territory, simply hadn't been much of a concern in years gone by. Germany lined up so deep against any half-decent opposition that they had fifty, sixty metres of green ahead of them. Space was seen as a predominantly negative commodity, something that needed to be denied to other, more technical teams, to starve their game of oxygen.

Older football fans remembered a brief, happy time when attacks from deep positions in quick, elegant waves spawned the term '*Ramba-Zamba-Fußball*'. That's what *Bild* called West Germany's historic 3-1 at Wembley in the quarter-final of the European Championship in 1972. The neologism was a necessity: Franz Beckenbauer and playmaker Günter Netzer had overwhelmed Alf Ramsey's side in such exhilarating fashion that there were no German words to describe it. Literary scholar Karl-Heinz Bohrer, too, used the English word 'thrill', writing about Netzer's charging forward from the 'depth of space' in *FAZ*: 'Thrill is the transformation of geometry into energy, an explosion in the box that makes you mad with happiness.' 'Dream football from the year 2000,' *L'Equipe* called the performance in northwest London.

Helmut Schön's *Nationalmannschaft* won the World Cup two years later, but pace and excitement had been dampened in the course of the rain-soaked competition. 'Ramba-Zamba', as an expression and a style of football, only made a return in 2010, when Philipp Lahm declared that he'd never played in a better German team before and *Berliner Morgenpost* hailed 'the new Ramba-Zamba feeling' after the 4-1 and 4-0 wins over England and Argentina, respectively.

Müller, with his infallible GPS, his Bavarian *Naturbursche* (nature boy) stamina and the ability to see gaps before they appeared, played a big part in the revival in South Africa. Without his particular unconventionality, Germany lost the semi-final against Spain rather meekly, mustering a single scoring chance worthy of the name. Müller was suspended for the 1-0 defeat in Durban.

Now, four years later, Löw's men had evolved into a team that monopolised possession. Getting behind deeper defences had become the key problem for the attack, and so the unique skill set of the *Raumdeuter* had taken on even greater importance. 'I don't think there are many [opposition] players in the world who understand his runs and ideas,' Bastian Schweinsteiger said.

Both teams conserved energy in the second half in Salvador, content with the score line. A comically limp, eighty-fifth-minute free-kick from Cristiano Ronaldo that found Lahm, the sole constituent of the German wall, summed up the Portuguese superstar's miserable afternoon. Müller had completed his hat-trick a few minutes before. Patrício didn't deal with a low cross from substitute André Schürrle.

The ball was a little behind Müller but he adjusted his feet to stab it home, falling backwards in the process. A classic '*Abstauber*', a routine goal from short distance, dispatched in the slightly awkward manner that brought to mind Schön's famous verdict. 'Müller is a man of small goals,' the former West Germany coach once said.

He meant Gerd, not Thomas. But the observation held true for both of them. Just like '*der Bomber*', his much stockier namesake, tall and skinny Thomas Müller had developed the talent of forcing all kinds of goals from unlikely angles, sometimes with unlikely parts of his anatomy. Both Müllers were passionate goalmouth '*Wurschtler*': *Wurscht* is Bavarian for sausage, and *wurschteln*, as a verb, means muddling through, succeeding in a non-linear, messy but resourceful fashion. After Germany's win in the opening game, Thomas Müller beamed that 'every goal was more beautiful than the next', but he was being ironic, obviously. His was a *Wurschtler*'s hat-trick and he knew it.

Portugal's collapse made it difficult to accurately gauge Germany's strength. But Löw had found that he could once again rely on Müller's sixth sense in Brazil. In him, he had a player who never stopped running ('He did a great job up front,' Löw said, 'he kept on creating openings for others') and hassling defenders until they lost the ball or their head or both. He never got injured ('I don't have any muscles so I can't get hurt,' Müller laughed) and, most importantly, he never seemed to feel any pressure. Löw: 'He has the unbelievable quality to never choke or show a nervous reaction in front of goal.'

False nine Müller was turning into a real Müller, *the* real Müller in that respect – efficiency incarnate. Thomas Müller himself wasn't surprised. He had confidently opted to wear *der Bomber*'s famous number thirteen shirt before the 2010 World Cup ('I had the choice between 4, 13, 14 and I then remembered that Gerd wore the 13 and couldn't resist,' he explained) and chosen @esmuellert_ ('it müllers') as his Twitter handle. His account name echoed the use of Gerd Müller's surname as a verb to describe his otherworldy prowess during

West Germany's golden period of the seventies. Something, a thing, an unstoppable, supernatural force, scored all these goals – not him.

On TV, Mehmet Scholl was a convert after the final whistle. There was no more need to talk about Germany playing without a real striker. 'Thomas is not a false nine, he is the wild thirteen,' he said.

Bierhoff: 'Portugal? I'm bad on these things, sometimes I even forget the result. 4-0? Okay. All I remember about this game is Müller. He comes across like a joker but he's very ambitious, and he was focused from the word go. As the penalty went in, I knew we'd win this game.'

The hat-trick in the Arena Fonte Nova had put Müller on course to become the first ever leading goalscorer at World Cup finals to defend his trophy. He dismissed the idea with a shrug. 'I already have one Golden Boot, what should I do with a second one?' His eyes were on a bigger prize.

GO WEST

'Coincidence. A series of coincidences.'

Jürgen Klinsmann is nursing an iced tea. We're sitting in the half-shade, on the terrace of a Starbucks coffee shop, less than a couple of hundred metres from the rugged Pacific coastline, halfway between his California home in Huntington Beach and the wealthy boho-surfer haunt of Laguna Beach, and neither the faux-antique, 'money, money'-screaming over-the-topness of Crystal Cove shopping parade nor the endless rows of vehicles in the adjacent car park can do anything to spoil the golden afternoon beauty of this spot.

It feels somehow inappropriate to talk football here. More wrong still to delve back into German football's sickly past, to drag up the bad old days. I find myself apologising to Klinsmann for the inconvenience. Rock musician Chris Isaak once quipped that on the West Coast you got up in the morning and thought about going to surf whereas in Germany you felt like 'printing a bible'.

But maybe that incongruence between the sun-kissed, palm-tree-lined setting and the heavy subject goes some way to explaining how the *Nationalmannschaft* were transformed from a joke to revered representatives of a new country in the space of two years by a non-native Californian. The optimism, freshness and can-do spirit had to be be shipped in from somewhere, from somewhere else, far away. From the end of this world.

Up the road in Hollywood they could work with this script: Klinsmann, the exiled, mistrusted outsider, comes in from the warm to rebuild a team that's dead on its feet. There's plenty of resistance, people don't believe in his reformist master plan. Insert a training ground montage – we need a montage – of Michael Ballack et al. doing strange things with elastic bands to the tune of the theme from *Team America*. Klinsmann nearly gets fired. Then they win, beautifully. The whole country falls in love with them during the 2006 World Cup – and with itself. A bittersweet, third-place happy ending in Berlin. And for the opening credits you can have Berti Vogts driving his campervan on the California State Route 1 outside San Diego with some indeterminable MOR rock playing on the radio.

Vogts, the former national manager, happened to be there on holiday with his son in mid-July 2004, heading for Las Vegas. 'He phoned me and said he wanted to say hello,' says Klinsmann. 'So I said, let's do it properly. He drove here, we had a barbecue and talked for hours about football and the national team. At one point he asked me whether I could imagine taking on such a task. Otto Rehhagel and Ottmar Hitzfeld had already ruled themselves out at the time. I said "Yes, but only if I could do it my way." It was more in jest. But they called me the next day.'

Vogts had told German FA secretary Horst R. Schmidt, a member of the task force, about Klinsmann's willingness to step into the breach. Schmidt passed on the message to FA president Gerhard Mayer-Vorfelder. A couple of days later, the three of them met in a restaurant in New York. Klinsmann: 'I had prepared a presentation with my two American business partners that detailed the changes I wanted to make because the old ways were no longer working. The public pressure on the German FA was enormous. I'm not sure they could have afforded yet another guy turning down the job. It was all head over heels. Then the project started.'

Klinsmann had retired to the West Coast sunshine in the summer of 1998 after a successful club career with VfB Stuttgart, Internazionale Tottenham Hotspur and Bayern Munich, and winning the World Cup (1990) and European Championship (1996) with the national team. The Swabian 'sonny boy', as German newspapers used to refer to him in light of his blond hair and unfailingly smily demeanour, had helped the FA in their campaign to win the FIFA vote for the 2006 World Cup at the turn of the century and worked as a pundit for German TV during the 2002 World Cup. But by 2004 he'd become a little forgotten in his homeland. He was concentrating on his work with SoccerSolutions, a sports marketing and promotions company formed by former Aston Villa midfielder Mick Hoban and New Yorker Warren Mersereau.

It was the 'woeful situation' the German FA found themselves in after Völler's resignation, as he put it, that brought him back into the newspapers. On the day of the Euro 2004 final, he systematically dissected the national team's problems and failures in an interview with *Frankfurter Allgemeine Sonntagszeitung*.

Germany didn't have players – Philipp Lahm excepted – who could play at the highest tempo. They didn't have players who could run past opponents with the ball. Others were playing attacking football, Germany only sideways. And where were Germany's Cristiano Ronaldos, Rooneys or Robbens? Why were the FA chasing all manner of big-name coaches (to succeed Völler) without first defining the specifications of the job? A 'kind of general manager' was needed to assist and protect the future coach. And a 'vision', too. 'Where do we want to be in the next six, eight years?' Germany, he warned, had a chance to represent herself at the World Cup on home soil, a chance that wouldn't come around again for another thirty or forty years. 'That's why we simply can't afford to make such an unholy mess of things.'

Klinsmann's 4th of July declaration of independent thought hardly registered. It was only when he repeated his criticism in starker language and more precise terms in *Süddeutsche Zeitung* twelve days later that those at the association headquarters in Frankfurt started listening. Klinsmann called for a 'revolution' that followed the example of Aimé Jacquet's successful work with 1998 World Cup winners France; 'the whole training curriculum is in need of reform,' he told *SZ*. 'A team of specialists' was needed for 'every single area', including sport psychology. 'The players experience stress situations that they have never been prepared for. I feel as if the machinery in Germany has been at a standstill for twenty years.' A 'ten-year-plan' needed to be developed; everything had to be 'X-rayed, down to the youth team'. Klinsmann's critique culminated in the demand that 'the whole shop' needed to be 'taken apart'.

Christian Zaschke, the *SZ* reporter who conducted the interview, remembers being excited about Klinsmann's candour. He was afraid Klinsmann would tone down the belligerent rhetoric during the authorisation process. In Germany, it's customary to give interviewees the right to double-check the quotes attributed to them before publication; in practice, quite a few controversial statements tend to get watered down or removed altogether at that stage. 'But, to my surprise, Klinsmann changed some lines to make them even stronger, more cutting,' Zaschke says.

Klinsmann ruled himself out as candidate to become the next *Bundestrainer*, 'for the moment'. But the *SZ* piece concluded with him casually confirming that he had coaching licence. 'It's good to know that I have it in my pocket.'

'Coincidence', as Klinsmann insists, did play a big role in his appointment. The *SZ* interview did not constitute a job application, he stresses, 'it was only an emotional statement from a distance'. But the former striker had done what any striker worth his salt does: he had manoeuvred himself into the right position to take full advantage of the breaks.

*

The coaching badge in Klinsmann's pocket had been Vogts' doing as well. The 'Terrier' had wanted successful former internationals, the classes of 1990 and 1996, to stay involved with football and had arranged for them to do their 'Pro' licence in a condensed, but still UEFA-compliant course lasting only six weeks instead of the usual six months in 2000. Klinsmann, Matthias Sammer, Andreas Köpke and Andreas Brehme were among the nineteen participants. 'There were loads of debates, we were talking a lot, like footballers always do,' Klinsmann says. 'Even then, you could see that the foundations were crumbling. Erich Ribbeck and Rudi Völler were doing their best with what they had, but we felt that many things were going in the wrong direction.'

At the modestly furnished Sportschule Hennef, Klinsmann met a man who hadn't won anything as a player with Germany but who'd been allowed to take part in the truncated course because he'd already coached at the highest level at Stuttgart and Karlsruhe: Joachim Löw. 'I had been a professional player for eighteen years. In those eighteen years, not one manager was able to explain to me how a back four should move across the pitch,' Klinsmann recalled years later. 'But it only took one minute with Jogi for me to understand how it worked.'

After Klinsmann had agreed to sign a two-year deal to become national team coach on 26 July, Franz Beckenbauer wanted to push his former assistant, Holger Osieck, who was working as head of FIFA's technical department at the time, on him as the number two. Newspapers were briefed that Osieck's appointment was a formality. Klinsmann, however, had somebody else in mind.

The new general manager, meanwhile, had already been found. Oliver Bierhoff, team-mate of Klinsmann at Euro 1996, had been proposed by Bayern CEO Karl-Heinz Rummenigge for the role. 'He's a competent man,' Rummenigge had said.

Klinsmann agreed. 'He is somebody I can trust 1,000 per cent and get along with blindfolded,' the new *Bundestrainer* said at his and

Bierhoff's unveiling in Frankfurt on 29 July. Bierhoff described his own role as 'a link between team, Bundesliga, media and sponsors'.

Another of those coincidences had occurred a couple of days before in Stuttgart, according to journalist Udo Muras. Bierhoff was having lunch with his lawyer, at the same Italian restaurant that Löw happened to be in. They didn't see him but, as he left, Löw went over to say hello. Bierhoff phoned Klinsmann and mentioned Löw as a possible candidate, only to learn that the new *Bundestrainer* had already earmarked him as a strong contender.

The morning after, Klinsmann phoned Löw, who was about to go mountain biking in the Black Forest. Klinsmann asked him to meet him in Italy, where he'd gone to spend some time with friends. The talks at Lake Como went well but Löw wanted to go back home to Germany's south-west and sleep on his decision. Klinsmann couldn't wait. He had to come up with a quick alternative to Osieck. Pressed for an instant answer, Löw said yes.

'I'm happy with that decision,' Bayern general manager Uli Hoeness declared. 'Jürgen Klinsmann needs a coach, somebody who knows the Bundesliga inside out, not somebody who's been in Canada for ten years.' Osieck had coached the Canadian national team from 1998 to 2003. Hoeness also said that Klinsmann needed to be given 'a fair chance'. The approval of 'Mr Bayern' was in marked contrast to the overwhelmingly negative reactions from within the league. 'There are many arguments against [him]. The most important one was that Klinsmann has never worked with a team before,' said Klaus Allofs, the Werder Bremen general manager. Schalke boss Rudi Assauer was just as dubious: 'Klinsmann has never coached. Bierhoff has never coached or managed. Löw has experience, for sure, but he's only the assistant. These three are supposed to take German football forward. I find that hard to believe.' The German FA had acted 'like a rabbit breeders' club', Assauer added.

*

Bayern Munich's support for the new *Bundestrainer* was in part informed by the club's instructive experience of Klinsmann as player from 1995 to 1997. The striker's hard-nosed business acumen in the contract negotiations had impressed Hoeness. 'There was a battle over every comma in my office, for eight hours,' he said. Klinsmann's emotionally detached dedication to his job had also stood out during a tumultuous period in which Bayern had actively cultivated the 'FC Hollywood' brand by turning football into entertainment product, replete with storylines of personal confrontation, betrayal and forgiveness.

A total of six years abroad – three at Inter Milan, two in Ligue 1 with AS Monaco and one at Tottenham Hotspur – had broadened the Swabian's horizons. In Munich, Klinsmann was confronted with conditions and habits he considered outdated, not conducive to football at the highest levels. Bayern's insistence on public training sessions, spending the night before home games in a hotel at Lake Tegernsee a good ninety minutes away from the Olympic Stadium and the tactical limitations of new coach Otto Rehhagel were among the many things he openly criticised. And why were they still playing with a fifth defender as a sweeper? 'No wonder Bayern haven't won anything internationally for a while,' he said. At the time, his serial discontent and cool demeanour very much irked Hoeness, who wanted every player to become part of the (slightly dysfunctional) Bayern family. 'He gave us his body but not his mind – let alone his heart,' Hoeness told Klinsmann's biographer Michael Horeni years later. But in 2004, German football was in dire need of such purposefulness and professionalism. 'He's unspent, he's intelligent and he's got energy,' the Bayern boss said.

Politics came into it, too. Hoeness and Rummenigge were determined to prevent Beckenbauer's favourite, Lothar Matthäus, getting the job. The former Bayern midfielder had made himself an outcast after (unsuccessfully) suing the club over the proceeds of his testimonial in 2000. 'As long as me and Karl-Heinz Rummenigge are in charge, he won't even get a job as groundsman in the new stadium,' Hoeness vowed. Matthäus, the 1990 World Cup winner, didn't have too many fans elsewhere in the league, either. Lothar as *Bundestrainer*? 'That would have topped it. If that had been the case, Schalke would have withdrawn their professional team and registered to play in Holland,' thundered Assauer.

Klinsmann wasted little time taking the whole shop apart. National team head of logistics Bernd Pfaff, a man who had worked for the FA for forty-six years, was the first official to bite the bullet. Bierhoff took over his role, with the express brief to stop the mingling of sponsors and FA functionaries with the team before matches. 'We needed the players to focus on the task ahead, without distractions,' Klinsmann says. Bierhoff also had daily newspapers removed from the breakfast room ('We wanted them to talk to each other') and installed a players' lounge. 'We didn't want them to sit in their rooms by themselves on their PlayStation all day,' he says.

Ahead of his first game in charge, a 3-1 away win in Austria, Klinsmann demoted captain Oliver Kahn and handed the armband to midfielder Michael Ballack. The *Bundestrainer* argued that a field player was in a better position to lead the team, emotionally and tactically. The move was replete with symbolic meaning, too. The new manager wanted the German team to trade in the passiveness of recent years for 'a high level of aggression' and a dominant playing style. Kahn was the world's best at making goal-line saves to prevent defeats, but his rise to the level of national hero mirrored the demise of Germany as an attacking force. Klinsmann wanted the centre of gravity to shift from the last line of defence to the final third in the opposition half.

Kahn didn't just lose the captaincy. He was no longer untouchable, no longer the first man on the team sheet. Klinsmann named his arch-rival Jens Lehmann, who had just won the Premier League with Arsenal's Invincibles of 2003–4, as 'the challenger' against whom

Kahn needed to 'defend his position'. Both keepers would be rotated over the course of the next couple of years.

Sepp Maier, the long-serving goalkeeping coach at Bayern and the national team, came out in favour of Kahn and against the idea of a competition for the gloves of the nation. The popular Bavarian was publicly reprimanded for violating his neutrality, then dismissed a couple of months later after sixteen years in the service of the German FA. Andreas Köpke assumed the position of the new goalkeeping coach. The appointment of Dieter Eilts as U21 coach completed the takeover by the class of '96. Nepotism, some detractors cried.

'Klinsmann is a killer. He axes people to advance his aims,' Matthäus commented in his *Sport-Bild* column. 'Humaneness hasn't been a concern at the [German FA] for long time – especially now that Jürgen is there.' Yes, this was personal. Matthäus and Klinsmann, two very different characters, had clashed over a number of issues during their time at Bayern in the nineties and the conflict had been magnified by the former's close relationship with Germany's all-powerful tabloid *Bild* and sister publication *Sport-Bild*. The two Axel Springer titles, which also counted Bayern president Beckenbauer as a regular contributor, took delight in revealing that Klinsmann's nickname among colleagues in the Bayern dressing room was 'pin-ball', due to his less than perfect ball control. Klinsmann's contractual details and salary were also published. The well-travelled international was portrayed as an '*Abzocker*', a greedy mercenary who couldn't put down roots and violated the much-cherished, romantic notion of football loyalty. Hadn't he promised his father Siegfried he would never go to Bayern? (He had. Ahead of his move to the Bavarians, the player had gone back to Klinsmann senior and asked to be released from this solemn vow.)

On top of that, his unwillingness to engage with the tabloid media, both print and TV, was cited as proof that he couldn't be a leader in the dressing room. True leaders took responsibility by speaking their mind, every time, into every microphone. Everyone knew that.

Before too long, many wondered whether his perma-smile was hiding an egotistical loner who only cared about his own interests. Matthäus went so far as to challenge Klinsmann to a live TV debate to resolve their differences. Klinsmann ignored the bizarre request. Germany's most capped player suspected that 'Klinsi' had slyly retaliated by talking Vogts into dropping him from the Euro 1996 squad.

'The storm is blowing from the same direction as in the nineties, when Matthäus was a *Bild* informant and Klinsmann wasn't,' *Süddeutsche* wrote about Matthäus' attack on the new national manager in October 2004. 'You would love to make fun of this conflict but that's hardly possible. It will shape the climate in which the new man has to prove himself.'

Süddeutsche's fears were not unfounded. Klinsmann and his staff's every move was treated with suspicion bordering on hostility. *Bild* had their own motives. Unlike other national team players, Klinsmann had been unwilling to pass on information for favourable headlines, and he was not going to change this stance as national team manager. On top of that, he expressly warned his charges about the dangers of 'information corruption', the leaking of dressing room information to the media ahead of games.

Back in 1996, he had also successfully sued the paper for illustrating a (completely harmless) story about the Euro team's visit to a hotel sauna with a picture of him. He hadn't taken part in it.

Prominent figures in the Bundesliga took exception for another reason. They saw in Klinsmann's revolutionary writing a thinly disguised attack on their own practises. 'He is supposed to call up players, coach them, motivate them, line them up. Borussia Dortmund will give him all their support for that,' said BVB general manager Michael Meier. 'But he has to stop questioning everything.'

That was precisely what he did, however. 'This was not about changing everything,' Klinsmann says. 'It was an exciting process to see where we were and where we could go. We wanted to try as many things as possible, doing it with a certain amount of stubbornness: if we were convinced something could get us ahead by a few percentage points, if it made sense, we were prepared to go with it. We knew right from the start that we needed broad shoulders to follow through, past established opinions.'

Or existing agreements. The German FA had signed a contract for the national team's use of the Bayer 04 Leverkusen training complex during the World Cup. The team were supposed to stay in the sleepy town of Bergisch Gladbach, a forty-minute bus drive away. Klinsmann thought that was too far away. In any case, he wanted to be in the capital Berlin, to feel the pulse of the country and the competition. 'Berlin is a better fit for my team. It also offers the players the opportunity to do some other things, like going to a cinema,' he said.

Leverkusen were not best pleased. Their parent company, pharmaceutical giants Bayer, had been among the earliest supporters of the German bid for the World Cup when nobody else had thought it feasible. 'Bayer drove the armoured reconnaissance car and pumped in a few millions to fuel the campaign,' the former Leverkusen CEO Reiner Calmund said. The total outlay was estimated at €2 million, and that included a party at the Confederations Cup in Mexico 1999, where Charles Dempsey was one of the guests. The FIFA Executive Committee from New Zealand's surprise abstention in the voting in Zürich gave Germany the edge over South Africa.

The FA were further in 04's debt because they had released (sporting director) Rudi Völler to take over the national team after Erich Ribbeck's debacle at Euro 2000. Hosting the *Nationalmannschaft* in 2006 would be Bayer's reward.

Klinsmann and Bierhoff rode roughshod over the deal, and didn't let up until they got their way after much internal wrangling. 'I didn't want to have any regrets, I didn't want to look back at the World Cup in August 2006 and feel that we should have been somewhere else.

So we said: let's not compromise. That was also good for the team. They saw that we did our thing, irrespective of the resistance.'

But was it really necessary to engage on so many different battlefronts in such a short space of time? Klinsmann is unapologetic. 'We knew who was having a go at us, and why. It was never our intention to start a fight on all fronts. We were simply determined to stick to our guns and make the best decisions, without worrying too much how they would play out in the media. Everything was presumed to be personal, including the goalkeeping question, but that simply wasn't the case. I can tell you that I have nothing but the greatest respect for Oliver Kahn, and this was not at all about him being a lesser keeper. It was only football. We spent hours debating with Andreas Köpke, who's the expert, about the style of football we wanted to play and what kind of keeper we needed for that.' Lehmann, a more active keeper who was able to cover behind a high defensive line, unsurprisingly won the race.

Klinsmann was aware that he was asking a lot of his countrymen. 'I never took criticism personally. I know how tough it is to change when you feel that you're doing okay. It was years before I understood the Italian way of thinking, which was completely results-based, for example. They wanted 1-0s, I wanted 4-3s. Then I went to France and England, and it was one culture shock after another for me. German football had its problems. But we were somebody. Did we really have to do things differently all of a sudden? The time Jogi, Oliver and me had spent abroad convinced us that the answer was yes. There had to be a new way if we wanted to beat the international competition.'

At the squad's first get-together in the team hotel, Klinsmann showed them a video of Germany's past World Cup triumphs and the 2002 team's triumphant return to Frankfurt after their runners-up place in South Korea/Japan. Eminem's 'Lose Yourself', an ode to taking chances ('One shot, one opportunity . . .') played in the background.

James Brown's *Revolution of the Mind: Recorded Live at the Apollo, Vol. III*,
with its iconic prison cover artwork, might have made for an appropriate
soundtrack, too. Klinsmann was leading his charges in a 'Revolution of
the Mind': before they played differently, they had to think differently;
retune the mentality, free themselves from the shackles of past attitudes.

'We took out a flip chart and said: let's define, with you, who we want
to be, the style we want to play. Words like "aggressive", "attacking",
"forward", "fast", "dominant" were mentioned. We said: "Let us stop
chasing after the ball. We want the ball now." I believe that football
represents the culture of a country. Germany was a doer country, but
we had stopped playing doer football. We wanted to get back to that
over the course of the next couple of years. That was our primer.'

'Personality development', as Klinsmann called it, became a fifth
priority, along with the four basic coaching pillars of technique, tactics,
physical and mental conditioning. 'We tried to activate the players'
brains, through computer courses, language courses, other things . . . to
get them to say "I'm in the driving seat here."' Suddenly, national team
meetings didn't so much feel like a holiday camp with some football
thrown in, more like management seminars. There were plenty of
motivational talks. Bonding sessions. Go-karting. Archery. Even a
course in watch-making. Klinsmann: 'We wanted them to understand
that it was their career, and they had to make the most of it. We
wanted them to take responsibility. Don't make ten sprints because
your manager tells you to. Think about why you're doing it. Demand
explanations. Part of that process was also learning from other sports.'

Three Olympic athletes from Athens 2004 were invited to visit
training sessions and have their say: Patrick Weissinger (water polo),
Robert Bartko (cycling) and Tibor Weißenborn (field hockey). Oliver
Bierhoff told me that footballers never do anything of their own
volition,' said Weißenborn, 'that surprised me.' Weissinger added that
in his sport, 'people were asking a lot more critical questions. We listen
to our bodies more. We spend a lot more time thinking about what
we're doing.' Klinsmann duly took note.

The challenge went beyond building a team that could compete at a World Cup. They had to be able to win a World Cup on home soil, a competition that transcended sport to take on huge national importance. This was the first major sporting event since reunification, a chance for Germans to show the world and themselves that theirs was a tolerant, friendly, modern country. 'That's one of the most amazing things about sport, and football in particular: it can change your perspective on things,' Klinsmann says. 'There was huge drive to present a new Germany, in both senses of the word, a Germany that wasn't about "Panzers" but a multicultural Germany that felt comfortable in the centre of Europe and thought internationally; a Germany that could enjoy itself. But that could only work if the team were playing good football. The expectations on us were brutal. Look at Brazil [in the 2014 World Cup]. They were expected to solve all the country's problems. That was impossible from the outset. They eventually buckled and broke apart under the weight of those expectations.'

The situation for the German national team was complicated by the fact that, paradoxically, the extreme pressure corresponded with rather low expectations and a generally pessimistic outlook. Most of their countrymen were far too busy worrying about another potentially disastrous showing to entertain any serious thoughts of the team winning the competition.

Inside the squad, true believers were few and far between as well. Klinsmann decided to aim as high as possible, regardless. 'We want to become world champions,' he said in his first press conference. What would have been a banal statement in years gone by sounded positively upbeat in August 2004, a month after German football had just reluctantly come to terms with its relegation to the second tier at the Euros in Portugal.

In his current job, as coach of the US men's national team, Klinsmann, too, has experienced the debilitating effect a lack of collective confidence can have on a team's chances. 'Because there is no history of success, American football doesn't have self-assurance, it puts itself down. It has taken a while to get to the point where we feel that we can at least dominate our region, that we can beat our local rivals Mexico. But then you come up against Belgium [at the World Cup in Brazil] with their famous players from famous European clubs, and your brain starts turning and then you feel quite small.'

Klinsmann hired sports psychologist Hans-Dieter Hermann, who had worked with Ralf Rangnick's Ulm 1846 team in the Bundesliga, to help German national team players cope with the unique situation. A shrink for the national team? German footballers were supposed to be mentally tough to the point of being autonotoms. When Oliver Kahn told the press he'd be seeking out Hermann, *Bild* had a field day. 'Kahn to see psycho-doc?' its headline screamed.

Klinsmann admits that he wasn't certain that the players would buy into the idea that feet and brain were closely connected. In between those body parts lay the guts, and gut instinct told many Germans that this was new-world, new-age hogwash. 'It hadn't been done before, nobody knew. It was strictly voluntary, a service that was available. It was the same with some of the other stuff we tried out. We thought it can't hurt. Only not doing it can hurt.'

Even well-meaning observers were unsure about the new regime's esoteric tendencies, their frequent use of English consultant-speak and terms like 'energy field' and 'inner inspiration' – buzzwords one would have rather expected to encounter at an Orange County yoga centre. Klinsmann, however, saw in his own career confirmation of the idea that football was first and foremost a mental exercise. He'd never been the most gifted player technically, but made up for that with total commitment and application on the pitch.

Milan's Stadio Giuseppe Meazza (more commonly known as the San Siro), the last sixteen against the Netherlands, World Cup 1990: the game of Klinsmann's life. Rudi Völler and Frank Rijkaard were sent off after twenty-two minutes. Klinsmann scored the opener and chased after every ball on his own upfront, like a madman on speed, until leaving the pitch totally exhausted eleven minutes before the final whistle in the 2-1 win. 'He ran for both of us,' said Völler. Coach Franz Beckenbauer felt that the striker had performed 'beyond his abilities' and Klinsmann explained that eating up so many kilometres in one of his 'most extreme matches' was a feat achieved 'at the mental level'. He 'incredibly' enjoyed running after all these balls, he said.

Six years after the winning the World Cup in Italy, Klinsmann led the German national team to a triumph at Euro 96, a trophy that proved to be the last for some time. Berti Vogts' team didn't have much by way of artistry and individual skill in England, and a series of injuries saw half the squad playing out of position to fill in the gaps. That pain and adversity forged them into a strong unit whose team spirit carried them past the hosts – via penalties in the semi-final – all the way to a handshake with Queen Elizabeth II on the Wembley steps. Klinsmann returned home a certified hero but he lacked the cuddliness of a Völler or the populist charm of a Beckenbauer to be taken to Germany's heart.

The aim of trying out a huge variety of new players was to find those 'willing to go to the extra mile' for Germany in 2006, he says. Klinsmann, in fact, was looking to assemble a team of twenty-three Klinsmanns. 'Are you prepared to suffer to reach the ultimate target? Are you ready to run up and down the pitch once more, fifteen minutes into extra-time? Do you completely identify with your task, are you prepared to sacrifice yourself for the team? Or will you only give 90 per cent?' These were not just questions for professional athletes, he says. 'I've always been fascinated by people who find satisfaction through total commitment in their jobs. They could be bakers, painters or footballers. The painter who comes up with a new colour he's truly proud of is as happy as the striker scoring goals. Maybe even happier.'

Football, he believes, remains a 'player-driven game'. Americans sometimes find that hard to understand, Klinsmann says, because most team sports are considered coaching-driven there. 'You'll often see players look to the coach for direction. But football doesn't work like that, because it's too fluid. You need players to take charge.'

Clarity of purpose was one thing, the capacity to deliver another. The new programme was nothing if players weren't physically in the position to give it shape on the pitch. Nobody thought that should be too much of a problem, however, because the production of players who could run a lot was considered one of the last core competencies of German football to have survived its millennial downfall intact. Klinsmann disagreed. Data from the national team, provided to him by Vogts, suggested that relative performance levels had continuously dropped since the mid-90s. Klinsmann: 'As long as everybody does more or less the same thing, you're okay. But when your rivals start training eight times a week to your five, when they regenerate better, eat better, sleep more, do a lot of the things off the pitch better than you, then you will see a difference over the course of a few years.' German football made the mistake of believing its own press, he adds. 'For decades, they told us that we never gave up, that we were super-hard working but, in reality, we had been pushed to the margins by the competition. There were was no success in European club competition, the pace in the Bundesliga was slow. And yet, the assumption was that we're very fit.' (He encounters the same misconception in his current job, he says. 'Americans believe they are fit, as a matter of course.')

Ahead of his second game, a friendly with World Cup holders Brazil in Berlin, Klinsmann brought in experts from the USA to sharpen up the players. Mark Verstegen and his team from Athletes' Performance (since renamed EXOS) evaluated existing performance levels and set benchmarks. 'Numbers don't lie,' says Klinsmann. 'It was important to see where we were in terms of stamina, acceleration, etc. The best footballer will struggle if he can only perform at his best for seventy or seventy-five minutes. That's why I made sure after the [1-1] draw in the Brazil game to stress that we could keep up for fifty-five minutes only, that we needed to get to the point where we could do well for the whole ninety minutes.'

Verstegen brought with him a ton of strange instruments of torture, like heavy sledges that players had to drag behind them while running. *Bild* ran pictures of the national team walking in crouched lines, wearing plastic bands around their ankles, legs spread apart – reminiscent of saddlesore cowboys after too much time on horseback. It looked funny, playground funny like 'Gummitwist' (French skipping), sniggered the tabloid.

The joke had some dark, chauvinistic undertones. Taking a lead from Dutch, Italians, maybe even French experts, men from proper footballing countries that had overtaken Germany, might have been acceptable. But surely not Americans? What did they know about football? Hiring these guys was an insult to German football culture and know-how.

Bierhoff recalls meeting with league representatives, wise old men who'd been in charge of clubs for decades. 'We sat there, told them about our ideas and they shouted back at us: "You and your fitness nonsense will be the end of German football." It was one of the lessons I had to learn very early. You can put on the best presentation of your ideas possible, with totally convincing arguments, like in the movies, where everyone listens intently and then says: "Yes, you go for it, man!" I did all that at the beginning and found that didn't work at all. The emotional factor is so strong, at least in our field, that you can't disregard it. You have to get people on board emotionally, not through facts.'

Bild columnist Paul Breitner wrote that 'the Americans might have worked successfully in American football, baseball or basketball but these US sports have as much to do with our football as the Pope [has] with the pill'. Note the possessive 'our' before 'football'.

*

On the pitch, results were encouraging. After the credible draw with the *Seleção* (Brazil) in Berlin, Germany beat Iran 2-0 in Tehran and Cameroon 3-0 in Leipzig. The first game of a tour to Asia was also won convincingly. 'Something great is coming together here,' Klinsmann said in the wake of the 3-0 win over Japan in Yokohama in December. His sixth game brought the first defeat – 3-1 v South Korea – but the year ended on a happy note, with a 5-1 win in Thailand.

And yet, broader support for his agenda was not forthcoming. Perhaps the timing was bad. The government of Social Democratic Chancellor Gerhard Schröder, who had taken over in 1998 after eighteen years of conservatism under Helmut Kohl, was on its last legs. Schröder had reformed the benefits system and employment regulations, liberalised the antiquated citizenship law to make it easier for foreigners to integrate. Schröder and Klinsmann had travelled the world together to win votes for the 2006 World Cup at the turn of the century, and the Swabian had told the football-friendly politician that the tournament would offer the chance 'to reposition Germany as a brand' on the international stage. By summer 2005, however, the country had had enough of Schröder's modernisation. Angela Merkel, a conservative, was about to win back the Bundestag in the general election that autumn.

Süddeutsche asked Klinsmann how far he'd come in his attempts to take 'the whole shop apart' a year before the World Cup. His answers sounded wary. 'We have to question all rituals and habits, not just in football. That's nothing to be afraid of. Reform is not a process that happens in episodes. Reform has to become a permanent state. Not just before the Word Cup, but after it as well.' Germans, he added, found that difficult to accept because they believed processes to be dependent on leaders. 'In reality, that assumption is one of the main reasons for the problems. The aim has to be to construct a structure that works independently of [leaders]. Otherwise, egos, vanities and jockeying for positions take priority again.'

A third place in the Confederations Cup, the test run for the World Cup, saw an outbreak of mild euphoria at last. His young, new Germany played with pace and panache, and in Bastian Schweinsteiger and Lukas Podolski it sported a couple of carefree daredevils who were feted as Germany's first football boy band. At the back, though, untested teenagers like Robert Huth from Chelsea and Per Mertesacker (Hannover 96), struggled to cope with a risky, gung-ho strategy that sometimes veered towards reckless abandon.

His 4-4-2-Germany played a cavalier, one-way style, not unlike the one that Klinsmann had enjoyed with Spurs in the Premier League ten years before. Every opportunity was used to attack in numbers. Conversely, every loss of possession was an invitation for the opponent to overrun a 'high' defence positioned without much protection near the halfway line. The public found the ensuing spectacle exhilarating and worrying in equal measure. Half a decade after the terrorist attacks of 9/11 had dampened the advent of '*Spaßkultur*' (fun culture), the celebration of all things young and pop in opposition to dour, unstylishness and political conservatism in Germany, his team were putting the fun back in football.

Beckenbauer declared that 'no one was in a position to criticise Jürgen Klinsmann' – in his *Bild* column, no less. But as was so often the case, *der Kaiser* didn't take long to contradict himself, to condemn the rotation in goal and intervene on behalf of Bayern keeper Kahn, who was losing ground to his Arsenal-based rival. 'Klinsmann is shirking a decision,' Beckenbauer said after the 2-0 defeat in Slovakia in September. 'It drives me crazy to see the best keeper in the world playing golf while there's an international game going on. How are the defence supposed to get used to a keeper?'

Murmurs of discontent reached a crescendo in March 2006, three months before the start of the World Cup, as the *Nationalmannschaft* lost a friendly in Florence 4-1 to arch-rivals Italy. *FAZ*'s take on the unmitigated disaster – 'Germany shrinks into a football minnow, they're a picture of sorrow' – was one of the more measured verdicts. The performance against Marcello Lippi's eventual world champions was so frighteningly inept that pundit Stefan Effenberg, formerly of Bayern and Germany, felt that Klinsmann should resign and let Ottmar Hitzfeld handle the World Cup: 'That would bring peace and stability into the squad.' 'Klinsmann, who has already shown a streak of egomania as a player . . . is a dreamer, a loner who is more of a guru than a strategist,' wrote *Focus* magazine. 'He bullies experienced pros out of the squad and unsettles the young ones . . . He could have sought the help of experienced Bundesliga coaches but wanted to do everything by himself. A novice and a know-it-all – a dangerous combination.'

Paul Breitner pleaded for a full-scale tactical counter-revolution and the reintroduction of a sweeper for the group games in June. 'The closer it gets to the World Cup, the greater the chaos in the national team,' Matthäus sniped. *Bild* went for the kill, accusing 'Grinsi-Klinsi' (from '*grinsen*', to grin) of smiling haughtily while he wreaked havoc on German World Cup dreams. His choice of non-traditional red for the away shirts, a colour that was supposed to represent aggression and passion, was derided as a superficial gimmick. A few overeager members of the Bundestag even threatened to haul him in front of a parliamentary committee hearing.

Klinsmann's long-distance commuting – he was still living in California and only flew in for the games – fanned the flames further. Two days after the Italy defeat, he flew home again, leaving behind an enraged Beckenbauer. 'It's a question of good manners,' thundered the head of the World Cup organising committee, as Klinsmann skipped a workshop of coaches from participating nations in Düsseldorf, 'we have to sweep up the broken glass on our own.' The quip resonated. Beckenbauer had grown up in the Munich working-class district of Giesing, dubbed 'the broken-glass quarter' for its many bombed-out houses from the Second World War. It was a 'disgrace' that the manager was 'having a good time in the Californian sun' while the football nation were smarting, *Bild* barked. 'It would be best if he stayed there.'

Klinsmann looks back at his darkest hour with a wry smile. 'The tension was real. We knew what was going on in the background. There were people who wanted to take the whole thing down. But this emotional debate also showed the relevance of this topic, how much people cared in Germany. Everybody feels that the national team is their team. That's actually very positive, if you think about it. Without that sense of ownership, I don't think we could have ridden this wave of euphoria and seen the team play the sort of football that people wanted to see.' Should he have spent more time in Germany, though, to deprive his critics of their most obvious line of attack? 'No. It was really important for me that I could always fly back home [in between games], that I didn't sit in an office in Frankfurt, caught up in little, irrelevant things like who's in charge of the U18s or U19s,' says Klinsmann. 'The view from the outside, the distance, enabled me to make continuous adjustments with minimal interference.'

'Plane back home today?' *Bild* asked gleefully ahead of the game against USA in Dortmund three weeks later. Germany won 4-1 against a side that didn't have their best players as the game hadn't taken place on an official FIFA date. Klinsmann and *Bild* called a truce. His work was essentially over by the time the World Cup began, he says modestly. 'The players understood that they now had to push through with this process, that they had to believe in it and in themselves, in order to write their own piece of history.' And history they did write: as the most popular losers the country had ever seen.

SECOND-GAME ITCH

'Was it hell or fun for you today, Mr Löw?'
'It was both.'

Before the advent of the dark ages of 1998–2004, Germany were known as a '*Turniermannschaft*', a tournament team. Successive *DFB* outfits had earned this honorary title through sheer staying power, peaking at the business end to eliminate fancy fairweather sides after (mostly) stodgy opening performances. Völler's 2002 runners-up, so reliant on the 'three K' principles of 'Kahn, *Kampf* and *Kopfball*' (Kahn, fight and headers), as TV commentator Marcel Reif put it, had played that same old, half-forgotten tune, faithfully like a tribute band, only hitting the wrong final note.

The *Nationalmannschaften* of Klinsmann and Löw, on the other hand, were grooving to an entirely different beat. They tended to start quickly, play enthralling, dream-like stuff early on, then falter meekly within touching distance of a trophy.

At the 2006 World Cup, Euro 2008 and the World Cup in South Africa, supporters forgave the team for not living up to the standards of their forbears because their pleasingly unGermanic football had been a reward in itself. By Euro 2012, however, the sheer amount of brilliant players at Löw's disposal had made his side's serial choking much harder to accept. Per Mertesacker, now playing in the Premier League with Arsenal, warned that the Portugal result had only increased the obligation to 'see this thing through' in Brazil.

The 4-0 win in Salvador had made it five out of five in tournament openers in the post Völler-era. 'Another rocket launch,' cheered *Süddeutsche*. 'This focused, technically strong success conveys more than a good feeling.' Inside Campo Bahia, Germany's remote base camp on the Costa do Descobrimento, the 'coast of discovery', the feeling was more than good, too. Mats Hummels was doubtful with a hamstring injury but nobody seemed overly concerned. Ghana, the next opponent in Fortaleza, were not considered quite the same team as in 2010, when the Black Stars had nearly dumped Löw's side out of the group stages and gone on to reach the quarter-finals. Reports circulated about a split in their camp; Kevin-Prince Boateng, the flamboyant half-brother of Germany defender Jérôme, was said to have been unhappy about being left out of their 2-1 defeat against the USA in Natal.

Bierhoff detected signs of overconfidence. 'Everyone was happy, and one or two players asked me "What's next?", "How does it work if we get to the final?"' says the general manager. 'Now you know why the Ghana game went the way it did.' Löw's message ('If you let up at this World Cup, you lose. Ghana will push us all the way') wasn't getting through to everyone, in spite of the team's recent experiences. In 2008 and 2010, rocket launch starts had seen the DFB eleven crash straight back down to earth in the next games, with defeats against Croatia and Serbia, respectively. (The 1-2 defeat against Slaven Bilić's team in Klagenfurt at Euro 2008 had marked a watershed for Löw: he ditched the 4-4-2 formation, a system that had become staid and easy to defend against, for a more fluid 4-2-3-1.)

'The second game has often been tough and afterwards, people were asking "Where's your plan B?"' says Bierhoff. Khedira, a man with a finely-tuned sense for dressing-room moods, too, advised caution: 'We don't want a final in the third game [against the USA].'

The Real Madrid midfielder had been one of the biggest winners of the Portugal game, providing support in front of both boxes on the pitch with tireless running for ninety minutes. Löw's pre-tournament trust in him had been validated.

Khedira was not really a holding midfielder; Löw didn't believe in purely destructive central players, much to the chagrin of his critics. The former Stuttgart player brought some vertical, plain old drive to a team who had learned to let the ball do most of the running, but he wasn't one of these players who strutted all over the pitch to get as many touches as possible. His movement followed fixed, meticulous patterns of 'active ball-winning', as Löw called it, an aggressive, high-pressing game that he had learned under VfB Stuttgart youth coach Thomas Tuchel, a disciple of tactical innovator Ralf Rangnick. Stuttgart won the youth championship that year, and Khedira led a Germany U21 team with Mesut Özil, Manuel Neuer and Mats Hummels in their ranks to a win at the European Championship in 2009. Khedira was the first leading Germany international who had been systematically versed in the art of this full-throttle back and forth football. Löw favoured a more measured approach but Khedira was his perfect man in the middle, able to reconcile the more possession-orientated game of the Bayern camp with Dortmund's high-tempo pressing style.

A *Der Spiegel* interview from 2011 described the then twenty-three-year-old as 'the model pupil of modern football, in all fields': technically proficient, well-rounded, selfless, willing to stretch his legs for the cause, capable of integrating into a group without becoming a mere also-ran. 'There are many players who have fantastic footballing ability but aren't mature enough to find their way inside a team structure,' he said.

At the 2010 World Cup, he'd been thrust into a central role in the absence of the injured Michael Ballack. Thomas Müller and Mesut Özil were the attacking players who caught the eye with their goals in South Africa, but Khedira was the heart and soul of the youngest German post-war World Cup squad as well as the face of the multicultural new Germany, in both senses of the world. Eleven of the twenty-three players of that team had a background of immigration.

'Of course we noticed that it's something new to have German national players with Turkish, Ghanaian, Nigerian or Tunisian roots, but for our generation it's very normal,' Khedira said. 'I have been playing [with these players] as long ago as the U15s. We have some players called Khedira and some called Müller. We don't know any differently.' Integration was the new story, Khedira was its poster boy. He had decided as a small boy to speak only German, like his Turkish and German friends. No more Arabic. (He employed a business consultancy firm to teach him Spanish using hypnosis, in order to arrive fully prepared at his new club Real Madrid after South Africa, only to find that most players were speaking English on the pitch.)

A key moment in his career was turning up late for the team bus as a teenager and being left stranded. He's been punctual ever since, a fully-paid up defender of the Swabian work ethic. 'You'll never get beyond a certain level as a professional athlete if you're sloppy,' he said. When a serious knee injury at eighteen threatened his career, he read books about leaders in business and politics in order to find the secret of inner strength. 'Successful people have similar strategies. Success always starts in the head.'

But so did defeats. Germany turned up at the Estádio Castelão in Brazil's hot, humid north-west with an unchanged formation. Reigning World Cup champions Spain were already eliminated after a 2-0 defeat by Chile, and so were England, courtesy of Luis Suárez's double in São Paulo two days previously. Italy, too, Germany's nemesis, stared an early exit in the face. All Löw's team had to do now was to repeat their almost perfect performance from the Portugal game – the line-up and tactics had worked out so well – to render the last match against former national manager Jürgen Klinsmann's USA a dead rubber and progress early.

Ghana had other ideas, however. They exposed Germany's attitude as presumptuous in no time. Philipp Lahm, the German captain, still as youthful looking as he was in his first World Cup game in 2006 as a twenty-two-year-old, suddenly looked his age within the space of five minutes. The muggy conditions, bobbly pitch and thirty-degree temperatures slowed Germany down from the kick-off. Ghana coach Kwesi Appiah's smart game plan made sure that they didn't pick up any significant pace in the first half, either. The Ghanians attacked the ball as soon as Germany crossed the halfway line, which forced Löw's team to play the ball out wide. That's where Appiah wanted it to be. He had spotted the biggest weakness of Löw's new back four, made up exclusively of centre-backs: they were neither comfortable nor quick enough to support the attacks. Jérôme Boateng on the right and right-footed Benedikt Höwedes on the left mostly passed the ball back again, at which point Germany's centre-backs were back to square one and often forced to play the sort of long balls that Löw abhorred. His team never truly settled, and a Ghana side seemingly less affected by the weather threatened Manuel Neuer's goal a couple of times by attacking from wide areas.

'*Ochsenspieß*', skewer of oxes, *Bild* called the row of four central defenders. This surprisingly negative option was seen as evidence of Löw's new-found pragmatism and determination to win at all cost at this World Cup but he felt he had no other choice but to play without any recognised full-backs at this stage. Lahm, the right-back and the best full-back on either side of the last decade, was needed in midfield in place of Schweinsteiger. Dortmund left-back Marcel Schmelzer hadn't made the trip due to injury and Löw didn't trust Schmelzer's club colleagues Erik Durm and Kevin Großkreutz either. The former was too inexperienced, with only one cap, the latter too . . . well, too Kevin Großkreutz, maybe.

*

The German front three of Müller, Mario Götze and Arsenal's Mesut Özil, who had been somewhat demoted from central playmaker to makeshift right winger by Löw, did carve out chances through some creative positional changes but they were isolated. Germany were reluctant to commit too many men forward, well aware of the heat and the Black Stars' pacy attackers. 'The idea was to play a patient game,' says Lahm, but the upshot was the DFB eleven resembling one of those 'broken' sides that unwittingly demonstrate the qualitative difference between top-level club football and international teams. There was attack and defence, and not much in between.

The last remnants of tactical cohesion melted away altogether after the break. Boateng, the fastest of the four 'oxes', had come off at half-time with a hamstring strain. Shkodran Mustafi was his replacement. Shkodran who?

'How do we pronounce your name?' was one of the first questions the defender had been asked by German journalists when Löw had called him up for the first time, for a friendly against Chile in March. Mustafi had been as surprised as his interlocutors to be sitting on the podium. 'I didn't even know that they were watching me,' the Hessian-born son of Albanian immigrants admitted with a shrug. Mustafi had played alongside Mario Götze in the German U19s but a move to Everton from Hamburger SV's youth team and subsequent switch to Sampdoria had taken him completely off the radar. Italian football was not regularly shown in Germany. 'I'm a bit of a favourite with the fans in Genoa, but in Germany, I'm Mr Nobody,' he laughed.

Mustafi had planned to go on holiday to Spain with some friends and watch the tournament there; he hadn't made it into Löw's World Cup squad. But late on 6 June he received a call. Would he mind coming to Frankfurt to join up with the team, now that the injured Marco Reus could not make it? The next day, he was on a ferry crossing the João de Tiba river for the fishing village of Santo André, where Germany were based. 'I stood next to Bastian Schweinsteiger and thought: That's crazy. It's really Schweini!'

The fantastic experience became more fantastic still. Mustafi was following Germany v Portugal in Salvador's Fonte Nova Arena from a seat very close to the action, until somebody politely asked him to vacate it on seventy-three minutes. He got up, stepped on to the pitch and calmly played as right-back for Germany, against Cristiano Ronaldo. Ten-men Portugal had mostly given up the ghost by then but their star player was still desperate for a World Cup goal, shooting frequently – and tamely – from impossible angles.

The scene was reminiscent of one of those dreams that many football fans are familiar with: your favourite team suddenly calling on you – yes, YOU – in their hour of need. But with a twist. Mustafi was actually there, in flesh and blood. 'I have to digest and understand this first,' he said in the mixed zone afterwards, clearly bemused by the circumstances of his first competitive international.

Unfortunately for Mr Nobody, he was nowhere to be found in the box when Ghana's Andrew Ayew headed in a cross from Sulley Muntari for the fifty-third-minute equaliser (1-1). Mario Götze had given Germany the lead only two minutes earlier, by heading the ball on to his knee and past keeper Fatau Dauda from a Müller cross. Ghana took the lead on the hour mark, capitalising on a misplaced Lahm pass in midfield. Asamoah Gyan was released by a precision pass from Muntari and shot powerfully past Neuer into the far corner.

Mustafi might have been living the dream personally, but his team found itself in the middle of a nightmare that some had seen coming. How many times had Löw and Bierhoff warned against the dangers of falling behind in the sub-tropical conditions in Brazil? Yet here they were, chasing the game against a physically superior side who thrived on counter-attacks. Spaces were opening up all over the pitch like sink holes, threatening to swallow up the men in white.

Both teams kept flooding forward in cavalier style, undeterred by their own fallibility. With each passing minute, the duel degenerated into an uncoordinated punch-up. Gone was the control of territory and the ball; the game was now controlling them. Germany and their opponents were being thrown around, side to side, in a maelstrom of innumerable scoring opportunities.

We never remember the things that didn't happen, only those that did. That's one of the reasons why defenders who prevent dangerous situations arising through clever positioning are undervalued. That's also the reason why the match's pivotal moment, a few seconds that could have blown Germany's whole World Cup off course, didn't feature in FIFA's official highlights reel. Substitute Jordan Ayew was bearing down on Neuer's goal on the left, supported by two more Ghanians against only two Germans. Ayew made the wrong choice, going it alone to shoot tamely at Neuer instead of picking out a pass that would have killed the game and consigned Löw's men to yet another second-game defeat.

But his side survived and rallied once more following the substitution of Khedira and Götze for Schweinsteiger and Klose with twenty minutes to go. Seconds later, Benedikt Höwedes headed a corner from Toni Kroos towards the far post. Klose stretched out a leg to make it 2-2. The veteran from Lazio had, at thirty-six, equalled the World Cup record of Ronaldo, the Brazilian forward, with his fifteenth goal.

Klose had vowed to keep his feet on the ground but the historic moment got the better of him. 'I didn't want to do it, it took hold of me,' he said sheepishly after the final whistle at the Castelão. 'I went for it. And you could see I'm out of practice.' Truth be told, his somersault wasn't that badly executed, save for a slight wobble on landing. The 'Klose salto' used to be his trademark celebration but he had stopped doing it a while ago, wary that his body could do without the extra strain of aerial acrobatics. Was he actually truly annoyed with himself for getting marked down for presentation? Klose's deadpan delivery made it impossible to say.

'I had the right nose, it was a nice goal, I was happy it was the equaliser, you write the rest,' he added, as if the strike's mundane nature precluded the mentioning of any wider repercussions. It took much prompting from reporters and TV interviewers in Fortaleza before Klose would elaborate on his achievement. His poacher's goal hadn't just equalled Ronaldo's record but broken that of national icon Gerd Müller (fourteen goals in World Cup finals), too. 'The record was intriguing, it was an itch I wanted to scratch. Twenty World Cup games, fifteen goals, not bad,' he shrugged. Ronaldo, who had asked Brazilian supporters in Fortaleza to 'use their energy against Klose and Germany' ten days earlier, congratulated him via Twitter. '*Willkommen im klub*,' the thirty-seven-year-old wrote – almost perfect German for 'Welcome to the club.'

Klose had already broken Müller's all-time record of sixty-eight international goals for Germany in the 6-1 friendly against Armenia a week before the trip to Brazil. Of course he was proud, but he rejected in no uncertain terms the idea that he had now somehow overtaken *der Bomber*. 'It's an absolute joke to compare me with Gerd Müller,' he said. 'No one compares to him. No one.' The Bayern Munich striker had scored his sixty-eight goals in only sixty-two internationals, whereas Klose had needed more than twice as many matches, 132, to get to the same tally. 'I would never mention myself in the same breath as Gerd Müller,' he protested.

He was happier to describe himself as a 'tough dog' in an interview with *Süddeutsche* earlier that year. 'I have always looked after my body, I'm fit and I'm fast,' Klose said. He revealed that he was the quickest player in the Lazio squad ('it's not so difficult,' he joked) and still 'among the top three' in Löw's team.

The son of Polish parents – his father, Josef, a former professional with AJ Auxerre in France, had managed to move his family from the Communist country to the Rhineland-Palatinate village of Kusel in 1985 because he could prove German ethnicity – Klose was a late bloomer. He grew up without ever receiving a specialist footballing

education, and, at nineteen, he was still playing for SG Blaubach-
Diedelkopf in the seventh division. Three years later, he made his
debut in the Bundesliga for Otto Rehhagel's 1. FC Kaiserslautern
at the age of twenty-two. An acute shortage of strikers won him a
national team squad place for Japan/South Korea, where he scored a
hat-trick (all headers) in the 8-0 win over Saudia Arabia.

'His career would have been so much bigger if he'd been able to
play with the players he's playing with now,' said Bierhoff, with brutal,
self-deprecating honesty. The general manager had been one of Klose's
team-mates at the 2002 World Cup, and the target of abuse from the
former Germany head coach five years later. Bierhoff had had the
temerity to suggest that German club players should be 'challenged
intelligently' when it came to training sessions and theoretical know-
how. Bayer Leverkusen sporting director Völler took great offence at
his erstwhile player's intervention. It got personal. 'I can't listen to it any
more,' Rudi Völler ranted. '[Germany's] so-called playing philosophy
is first and foremost a function of the good youth development by the
clubs. An appropriate philosophy for players like Bierhoff has yet to be
invented. A Brazilian philosophy with Maltese feet, that's impossible.'

Maltese feet? Bierhoff was born in Karlsruhe, not Valletta. Völler
was trying to land a blow below the belt: Bierhoff was never the most
technically proficient of players. Carsten Jancker was often preferred
to the AC Milan man in the national team, which said it all, really.
There was also a suggestion that, by 2007, Völler had become a little
miffed that his achievements – taking a below-average side to the
World Cup final in 2002 – were increasingly being overlooked amidst
the admiration for Löw's younger, much more attractive side.

The German word for 'draw' is '*Unentschieden*', undecided, and that is
exactly what the view of the national team was after referee Sandro
Ricci had brought the stirring match in Fortaleza to a close. They could
have gone on to win it after Klose's goal; they could have gone on to
lose it. Neither side had been able to land the final blow. 'It was an

incredibly exciting game, pure drama and tension,' Löw said, a little breathlessly. The game had rushed by at breakneck speed, like an art house horror film: moments of danger and scenes of relief followed fast on each other without rhyme or reason. And the ending was pretty indeterminate.

The coach took pride in his side's character, their strong mental and physical response in a very tough spot. That was one way of looking at it. 'We were strong, no doubt,' said Toni Kroos, the midfielder who was never short on confidence. 'The team understand that they have to "bite" when things don't go according to plan,' said assistant manager Hansi Flick. It was meant as a compliment. Many people thought the side didn't come with an 'epic battle' mode included. 'It was a good test for us today,' Mertesacker thought.

Not everybody had passed that exam with flying colours. Mustafi had been too slow to react when Ayew scored, Khedira's engine had stalled somewhat in the heat and Lahm's mislaid pass for the second Ghana goal left everyone thoroughly perplexed. The captain was nothing if not almost freakishly dependable. 'Usually, he makes very few mistakes but today it happened a couple of times,' said Löw forgivingly. 'These things happen,' Lahm said coolly, 'it's not generally a problem [with our game].'

But what felt like a mere accident for Lahm ('Five days ago, everything was good. Sometimes things go better, sometimes worse') looked like a frightful apparition to others. The 'frenzied midfield chaos' (*Frankfurter Allgemeine Zeitung*) raised again the spectre of that suicidal 4-4 draw with Sweden in October 2012, when Germany's midfield had lost its way just as badly from one minute to the next. Opponents with more quality and better decision-making would have surely ripped them apart in the Castelão.

'It was frantic harakiri football,' admitted Kroos of that earlier Sweden match. 'The game just went that way, it was an open clash. That wasn't planned,' Löw agreed, philosophically. His free-flowing passing football could have done with a bit of steel, a specialist defensive midfielder, adept at fighting the side's 'naive tendencies for open spaces', as Christof Kneer wrote in *Süddeutsche Zeitung* after the Sweden game.

'This wouldn't have happened with a Bender,' Schweinsteiger had reportedly exclaimed in Berlin's Olympic Stadium dressing room that night. The twins, Lars (Leverkusen) and Sven (Dortmund) were the closest approximation of destroyers who could also play a bit. They had missed the 4-4 draw. Sadly, injuries had kept them out of the World Cup squad as well.

The Ghana mayhem confirmed what many had felt: Germany had a half-fit Schweinsteiger, a three-quarter-fit Khedira and the reconfigured full-back Lahm (courtesy of Pep Guardiola) in the middle but not one true '*Sechser*' (player in the number six position), a natural water-carrier, eating up space, in the starting line-up. In Löw's reign, Deutschland, the team of holding midfielders, had metamorphosed into an '*Achterland*', as Kneer put it, a country full of 'eights', deep playmakers and box-to-box experts.

Lahm emphatically disagrees. 'I can understand the criticism of the Sweden game – you can't draw 4-4 when you're 4-0 up. But we were sensational in the first half. The problem later on wasn't us playing too pretty or trying to find nice, technical solutions in the middle of a storm. The problem was half the team going into hiding when it was 4-1 and then 4-2. Nobody wanted the ball any more. We were hoofing long balls forward, they came straight back. It wasn't about being too technical. We weren't technical enough because everybody had started shitting themselves.'

In that respect, the draw in Fortaleza did mark an improvement. Germany had teetered on the brink of defeat but at least kept faith with their own game going forward. Blown away without the ball, they had managed to rediscover their shape in possession. 'The volatility was hard to believe,' says Bierhoff. Later in the tournament, he came to understand that 'other experienced sides' were prone to the same sort of lapses in Brazil, however.

Another positive to take back to Campo Bahia – the point aside – was Löw's ability to influence the game with substitutions. The depth in the squad was vital. And yet, half a good game would certainly not be enough to get to the Maracanã for the final.

'Tactically, we weren't good,' said Khedira in the stadium's mixed zone. 'Our positioning was wrong, we didn't have the numbers where it mattered,' said Lahm. Hummels, intriguingly, pursued a different line. 'Our problems were personal in nature, not tactical,' the Dortmund defender said. Was he talking about Khedira? Or Mustafi? Maybe even Lahm? The captain's less then perfect performance in midfield ensured that he'd remain the main debating point ahead of the meeting with the USA in Recife. Germany missed the chance to qualify automatically, but a point against Klinsmann's team would suffice. 'The result doesn't really change much for us,' Klose said. 'We would have wanted to win the last game against the US anyway. Now we'll have more pressure. But the team knows pressure. They're used to it.'

GERMANY, A SUMMER'S TALE,
NARRATED BY THOMAS HITZLSPERGER

I had hoped to be involved in Euro 2004. I had been playing with Germany's U21s at the time, and the coaches had promised that two of us would join up with the seniors. But they picked Bastian Schweinsteiger and Lukas Podolski.

Euro 2000 was a semi-disaster. No: a total disaster. World Cup 2002, you thought: no, everything's okay, actually. But then 2004 brought confirmation that we couldn't simply go on. Something had to happen, right now. Then Jürgen Klinsmann came in, with new ideas and these Americans in tow. I saw the pictures of the Germany players with those weird plastic bands around their knees, there was this huge media debate about him not living in Germany, and all the emphasis was on fitness. Would that work? It was a huge change at the German FA, a revolution. I followed it from a distance, playing for Aston Villa, I thought: I want to be part of that.

I was disappointed that Schweini and Poldi had made it to Portugal in 2004 instead of me but people had talked about them a lot. They said the future belonged to them. Naturally, it was my aim to make it as well. I hoped that Klinsmann might appreciate what I could do, considering that I had gone abroad at a very young age, at eighteen, He had also played abroad and must have known how difficult it was to make it in England. Maybe I had that going for me.

I didn't get the call-up for the first two games, against Austria and Brazil. But then he phoned me. 'You've done well in England, you deserve to get an invitation, come to the game against Iran.' I had been warned by my agent that the call might come but I was still in shock. I opened a bottle of red wine to celebrate. It felt unreal. As a little boy, you dream about playing for Germany, suddenly you're there. Per Mertesacker was also called up for the first time for that game.

We met up in the hotel in Munich and Oliver Kahn was sitting on a table, next to Michael Ballack. I was a bundle of nerves. I was eating some soup and my hand was shaking. I wasn't sure they even knew who I was. I was playing abroad. I was hoping they knew me. Did they? But they were all super-nice. They said hi and that I wouldn't have any problems. 'Nice that you're here. How's the Premier League? I saw you on the *La Ola* [highlights] show!' I was made to feel welcome. Thank God I knew some of the younger players like Philipp Lahm, Kevin Kuranyi, Andreas Hinkel . . . So I had people to talk to. It felt very easy to integrate.

Then you take your first training and you run next to Oliver Kahn. Oliver Kahn! I was in awe of him, he was a superstar. Training was very well structured. It was clear from the outset that Jogi was in charge of all the tactical stuff. Jürgen kept saying 'We have to continue improving, our goal is 2006, that's when we will peak.'

That message was being repeated all the time. It all felt very professional. The team were relaxed off the pitch but they never let themselves go. As soon as the work started, the focus was there. The established players all admitted it was a new regime for them, too, which it made it easier for me to shake off my nerves. In any case, we didn't have much time because of the long trip to Tehran.

The sessions mostly consisted of short passing games. We had to keep the ball on the ground. Jogi would say it, incessantly: 'I don't want any high and long balls. It's much easier to do something with the ball if you keep it on the ground.' I knew that type of instructions from club football. In pre-season, coaches would bark at you, but, after a while, bad habits would always creep back into the game, and eventually, they just got tired of correcting you and let it go. With Germany, though, the training games would be stopped every time someone played a long ball. Every single time. There were clear instructions to build from the back, through the two centre-backs and midfield, and then to move out as a team. Jogi didn't stand for it if somebody didn't follow that plan. That kind of rigour was new to me. I had never experienced it before. Eventually, playing that way becomes second nature to you.

At some stage, we started to concentrate on the attacking game. Every half-decent team had learned to defend by then, they knew how to shift a back four across the pitch. But what about having a plan going forward? We were split in two. Jogi worked with the defenders – I was part of those as a holding midfielder – and Jürgen took the attackers. One thing I hadn't seen before was the systematic pressing. We were constantly working on keeping small distances between strikers and midfielders, to move together, so that we could attack the ball when there was a bad pass from one of the defenders. That needed a command structure, as well; someone who shouts out the order to press. They showed us the stats: teams were most susceptible straight after losing the ball. We concentrated on those moments of transition. It was imperative that we all moved up as a unit, it was just as important as all of us coming back to defend. Those drills were being repeated again and again. That tenacity was unique. There was a plan in place, and it was being followed, independent of results. After matches, we would analyse collective and individual mistakes in great detail. But the plan never changed.

Club football, as I experienced it, was very different. If you lost a game because you hadn't scored enough goals, there would be crossing and shooting practice the next day in training. At first, with a couple of defenders, then, after they'd headed everything clear, the strikers would be left alone to find the net and build up some confidence.

You didn't follow some overriding strategy. You were always trying to resolve problems that had turned up a couple of days before.

We needed to be very fit to play such a demanding up-and-down game. Mark Verstegen and his guys from Athletes' Performance told us that acceleration comes from the biggest and strongest muscle, the buttocks. We learned how to run differently, to be faster and more powerful. There were also many exercises for core stability. I knew some of these things from England; they were a bit ahead of Germany at the time. We were given individual training programmes that we had to follow back home with the clubs. Our coaches tried to talk to the club managers; some agreed, some didn't because they felt that it wasn't the German FA's business. I did some additional sprinting exercises and weights but it was hard to combine that with regular sessions at Villa. Other players had problems as well, their club coaches were offended by the unspoken suggestion that they weren't training properly.

I had first experienced video analysis at Villa. But Urs Siegenthaler, the man in charge of scouting and analysis, was something else. I had never seen a guy like that, he was a complete tactics freak. He would fly to Venezuela to see a league game there. He travelled to those countries to find out what made them tick off the pitch, what kind of mentality they had. He spoke to the cab drivers on the way to the stadium, he spoke to everyone. That kind of research played a big part in the World Cup. I remember he was saying that the Ecuadorians were very hard workers, strong athletes, but that they were prone to losing their heads. They had a tendency to become impatient and didn't react well to pressure. So you had to keep them busy all the time.

This guy was breathing football. I found that fascinating, inspirational. Löw was the same, and that's why they got along so well. At the time, you couldn't really see Löw in his track suit and the whistle in his mouth becoming a national manager, you need a bit more than that. (He would grow into the role after taking over.) It was a good way in for him, however – as Klinsmann's tactics guru who didn't really have to deal with the press. He knew his stuff, that much was obvious. I'd say he was best football coach I've ever had. Him and Siegenthaler had very clear ideas and they were adamant that any team following them would become a better, more successful unit. It was true. And even after big defeats, they didn't change. They just kept trying to make it right, to look at the best teams in the world and see why and how they were ahead of us.

But there were some players in the team who were less interested in looking that deeply into things. They wanted to be left alone. They were used to having a good time going away with the national team. Some adjusted to the change, some of the established guys also resisted it, because they were used to doing it differently before. Under Klinsmann, you were more or less forced to take part in the thinking process.

We flew to Iran. It wasn't an ordinary trip. We had been given brochures with information about the country: its size, the political situation, religion. Oliver Bierhoff came over for a chat and also said: 'Everything will go well for you.'

There were many Germany fans there, people knew who we were. We drove to the hotel in Tehran, you see enormous roundabouts but they don't have any fixed lanes, so people drive in all different directions. Traffic chaos. A completely different world.

There were 100,000 people in the ground. They were playing loud techno music. We had heard that people were arriving six, seven hours before kick-off to take their places, and that women – who weren't officially allowed to attend – would sneak in. My first international. Madness.

I came on fifteen minutes before the end. We were winning 2-0. The crowd were still screaming. It was a memorable occasion.

I was invited for the next game against Cameroon in Leipzig. I came on again, and had a hand in a goal, with a free-kick. The coaches liked me. I was an excellent trainer, I always went full throttle, that's how I was as a player. They noticed that. They wanted guys like me to be around.

Unfortunately, Klinsi had this idea that I should play as a left-back. I could pass the ball well, I could cross it, but I wasn't a defender. I had to play a friendly against Argentina, Javier Saviola was my opponent. That was one of the better games. But in the long run, you can't disguise your weaknesses at that level. I got a lot of criticism. People weren't saying that I should play in midfield, in my natural role, they said I shouldn't be playing at all because I couldn't defend.

But Klinsi didn't care about that, he was very stubborn. I think he saw that I fitted in well with the group, that I was motivating others. That was more important to him than my shortcomings as a full-back. He had enough midfielders. I was happy to be there but after a while it got difficult. I didn't play well. But, I thought, I can't tell him that I didn't want to play in that role any more. I wasn't in any position to make such demands. I was hoping that I'd eventually get better at defending. Philipp Lahm, our regular guy on the left in defence, was out with a cruciate ligament injury for a while. That presented an opportunity.

At the Confederations Cup in 2005, I played all group games as a defender but I was out for the semi-final against Brazil and the third-place play-off against Mexico. Should I say something to the manager? I didn't do it. I was still getting regular call-ups, and I was doing well in training. The Confed Cup showed everyone that we could play good football, there was excitement in the air, but our problems in defence made people jittery, too. The horrors of 2004 were still fresh in people's minds. No one really knew what to make of it all.

Then there was that awful friendly in Slovakia in September. We lost 2-0, and I had a bad time in defence, again. Time was running out for me, there weren't many games left to show what I could do, in my natural position. I was bricking it at this stage, really afraid that I wouldn't make the World Cup squad. I missed the low point of those two years, the 4-1 defeat by Italy in March 2006, maybe that was lucky for me. But all of German football was in uproar and it looked as if Klinsmann might get fired any second.

I was sure I'd be out when I didn't get a call-up for the last game before the squad was announced, against the USA. My last remaining chance was to do well at club level. I had moved to VfB Stuttgart from Aston Villa in the summer, but things weren't going well for me there, at the time. Manager Giovanni Trapattoni was fired, then Armin Veh came in. I decided to run myself into the ground, to be the fittest player ever, because there would be one more fitness test in the national team before the squad was announced. I had done my homework. Nobody would be better prepared.

I took part in a photo shoot for sponsors and advertising partners, so I had my own chocolate bar sticker. Congratulations. But so did twenty-nine others. That was a mere precaution on the FA's behalf, we knew that not all of us would make the final cut. Well, at least I was still in the running.

On the day of the selection, we were told to stay off our mobile phones between 10 a.m. and 12 p.m. You sit there, staring at the display, checking every couple of minutes that your reception is okay. Then his name lit up: Jürgen Klinsmann.

'So, Hitze, how are you?' 'Good, coach.' 'Pack your bags, you're in. Don't tell anyone.'

It was a surprise. I wanted to show him that it was the right decision.

Sardinia, the training camp, was tough. I found it a bit easier, because I was already in top shape, but there were many runs, long ones, short ones, sprints . . . Verstegen is a bit of a madman, you just have to go with it and allow yourself to get swept along. There were plenty of extra-curricular activities to take the edge off: bowling, go-karting, always with an element of competitiveness. I didn't win all the time – I came second in go-karts, as far as I can recall. It's important to have that competition. Winning is something you can learn. They said to us: 'You need to really believe that you will win, trying to win is not enough.'

The tension between Jens Lehmann and Oliver Kahn was quite noticeable. Kahn having to fight for his place sent a message to everyone: no one is safe here. At one of those performance tests, we had to do push-ups. Jens went first and managed, I think, fifty-two. Kahn asked how many Jens had done, then made sure he did one more, fifty-three, with one final, painfully slow effort. Pull-ups were also on the agenda. I was pretty good, others less so. One player couldn't muster a single one . . .

The team hotel during the World Cup was in the centre of town in Berlin. There was a media debate – why there? – but it turned out to be a very good decision. We had the whole place for ourselves. It was beautifully furnished, everyone had space to be alone but there were also rooms to come together in.

Philipp Lahm was doubtful for the first game in Munich. He'd been injured in a friendly against Luxembourg. Would I take his place? I was hopeful but, deep down, I wanted him to recover because he was tremendously important for us, even then. Balle – Michael Ballack – also had a problem, with his calf. The 'calf of the nation' they called it. Everyone was very worried he couldn't play. He and a few other players went to some faith healer who was dispensing 'swinging water'. It didn't work for the first game, though, 'the calf of the nation' was being obtrusive. Klinsi decided that Balle should sit out the opener against Costa Rica in Munich. That was a brave decision if you considered that quite a few people thought we might not make it out of the group.

Now it got interesting. The mood was quite positive. The training camp had been superb. We knew that we were in peak condition. We had done everything. We knew everything. We were ready. Klinsi said: 'Look what's going on in this country. Everyone's waiting, everyone's desperate to see you play.' Philipp was fit for the game, Balle wasn't. Of course that was a loss but we trusted Tim Borowski to come in and do a good job. For the opposition, it was perhaps more difficult: they could no longer concentrate on our main threat.

It was a dream. Philipp scored an early goal, the weather was great all of a sudden, the atmosphere took off. Something extraordinary was happening: 4-2, three points.

But two goals conceded – against Costa Rica. That shouldn't have happened. There were long discussions back at the team hotel in Berlin, a constructive debate. What are we doing, why are we so open at the back? You can't concede two against Costa Rica! Paulo Wanchope had scored twice. We all sat down together to talk about that. And at that point, we came together as a unit, as a team.

Analysis showed that there was too much space between midfield and defence, that had allowed them to play the through ball. After that game, everyone understood that they had to close down the guy with the ball immediately, especially after a long ball. You couldn't look to somebody else to do that for you. You had to take responsibility. Something clicked that night, as we were learning the lessons of Costa Rica. People realised that this wasn't about doing well individually at this World Cup, it wasn't about coming away with an enhanced reputation. We had to do it together if we wanted to avoid an early defeat.

In the second game, against Poland in Dortmund, we got lucky with the way the 1-0 went in, so late in the game. It was a close, tetchy affair. David Odonkor comes in. Nobody thought he would make the squad, but he had pace, that was his asset. So he goes down the touchline with a few minutes to go and he fires in the kind of cross that he had never fired in before and never fired in again after that, at the exact right moment, and Oliver Neuville slides the ball home. There was an eruption of happiness, on the pitch, on the bench, in the stands. The stadium was literally shaking. I had never heard so much noise in my life. It was one of those games that you never forget, because it was more than a game. All the negativity from the Italy friendly and everything else, the last remnants of doubt, had just disappeared, at that very second.

The emotions of that moment magnified everything, most of all us. We had improved as a team, and we did have more confidence but I'm pretty sure the whole World Cup would have gone down a very different route if that goal hadn't gone in. It could have all gone to the dogs, I think. But that goal . . . that was it. Crazy.

Ahead of the third game, against Ecuador in Berlin, we felt that the whole country was on our side. It had become bigger than football. We had already qualified for the next round as group leaders, there was nothing at stake, but we wanted to make a point and boot these guys out of the stadium.

3-0.

The stadium was shaking, again. And what was going on in the rest of the country was incredible. We were aware that we weren't this good because of our tactics. The crowds, the whole of Germany, had lifted us to another level. We had been quite worried about disappointing everyone, about going out at the group stage and now most of us thought: 'We can win the World Cup.' What's going on here? We had the basics – good positioning, we can score goals, we are fit. And the support carried us much further. The fear of failure was gone.

It became one big party. People who had never watched a football match before in their lives didn't want to miss out. The sun didn't stop shining, visiting fans from abroad had a great time, Germany discovered itself as a welcoming country, a fun place. Everything came together. 'A time to make friends' was the official motto, and that's how it really was. The summer of 2006 was Germany's Summer of Love, our generation's Woodstock.

The cars all had German flags attached to them. I had never seen that before. Patriotism was suddenly okay, cool even. For a few weeks, nothing existed apart from football. Thousands of people lined the streets to see our team bus travel from the airports to the stadium. It was like being in a strange film. You realised: there's a bigger dimension to all of this. No one could escape that feeling: how amazing is it to be a part of that? It was much better than anyone could have hoped for.

'Public viewing', one of those made-up English terms that only us Germans use, was the biggest thing. There were screens out in the open, everywhere. Friends called me: 'We've put up a screen, hundreds of people are coming, it's a shame you can't be here.' Yes, but I'm with the team. That's not bad either. 'No, no. You'll have much more fun here.' They meant it.

All you saw was niceness. I think there was some trouble in Stuttgart, at England's game versus Ecuador, when David Beckham threw up on the pitch, but that was it, one of the few exceptions. Germans travelled throughout their own country and they found a new . . . maybe not love, that's too strong, but a new affinity for their country. It was the first time since the war that people could say, 'Yes, I am happy to be here, I am proud of my country. I can fly the flag.' Before that, you were uneasy about these sentiments. The World Cup made it possible to support your team and your country and feel good about it. You were comfortable with your own identity.

That spring, some neo-Nazis had run a campaign against two of our players, Patrick Owomoyela and Gerald Asamoah. They were black. 'You are not Germany,' they said. But these idiots had no chance. Football proved them wrong, without trying too hard or going too far, to the point where support morphs into chauvinism or anything like that. It was just right. A positive celebration. Not putting anyone else down.

My own, personal World Cup story? It was difficult. I was doing so well in training, I would have definitely picked myself to play. But Asamoah came in against Ecuador, and I wasn't in the frame for the last sixteen against Sweden, either.

Klinsmann was giving all these big motivational talks – the most famous one is from the Poland game, where he said: 'We'll smash them through the wall' – and the substitutes were asked to make speeches as well. I was always sitting there. 'Don't pick me, don't pick me.' I would have been too nervous. At lunch on the Sweden match day, he came over to my table.

'Hitze, today, you'll say a few things.' Shit. Only a few hours to go. What am I going to say? I knew I wouldn't play but this was my game now, the only way to contribute significantly. This had to be something special. My team-mates had done all right with their lines, they had been nervous as well, but I wanted to be outstanding. It had to be very emotional. I had to be loud, I had to be fast. I had to nail it. They had to be gripped. The boys needed to be foaming at the mouth.

There's a circle. You step in. And then you go. My speech didn't make the official World Cup documentary. It was one of my best moments. I nailed it. Unfortunately, I can't remember what I said in any detail.

I talked about the atmosphere, about playing at home, in our stadium, our World Cup. I think I said the Swedes had no business being there. I screamed. A few players came up afterwards and said, 'That was great, that was different.'

And we did score two quick goals. Poldi, twice. We went out and took them apart. We overran them. We played them off the park. Siegenthaler had explained to us that their holding midfielder was never properly supported by his team-mates so we ganged up on him. They missed a penalty later on but we were very good.

After the Sweden game in the last sixteen, I knew I wouldn't get to play, but I can honestly say that I continued to do my absolute best in training. I decided that I wouldn't stop now. The staff told me they had trusted me to do that, that it was one of the reasons why they had included me in the squad. But everyone was like that. All the players did their utmost for the team's success.

The Argentina game brought a lot of pressure. We hadn't won against a big team in ages. We had put in some good performances against those kinds of sides but never beaten them. Klinsi said: 'Boys, that's not enough. We didn't come here to get knocked out in the quarter-finals.'

1-0, Ayala. 1-1, Klose ten minutes from the end. Extra-time. Penalties.

We had practised them, even during the training camp. They had us lined up at the halfway line, so that everyone had to go on that long walk. Every player had to tell the psychologist where he would put it in advance. Borowski went up once and all the players were showing the goalkeeper where to jump because they had overheard his prediction. But that bloody guy still scored anyway. Respect. I was amazed how well the five guys who were picked in Berlin took their penalties.

Many people remember Lehmann taking out his notes from his socks ahead of the Cambiasso penalty but the few seconds that are frozen in time, in my mind, was the hand-shake between Kahn and Jens before the shoot-out. Kahn went over to wish him good luck. It was an almost tender moment, shown on the video screens inside the stadium and around the world. Everyone knew about their rivalry and here they were, making up. It was dramatic, almost like a small miracle, you couldn't help but feel touched by it. Later, supporters put screen shots of that image on banners. It became a symbol for everything that was happening here, for the awesome positive power of football. Kahn had left behind his ego to go over, embrace his foe and help the team.

Semi-final. Italy in Dortmund. It was hard for me, again. Everyone was happy but I wasn't playing, I hadn't been allowed to really do my part. The suspension of defensive midfielder Torsten Frings hurt us. He had been banned on video evidence after a scuffle against Argentina, which was a bit of scandal, really. They had attacked us after the final whistle. The German FA tried to appeal right until the end but it couldn't be helped.

At first, I hadn't been convinced by Frings. He was playing in my position in front of the defence and you always pick up on your rival's mistakes. But then I realised during the tournament how good he was. I had to take my cap off to him. We knew it would be hard to compensate for that loss against the Italians. Borowski came in again. Despite that change, confidence was still high. Things were going for us. We will do this.

What did dampen spirits, though, was our terrible record against Italy. They're our '*Angstgegner*', our bogey team. We had never beaten them at a big tournament. Not once. Now it's them again. But now, they were going to get it. It's our World Cup. Our final. Our target is Berlin. We saw ourselves playing there on 9 July.

Pirlo made life difficult for us. We were completely spent by the end of regular time. Everyone was on their last legs, but we had fought bravely, and kept the game scoreless over nearly 120 minutes; that was a success against this Italy. They had many players at the peak of their powers. You already see yourself taking penalties, and winning. We win at penalties. Because we are Germany. We just have to get there.

And then they scythe you down. Grosso's goal: it was a death blow. It's over. The World Cup is over for us. It was very tough to deal with that because nobody had prepared for such an outcome. We had tried everything, the emotions had carried us but it hadn't been enough. They had been that little bit smarter, sharper, cleverer. It was an absolute tragedy for us to lose that game.

We knew it would be difficult. But this was our time. It's made for us. This can't happen. And yet it did. You don't know what to do with yourself. You just want to go home. The motivation was gone.

There were loads of discussions. Why even play this third-place play-off against Portugal? Why do FIFA make us do that? Should we say goodbye after the game in Stuttgart or come back to the Brandenburg Gate the next day? Some wanted to go straight on holiday, others felt we should bid the supporters farewell properly. We had a vote and decided to go back to Berlin because this hadn't been an ordinary World Cup. I'm pleased we did that. Five hundred thousand people turned out to see us. It was astonishing.

Before that the game in Stuttgart. Kahn played, Jens Nowotny played, Robert Huth played. But I didn't. Klinsi still didn't play me. That made me a little bit angry.

We were 2-1 up in the second half and I thought, maybe I'll get on. He left me standing on the touchline for ten minutes; the game was very open, he must have felt that it was quite dangerous to put me on. A bit of a risk: you don't want to be in that position as a player. Then Schweini scored: 3-1. Klinsi signalled for the substitution. It was the seventy-fifth minute. I was on. For that last quarter of an hour, I tried to tear myself apart on the pitch. I ran everywhere and soaked up the atmosphere.

I struggled with myself quite a lot later; I asked myself if that World Cup had been a disappointment or a success. But I had done everything I could, no regrets. And that was it. It was a happy ending.

NOT THE END

Jürgen Klinsmann: 'All of us were overwhelmed by the emotions thrown up by the "summer's tale", as people called it. Sometimes I think back to the game against Italy, to a specific corner or some free-kick that we could have scored from, perhaps we would have won the World Cup. That nagging feeling took quite a long time to go away: we had the chance to win the World Cup, there and then.

But a lot of people told me it was perfect that we didn't win, perfect for the image that Germany as a country projected. If we had won, on top of all of that, it might have been a little too much for the other nations to stomach. I felt that the team knew deep down that they had given their all, whatever that was at that moment, and that every player believed that they had dedicated themselves to those weeks, to those two years, to that process. That was very reassuring for all of us. It made it easy to hand over to Jogi for him to continue.

It was a wonderful feeling to let go for me. I was convinced that the transition to Jogi would not be a problem at all. He had already worked as head coach before, it was obvious that he'd be okay. I was glad, too, because I really wanted to come home. To be away from your family and to run into brick walls for two years leaves scars after a while. I had come to the point where I said, "It's enough, I need a break now." The thought of "What might have happened if you continued" never came came up. A lot of people said: "You should have reaped the rewards of your work" . . . No. It's not about a coach reaping rewards. It's about the development continuing, until it comes to fruition.

I was certain that Oliver and Jogi would see this through. They fine-tuned and improved many things, they built on the foundations that we had built, bit by bit. What the 2006 team didn't have was the *Spielkultur* [playing culture] of the 2014 team, nor their players. At the end, it comes down to the players again. Okay, I'll admit it: if I had known then that players like Reus, Özil and Khedira were in the pipeline . . . Damn. Every coach wants to work with such awesome players.'

WE AGAINST US

'*Gelegenheit macht Diebe*' they say in German, opportunity makes thieves. The final game in Group G in the north-eastern coastal town of Recife made it tempting to engage in a spot of daylight robbery. Extremely tempting.

A draw between Löw's team and second-placed USA, coached by his former Germany colleague Klinsmann, would see both sides safely through to the last sixteen. The two friends had secretly hoped that nothing would be riding on this game, their reunion. They could still make it a non-event if they wanted to. Sharing (the points) was caring, wasn't it? Mats Hummels knew that the idea of collusion between the coaches would loom large, at least in the public's mind. 'I don't think I'll try to dribble past four Americans in the ninetieth minute if it's 1-1,' said the defender. The joke did little to allay the fears of Ghana and Portugal.

'*Biscotto*', a cookie: that's what the Italians call that kind of sporting conspiracy. Germans use a Spanish word: '*Gijón*'. It's onomatopoeia, fittingly enough – disgust made sound. The correct pronunciation agitates the phlegm at the back of the throat.

The northern city on the Bay of Biscay was the scene of the worst footballing atrocity ever committed by the *Nationalmannschaft*. At the

1982 World Cup, Jupp Derwall's mustachioed, mulleted, money-motivated gang staged a pantomime of a match, a 1-0 win, not against but with Austria. The farcical non-contest – which became eventually known as 'the shame of Gijón' – was effectively over after ten minutes, when Hamburg striker Horst Hrubesch scored. Since Algeria had beaten Chile 3-2 earlier that day, both teams knew that a narrow defeat for the Austrians in the last group game would see them advance to the next round. The twenty-two men on the pitch spent the entire second half passing the ball around among themselves in a zombified stupor, occasionally running in the wrong direction like the pixellated blockheads who populated early football video games. Sweeper Uli Stielike had the temerity to obfuscate cause and effect, blaming the horror on the crowd's angry reaction. 'The jeering didn't help,' he said.

Only Walter Schachner, the Austrian forward, was apparently not in on the fix. He was threatened with being substituted by coach Georg Schmidt if he continued trying to score a goal, it later emerged.

'What is being offered up here is disgraceful, there's no other word for it, these two teams have lost all sympathy in the football world for years to come' said ARD TV reporter Eberhard Stanjek. He remained silent throughout large spells in protest.

What made this blatant fraud worse was the arrogance and total lack of repentance on the part of the perpetrators. 'I can't care about the crowd's reaction. It's their problem if they fly here to watch this game,' said Bayern midfielder Wolfgang Dremmler. Uwe Reinders (Werder Bremen) wasn't concerned about viewers back home either: 'I'm not interested if Aunt Frieda gets upset [in her living room].' The Spanish paper *El Comercio* famously printed the match report in the crime section.

The non-aggression pact between the central European neighbours, also called the 'Anschluss game' by the international press in reference to Nazi Germany's annexation of Austria in 1938, wasn't the DFB team's only affront to sporting decency in Spain. After the game,

Algerian fans enraged by the stitch-up descended on the German team's hotel and were pelted with water balloons from the eighth storey, where the squad were staying. Keeper Harald 'Toni' Schumacher made things worse when he brutally pole-axed Patrick Battiston in the semi-final against France. He clattered into the Frenchman neck high outside the box; Battiston damaged a vertebra and lost two teeth. While the victim of assault (which went unpunished) was being tended to by medics, Schumacher played keepy-uppy. After the final whistle – West Germany won on penalties after a thrilling 3-3 tie in extra-time – the keeper sarcastically offered to pay for the Frenchman's crowns.

The Battiston incident sparked a full-blown political crisis. In a poll in France, Schumacher squeezed out Adolf Hitler as the most unpopular German, and Chancellor Helmut Kohl and President François Mitterrand had to release a joint declaration to cool tensions before a friendly game in Strasbourg in April 1984.

The egotistical brazenness of the 1982 team marked a turning point in the post-war (footballing) history of West Germany. The Federal Republic had tried hard to present itself as a liberal, forward-thinking country; decency on the football pitch, in triumph (1954, 1974) and defeat (1966), was an unofficial part of the denazification programme. The World Cup in Spain, though, brought the return of yesteryear's 'ugly Germans': a generation once again prepared to do unspeakable things if it furthered their own interests. Dietrich Schulze van Loon, the chairman of a public relations association, called the appearances and interviews of the West German footballers that year 'the worst PR disaster since the Second World War'.

So powerful was the stench left by the side led by the faux-socialist rebel turned hard-boiled capitalist Paul Breitner – he had shaved off his famous beard for a 150,000 DM advertising fee ahead of the tournament – that later teams wearing white and black were presumed to smell just as bad as a matter of course.

España '82 created a lasting stereotype. German (national) teams were ill-disciplined and prone to infighting off the pitch, forever 'ruthless' and grimly executing orders like stormtroopers on it. César Luis Menotti's theory of 'right football (negative, conservative, authoritarian) versus 'left football' (positive, creative, democratic) was impossibly crude but, in the case of the *Nationalmannschaft*, the Argentinian coach seemed to have a point. The class of 82's joyless, purely results-orientated game was the fitting precursor to the conservative counter-revolution of Christian Democrat Helmut Kohl, who became Chancellor in October that year.

Klinsmann and Löw knew of the sins of their predecessors. More than that: their rebranding of the *Nationalmannschaft* after 2004 was a conscious attempt to deep-clean the team's image after a mass of awful connotations had coalesced like grease under the toilet seat over the past few decades. Keeping public opinion and supporters onside was a main component of the new, spotless way of life, to the point where the team's bosses occasionally overdid it.

A deeply disappointed Michael Ballack clashed with Bierhoff when the general manager instructed the captain to hold up a 'Thank you' banner in the aftermath of the 1-0 final defeat by Spain at Euro 2008 in Vienna. Ballack refused. The next day, Germany were at the Brandenburg Gate again, partying with the crowd and a comedian – yes, 'my' comedian from 2004 – making an embarrassment of himself on the stage. It was all too much fun.

Of course it was entirely possible that Germany and the USA would settle for a draw late on in the game in Recife but a preordained result would have fatally undermined all of Klinsmann's and Löw's efforts in the last decade. Another Gijón was out of the question. Both teams also wanted to win the group, to avoid Belgium in the next round and to be above all suspicion. The two coaches vowed not to talk to each other in the run-up to the game to avoid even the slightest hint of collusion.

The big win against Portugal put group leaders Germany in a very strong position. Their elimination was extremely unlikely, even if they did lose the final game. That made things easier for Klinsmann. There was now little danger that he would risk 'ending the era that he had begun himself' (*Süddeutsche*) by knocking out his former assistant from the World Cup.

But the match still had the potential to be awkward, especially from the Huntington Beach resident's perspective. The US manager was under immense pressure to qualify for the knock-out round after his team had caught the imagination of the US public like never before. And there was also another point to prove to his fellow countrymen. Sönke Wortmann's 2006 World Cup documentary *A Summer's Tale* had portrayed Klinsmann as little more than a shouty motivator while Löw was feted as the tactical brains behind the operation. The domiciled Californian later voiced his displeasure with that oversimplified characterisation. 'I shouldn't have authorised those scenes,' he told *11 Freunde* magazine.

His unsuccessful, short-lived stint as head coach at Bayern in 2008–09 – 'we only did fitness drills, the players had to get together to discuss how we were going to play each game,' Philipp Lahm wrote in his autobiography in 2011 – had chipped away at his professional standing, too. Recife offered the opportunity to redress the situation. 'The motivator tag doesn't do justice to Jürgen, he's become more of a coach over the years,' claimed Bierhoff.

But the closer it got to the game, the more it became apparent that Klinsmann had already won perhaps the biggest battle of all – that for recognition of his previous work for the *Nationalmannschaft*. All serious German newspapers used the opportunity to look back at the impact his reforms had had on the national team and German football as a whole. The verdict was unequivocal: Klinsmann had left behind a legacy of better practice.

A few days after the heady thrill of the 2006 tournament, *Bild*, the tabloid that had done more than most to mock his new methods, had gone into full reverse mode. 'How much Klinsi is in the [next]

Bundesliga [season]? Will the clubs copy his successful World Cup tricks?' the paper asked. The answer was an emphatic yes. 'You'd have to be blind not to have seen what happened here in the last weeks,' said BVB CEO Hans-Joachim Watzke. 'We will analyse and revisit the tournament and take a few things on board.' Individualised fitness training and the methods of Mark Verstegen's team were adopted throughout the league in the next few years, as was the in-depth scouting of opposition teams, a holistic attitude to man management that included the contribution of mental coaches and sports psychologists, and the delegation of various tasks to specialists. 'Jürgen has left his marks, a lot of them,' said German FA president Wolfgang Niersbach in Brazil. 'The whole [process of] professionalisation started with him. Look at the training pitches in the Bundesliga today. Jürgen introduced things that are taken for granted now.'

It was worth recalling Lahm's pretty damning appraisal of life in the national team under Rudi Völler to appreciate the difference. 'The practice sessions are surprisingly relaxed,' he wrote in his book. 'It was like a bunch of friends going away on holiday to play a bit of football. We trained perhaps for an hour a day . . . We don't practice anything specific at all, apart from crossing the ball, with someone shooting at goal unmarked. Good fun, but totally random . . . There were no tactical talks, no video analysis of the opponents, no analysis of our own mistakes.'

'All of us, the whole team, were inspired by Klinsmann,' says Per Mertesacker. The former manager's trust in younger players had started a new trend that other followers, adds the defender: 'he put his confidence into a very young generation, he created an environment in which playing young players became the natural thing to do. He's played a big part in freshening up German football. We are still benefiting from that today.' One of his most controversial decisions as a coach, the benching of Oliver Kahn, the best shot-stopper, for the more agile and proactive Jens Lehmann in goal, had a far-reaching effect, too. The ability to rush out and pass the ball competently with your feet has since become a key criterion for all Bundesliga keepers.

Lahm, Schweinsteiger, Podolski, Klose and Mertesacker had been there, at the start of German football's renaissance. The team that Klinsmann had installed behind the team hadn't changed much at all. Scout Siegenthaler, fitness coaches Mark Verstegen and Shad Forsyth, psychologist Hans-Dieter Hermann were still around. The game at the Arena Pernambuco pitted the *Nationalmannschaft*'s past against their present, 'Klinsmann against Klinsmen' (*Der Spiegel*), 'We against us' (*FAZ*), the father of the revolution against the son, Swabia v Baden.

Despite the warm words for the former mastermind, Germany's main aim was to avoid another relapse into the fast and furious Klinsmann football, another Ghana, in Recife. Löw's achievement, helped by the ever-increasing skills of the players available to him, had been to ease his team's attacking instincts into more refined, calmer channels. He preferred the more measured, calculated approach of Bayern Munich under Pep Guardiola and Jupp Heynckes to the 'heavy metal' (Jürgen Klopp) ferociousness of Borussia Dortmund that necessarily entailed some loss of command. He looked for a repeat of the Portugal performance.

Every game is played out in response to the previous one in tournament football, so the hustling, bustling Khedira had to make way for the more strategically minded Schweinsteiger. Löw hoped that a Bayern midfield of Lahm, Kroos and Schweinsteiger, the trio that had taken the club's passing game to new, exalted levels in the first half of the 2013–14 season, would reinstate calm against a US team that the Germany manager considered a physical challenge. Löw's reasoning followed a similar line to that of former Spain coach Luis Aragonés, who had come to realise that the *La Roja* were never going to succeed against bigger, stronger sides unless they kept the ball off them for as long as possible.

One slight complication: Schweinsteiger didn't feel quite ready to start the match in the tropical heat and incessant rain of Recife. He would only last twenty minutes at most, he told Löw and his teammates. The man from Kolbermoor, a small city at the foot of the Alps (and Paul Breitner's home town) had missed the DFB Cup final against Dortmund at the end of May with a knee injury. Two senior players cornered the Bayern linchpin near the base camp pool. They talked him into declaring himself fit for his first start at this World Cup. Schweini's old partner in crime, Lukas 'Poldi' Podolski, too, played from the beginning. Götze lost his place to the Arsenal striker.

Löw had ignored the swelling chorus of critics at home and stuck with his back four of centre-backs. It was obvious that he was now beyond caring what others thought. He and his players respected the opposition but were assured of their superiority. Bierhoff: 'It was a matter of prestige, that game. But we were totally convinced that we were better, that we would beat them. The rain and the heat made it quite hard, though. We were sitting there with rain capes underneath the roof but it was impossible to keep the water at bay.' The deluge had one welcome effect: Löw's pudding-bowl haircut looked much slicker than usual. 'There are probably quite a few people out there who'd agree with that,' Bierhoff laughs. 'But you can't get him to change.'

The Americans were tackling as hard as expected but they only pressed the ball inside their own half. Germany's midfield were able to dictate the pattern of play without too much trouble against the passive opposition. Klinsmann's team weren't in a hurry to start quick counter-attacks either. The match ebbed and flowed gently over the sodden pitch, both teams apparently happy with their respective lot. A goal for Portugal in their game with Ghana lessened the impetus for the 'US boys', as the German media called them, further still. They now had an additional safety cushion and no clear desire to force the issue themselves.

Schweinsteiger and former Schalke midfielder Jermaine Jones clashed over a couple of mistimed challenges but the first forty-five minutes drifted by without any major goalmouth action. After the break, Löw took off the disappointing Podolski – 'that was the old Poldi today,' one exasperated member of the coaching staff said later – and brought on Klose. Müller moved out wide to make room for the Lazio forward.

Germany took the lead not long after. A short corner by Mesut Özil found Mertesacker, whose header was parried by the excellent Tim Howard in goal. The ball eventually ended up outside the box where Müller side-footed it with great precision into the bottom right corner for his fourth goal of the campaign. 'It was my special moment. I don't score too many from outside the box,' he said later.

German domination increased in the wake of the fifty-fifth-minute opener. The USA couldn't switch gears. They were torn between going for an equaliser and keeping their defensive shape; indecision paralysed them. Their most noteworthy action was purely accidental: Alejandro Bodeya and Jones tackled each other by mistake.

Löw subbed Schweinsteiger after seventy-four minutes of an imperious performance. But this time, there was no job-sharing with Khedira in central midfield. Götze came on. The game refused to catch fire, however. Ninety-four minutes ended without a meaningful attack on Manuel Neuer's goal. Germany had done it, rather effortlessly. And the US also advanced, as runners-up, thanks to Portugal's 2-1 win over Ghana.

Löw praised his team's 'control and order in midfield', the defensive stability. 'It was our best game, in my opinion,' says Lahm. 'They were very aggressive, but we were in charge, we totally controlled the game and didn't give anything at all away at the back.' Müller: 'We showed them who was boss right from the beginning.' It all sounded remarkably like a Bayern Munich post-match press conference, for a reason. It was very much a Bayern win: 1-0, business-like, with a player from Munich scoring and the team pushing around the opposition without expending too much energy.

The Bavarian midfield, in particular, had worked out so well together that the under-fire Lahm would be afforded a respite from the criticism for the next few days. The most praise was reserved for club colleague Schweinsteiger, however. 'He was a revelation,' wrote *Kölner Stadt-Anzeiger*. 'He was excellent,' said Löw. 'It was a good decision to give Sami Khedira a rest today.'

Schweinsteiger's victorious return to the control centre was seized upon by his club-mates to strengthen his case for future inclusion. 'He is a general on the pitch,' said Manuel Neuer. 'You see him setting the pace. It's good for us [as a team] that there's someone who calls the shots. You notice straight away that he's back. I find it brilliant, the way he's playing.' Just to drive home the pro-Schweini message, Kroos emphasised that he, Bastian and Lahm had played together 'very often at FC Bayern'. The subtext was loud and clear: the strong Bavarian faction wanted to see a bigger dash of red being added to the national team's white.

Dortmund's Hummels wisely avoided taking a position in favour of either midfielder. 'If I say something positive about one of them now, it'll be interpreted in a negative way as far as the other one is concerned.' Another observer was far less diplomatic. 'We played too slowly against the Americans, we made it easy for them,' Khedira said in the mixed zone. 'If we want to go far in this competition, we have to speed things up and have more presence in the box.' More speed and more presence in the box: more Khedira is what he meant.

The Madrid player's comments caused a couple of raised eyebrows in the dressing room. There's an unwritten law that you don't talk about a game you didn't play in, let alone say things about those who did that can be interpreted as negative. At Euro 2012, brisk public demands for more game time from unused subs had caused much upheaval in the camp. But in this instance, the players' council let Khedira's complaints slide. They had learned that not every difference of opinion needed official intervention. It was better just to shrug and move on sometimes.

Khedira wasn't some troublesome upstart with ideas above his stations either, but a senior member of the squad with plenty of friends and team-mates who appreciated his many qualities. For the sake of harmony, his mixed-zone lament was considered an attempt at self-promotion that fell just within the bounds of what was deemed acceptable.

It was obvious that Löw was happy with the poise of the Bavarian triumvirate at the centre; 725 completed passes had set a new record in the competition. 'Schweinsteiger was very strong, for as long as he had the energy,' the coach said. The wording of the appraisal left the door ajar for Khedira. Löw had to handle this delicate situation with great care. He couldn't rely on Schweinsteiger recovering in time for the last sixteen game against Algeria. Khedira had to be kept onside.

At Campo Bahia, to be sure, the sudden jockeying for position at the heart of the team was seen as less problematic than Löw having neither of his two seasoned campaigners available. The public perceived the situation to be highly explosive, however. Schweinsteiger boycotting all interaction with the media in Brazil added to the sense of tension around the issue. He was the one member of the German delegation to resist all calls and efforts of gentle persuasion by the German FA to speak to print and television journalists. His attitude was described as 'arrogant' and 'diva-like' by *Frankfurter Rundschau*, who noted that Schweinsteiger's sulking 'in an imaginary snail's shell' ran counter to the open, uncomplicated demeanour of the rest of the squad.

His relationship with the Springer papers had been fraught for some time. A few years ago, *Sport-Bild* reporter Christian Falk had derided him as a '*Chefchen*', a mini-boss, in a cover story. Schweinsteiger hit back in a Bayern press conference, calling the journalist a 'liar', an 'arsehole' and a 'pisser'. Raimund Hinko, another *Sport-Bild* columnist and Bayern insider, penned a very harsh piece titled 'The End of a Football God' a couple of weeks before the tournament started. Hinko wrote that Schweinsteiger was 'too slow' and 'too inflexible' to fit Pep Guardiola's system: 'But he's flexible enough to lift the team's mood by organising a party . . . nobody is more talented at smiling in front of the cameras after wins.' When Podolski pushed Falk into the team hotel pool on one of the media days, it looked suspiciously like a premeditated hit on behalf of his silent buddy.

Löw had a few days to chew over the midfield conundrum ahead of the last sixteen game in Porto Alegre. Vahid Halilhodžić's Algeria were the surprise opponents after beating Russia in their final game of the group phase. The 'shame of Gijón' could not yet be consigned to the grave of history. The North Africans were out for revenge.

THE BEGINNING OF THE BEGINNING

Dietrich Weise lives in Heilbronn, in former US Army barracks that have been converted into a modern housing estate. 'The best thing about my apartment is that there's no one above me,' he says. 'I can't stand it when somebody throws parties above me late at night. This way, I have peace. That's what I have always wanted. It's nice when you're happy and content in old age.' Weise turned eighty in November 2014.

He has bought cake for his visitor. *Käsesahne* (cheesecake, but the lighter, central European variety). Four slices are lined up on a little table in the living room, which doubles as his office. Built-in cabinet: cherry. You can hear the coffee dripping through the filter. 'Shoot. What do you want to know? Do you want milk and sugar? Help yourself, it's all here.'

Weise suffered a severe heart-attack in 2013. His life was saved with seconds to spare. He's recovered well since. He still goes to watch amateur football regularly, in Heilbronn or Neckarsulm, talking to pensioners on the touchline. Bundesliga stadiums are not his world any more, the travelling takes too much out of him. 'The engine is getting weaker all the time,' he says, and looks at the floor. 'Maybe I've worked too much in my life. And I've probably kept too many things bottled up, sadly.'

*

Weise moved to Swabia from the GDR in 1958. He left his club, Fortschritt Weißenfels (*Fortschritt* means 'progress') behind him, and his Saxon accent made the journey west, too. Weise studied for his A and B coaching licence at the *Sporthochschule* in Köln while coaching VfR Heilbronn and Neckarsulm as a player-manager. He became an assistant to Bundesliga coaches at Kaiserslautern. One of them was Gyula Lóránt, a former member of the legendary Mighty Magyars, the Hungarian national team of the fifties. 'Under him, I learned what I would never do as the boss myself. He talked to players in a harsh, lordly manner – as if he was the *Übermensch*. I always thought: these are adults. You can talk to them normally, not just order them around. We worshipped the Hungarians. But the stuff Lóránt was coaching . . . dear, oh dear.' Weise followed Lóránt in 1971 as head coach of the 'Red Devils' at Lautern and later took charge of Eintracht Frankfurt. He was an early prototype of the modern trainer. Not a dictatorial patriarch, more like a sensitive teacher, willing to listen to key players before coming to a decision. He was a man of hard work and details; sideline theatrics were not his genre. 'In Frankfurt and Kaiserslautern the fans sometimes said: this guy is falling asleep on the bench.' He chuckles.

In 1974, Weise won the World Cup for West Germany. One of his Eintracht players did, anyway. Kind of. 'It was my idea to make Bernd Hölzenbein a left-winger,' he says, suddenly. 'We had many good right-wingers in the Bundesliga at the time. Uli Hoeness ran up and down the touchline, and Jürgen Grabowski was the god of crosses. So I said to Bernd: look, what happens if you come in from the left?' Weise jumps out of his armchair, spreads his legs, ready to take on an imaginary opponent. He drops his shoulder, turns inside on his right. 'When you cut in from the left as a right-sided player, you attack the weaker side of the right-back.' Weise takes two steps forward. He turns around to pretend that he's the defender now. He hits his left thigh and makes a face as if he's just been 'done'. Now he's the striker again. The carpet is slipping. He takes aim. His right slipper comes off and hits the wall. 1-0, Weise.

In the 1974 final, Hölzenbein attacked the Dutch box, employing the Weise move. He cut inside on his right foot, then went down after a sliding challenge from Wim Jansen. A dive, in all likelihood. Penalty by left-back Breitner, another right-footed player playing on the 'wrong side', 1-1. These days, fielding so-called 'inverted wingers' on the flanks has become a standard ploy.

West German football was at the peak of its powers in the mid-seventies but Weise noted something odd. Why were the youth teams never winning any trophies? 'We were by far the biggest football association in Europe but we didn't even make it to finals in the youth tournaments. I believe that was down to politics. The DFB was a huge machine then, with representatives from all the regional federations. They all wanted to see their players getting picked. That meant that much better players from the bigger states were left behind because somebody, somewhere, insisted on the inclusion of his guy.'

After his appointment as youth coach by the German FA in 1978, Weise set out to find talents in places where others hadn't bothered to look. He went to see hundreds of youth games all over the country, turning up unannounced at training sessions. 'Sometimes I looked at a player five times. I wrote everything down in a large file.' He carefully takes it off the shelf. The German FA have plans to include it in their newly built football museum in Dortmund, he says.

Most youth games kicked off on Sunday morning at eleven. There were no videos or DVDs then. But Weise decided that all competitive games should be covered. He recruited senior professionals to join in the hunt. 'Gerd Zewe, Wolfgang Seel, Ernst Diehl all worked for me in various parts of Germany. Klaus Allofs was doing the games in the west of the country for me. The trick was never telling them which players I was interested in. I wanted them to have an open mind. In return, the German FA paid them expenses, mileage.' Fortuna Düsseldorf striker

Allofs was a fully-fledged West Germany international, a European Championship winner in 1980. Different times.

Weise's network unearthed players who managed to win the U18 Euros in 1981 under his guidance, West Germany's first ever international trophy at youth level. 'In the semi-final, we beat France, at last. Their development work was exemplary'.

That same year, Weise also won the U20 World Cup in Australia. He takes a framed team photograph from the cupboard and gently puts it on his lap. 'Michael Zorc and Ralf Loose were key players, Roland Wohlfarth was an important forward. We had Ralf Falkenmayer. Rüdiger Volborn was in goal.' All those went on to become very successful Bundesliga professionals. Zorc works as Borussia Dortmund's sporting director now.

Weise also coached the generation of the 1990 World Cup winners. 'I worked with Lothar Matthäus, Jürgen Klinsmann, Thomas Berthold and Olaf Thon. Hansi Flick [Jogi Löw's assistant at the 2014 World Cup] was one of my boys, too. He played in the U18s at the 1983 Euros.'

Weise had achieved everything in the space of three years but youth development was still not being valued by those in the higher echelons. 'I was able to introduce a second A youth team, so that we had an A1 and A2 going forward. The French copied that. But that was all I could do, really.' Weise left his post to coach first Kaiserslautern and then Frankfurt again. With the exception of the U16s in 1984 and 1992 (European championships), no German team would win another youth competition until 2008.

The call came in August 1996. National coach Berti Vogts had urged DFB president Egidius Braun to do more to foster youth development. The German FA were only concerned with the youth national teams then. The real footballing education was in the hands of the powerful '*Landesverbände*', the regional federations, and the clubs.

Vogts' idea was to install one German FA coach inside each regional federation to conduct additional sessions for gifted kids who weren't part of the club system. That suggestion was turned down out of hand. It was considered unrealistic. The regional federations didn't want interference from Frankfurt.

Braun called Weise, who was the national manager of Liechtenstein at the time, and instructed him to come up with a more viable blueprint. Weise: 'He said that Germany would be bidding for the World Cup in 2006 and that we needed to have a competitive team in place in case we would win the vote.'

The decrease in talents was then widely seen as a sociological issue. Football was suffering thanks to the appeal of video games and individual activities, like going to the gym, the theory went. There were also mutterings about the current generation of teenagers being maybe a little too comfortable and well-off; too soft to defend their birthright against the post-Bosman influx of foreigners. 'In Germany, there is very little social pressure to improve your position in society through sport,' said German FA youth coordinator (and later assistant to national coach Rudi Völler) Michael Skibbe in 2001.

Nonsense, said Weise. 'I told Braun that there was enough talent in Germany. We just didn't get to them. And the ones we did get to didn't spend enough time training with the ball.'

Together with his assistant, the fresh-faced former Darmstadt pro Ulf Schott, who'd just graduated in sports science, Weise visited all the regional federations, and other national associations; they spoke to managers in other sports, too. What they found in nine months of research was that youngsters who didn't happen to play for one of the professional clubs were falling through the cracks. They had to rely on the federal associations, the FA sub-branches in every state, for recognition and development. If they called you up for the '*Länderauswahl*', the elite selection of the federal association, you had a decent chance of being spotted by a big club and moved on from there. But if they didn't, you didn't. Schott: 'There were big differences as far as the federal associations' ability to look after these kids was concerned. Some didn't have the finances, some didn't have the manpower. We thought that was unfair. Every kid playing in Germany should have the same opportunities. We also found that not all big clubs were doing as well as they could, in relation to their financial resources. Our proposed first step was the introduction of a comprehensive talent-spotting and development scheme, with the help of a network of 115 regional centres. These were supposed to develop thirteen- to seventeen-year-olds. We also wanted to support the *Landesverbände*, so that they could work more regularly with the best eleven- and twelve-year-olds.'

That was in spring 1998. The German FA said no. Too expensive. 'I told Braun we needed at least DM 2.5 million [€1.25 million],' says Weise. 'He went mad and looked at me, his eyes popping: "Where are we supposed to get that from?" Weise explained that youngsters needed good coaches. A whole new bus-load of coaches was needed, in fact. 'It wasn't enough to have a few coaches at the regional federations. And the fathers who were coaching youngsters in their spare time in many clubs didn't have any real qualifications either. That's not sufficient. Papa can't be the solution!'

'Pater Braun', Reverend Braun, as the parochial president's nickname went, was immovable. 'Let's see what the World Cup brings, they said,' recalls Schott.

A disastrous quarter-final exit against Croatia, the end of Vogts as national manager and a win for the hosts, who had systematically re-engineered their talent development in the years leading up to the competition: that's what France 98 brought. And a window of opportunity. Within four weeks of Germany's 3-0 defeat in Lyon, the German FA board approved Weise's concept. DM 3.2 million (€1.6 million) was made available to set up 121 regional centres ('*Stützpunkte*') that would provide two hours of individual, technical coaching for 4,000 thirteen- to seventeen-year-olds once a week. In addition, up to 10,000 boys under twelve would receive lessons by the *Landesverbände*. Total cost: DM 5.2 million (€2.6 million) per year. 'The plans had been in the drawer for a while. We have now dusted them off and improved them,' said German FA vice-president Franz Beckenbauer, under whose remit youth development fell. *Der Kaiser* had dramatically warned of an 'Albanisation' of German football after the disappointment in France. 'The public pressure on the FA to react was already quite strong,' says Schott. 'It helped us to get the plan implemented.'

Weise and Schott criss-crossed the whole of Germany for an entire year, looking for suitable locations for their new network. They saw hundreds of clubs in the most remote, provincial spots imaginable. Weise sweet-talked village councils into making their pitches and sports halls available, hired dozens of former professionals to work as coaches, provided equipment and even petrol money to enable parents to drive their children to the centres. Growing up far away from any footballing hot spots should no longer be a bar to enjoying a first-class football education for any German youngster. 'Everyone was supposed to have access to a regional centre within twenty-five kilometres of his home. That was the idea,' says Weise. Some of the federal associations were opposed. They felt that the meddling from Frankfurt implied a criticism of their own methods. 'It wasn't about taking anything away from them,' insists Schott. 'But we wanted to have equality for all youngsters, which was only possible by introducing national structures and benchmarks, in terms of numbers, frequency and level of individual coaching for these talents.'

The DFB-*Stützpunkt* programme introduced a permanent, systematic scouting system at the national level. But the part-time training for young players without any professional club affiliation could in itself do little to raise standards. Elite players needed better and more frequent coaching. In FA-run academies, like those that had brought success for *Les Bleus*, perhaps?

Weise and Schott called on the expertise of Franco-German Gernot Rohr, the general manager of Eintracht Frankfurt, and Alsatian FA president and former coach Ernest Jacky, to gain some insight into the

French model. (Rohr, a successful coach at Girondins Bordeaux, was the grand-nephew of Oskar 'Ossi' Rohr, the twenty-year-old Bayern Munich player who had scored in the 1932 final against Eintracht Frankfurt to help the Reds to their first ever national title, then moved to Switzerland and France to play professional football. His opposition to the Nazi regime saw him interned in a concentration camp and later sent to the Eastern Front. Rohr survived the war to play for a number of clubs in the south-west of Germany.)

'The French model was all the rage at the time,' says Schott. 'Rohr and Jacky explained the set-up to us and recommended not going down the French route of having FA academies, but to compel the big German clubs to build their own academies straight away. In France, they had started with FA academies, like the one in Clairefontaine, and then set specific requirements for the clubs to follow suit. After a while, the clubs' centres overtook the FA ones, and the latter became obsolete. Nobody lived there any more because all the best talents were playing for Ligue 1 clubs.'

Weise and Schott, in conjunction with German FA official Bernd Pfaff – the same functionary axed by Jürgen Klinsmann in 2006 – 'translated' the academy model and managed to earn a testimonial from Beckenbauer. A commission was formed. It included FA coaches and Werner Kern, the head of youth development at Bayern, as well his SC Freiburg colleague Andreas Rettig, who represented the smaller clubs.

The highly specified certification process the French had developed, a series of conditions and incentives in relation to transfers and contracts, was not adopted, to make things less complicated in the first instance. The clubs would be limited to schooling a defined number of talents, so that they didn't hoover up all youngsters in their surrounding regions. 'We didn't want the amateur clubs to lose all their best players to the new academies – only their one, very, very best player,' explains Schott. 'The good amateur players were better off staying with their home clubs and receiving *Stützpunkt* coaching.

They could always make the switch later, if they proved good enough for a professional career.'

Football stories are constantly being written and rewritten, canonised and revised, long after the final whistle has been blown. Run-of-the-mill incidents become key moments. Key moments become key goals or key non-goals. Key goals or key non-goals become scorelines. Scorelines become results. Results become *the result*. The watershed. The end of an era, the start of an era, a seminal point in the transition between the two states, either way. The darkness before the light. The light before the darkness.

The 'meaning' of Euro 2000, Germany's shambles of a tournament – the DFB team had failed to make it past Albania in the preliminary round of the 1968 competition but the European Championship didn't have much prestige back then – has significantly evolved since a Portuguese B team put three past Oliver Kahn. The greatest peace-time humiliation has turned into the best possible worst thing that could have happened: a healthy shock to the system to shake the last few dreamers into long overdue action. 'The bitter first-round defeat at Euro 2000 was the key moment: at the turn of the millennium German football stared disaster in the face – it completely lacked a professional foundation. What followed was a revolution in youth development,' an official publication by the Bundesliga (DFL) put it in 2011.

There are a couple of reasons why that is now the officially commemorated version of events. One, painful failure is much easier to stomach if you can convince yourself it all happened for a very good reason, as hard as that may be when the sporting disaster in question includes a 1-0 defeat against Kevin Keegan's England in Charleroi, an all-round embarrassment of footballing poverty. Two, and more importantly, the memory of the most relevant reforms begins in that fateful summer of 2000 because there exists no memory of any reforms that had been put in place before.

Weise vaguely remembers speaking at the first-ever convention of youth coaches in 1999 but nobody reported his comments. 'There was no real interest in the whole subject then,' says Schott. 'Everybody paid lip service to youth development, it was one of those things that people were happy to be associated with but when it came to putting ideas into practice, it was tough.' Nevertheless, the Bundesliga clubs realised that the establishment of academies was the necessary next step. They agreed to Weise's and Schott's programme – a couple of months *before* Euro 2000, as it happens.

The DFB made it compulsory for the eighteen top teams to build performance centres by 2001–02. 'It was for their own good, but we had to force them to do it, to an extent,' recalled Rettig. Money was the main obstacle: 'How much will it cost? Is that really necessary?', those were the reactions, says Schott. But there was also some resistance at the ideological level against fostering the elite. 'Werder Bremen doesn't want to follow the principle of selection,' the former SVW general manager Willi Lemke, a Social Democrat politician, said in 1998. 'We have a social responsibility! We are obliged to provide leisure activities for children, promote the motivation to perform, teach them solidarity and team spirit.' By 2000, the majority of professional clubs knew that change was necessary, however, says Volker Kersting, who has worked as youth director at FSV Mainz 05, one of the country's most innovative clubs, since 1990. 'We saw that we were getting behind internationally. The German FA were kicking in open doors.'

The *Nationalmannschaft*'s ineptitude at Euro 2000 had pulled the rug from under the last doubters' feet. 'After that tournament, the outcry was huge,' says Schott. 'Everyone was demanding reforms, especially after the right to host the 2006 World Cup was awarded to Germany in July. What they didn't know was that a lot of things were already happening on the ground, because the media had taken very little interest in the subject before.' Looking back, 1998 was the pivotal turning point, not 2000.

The changes were formalised in October 2000, when the DFL, a body of the thirty-six Bundesliga clubs in divisions one and two with a large (but not total) degree of financial and regulatory independence from the German FA, was formed. The Bundesliga 2 clubs at first resisted the academy system, due to its high cost, but they, too, were eventually persuaded. Running an academy became a condition of obtaining a licence to play professional football in both divisions from 2002–3 onwards. In the first two years of the new regimes, the thirty-six clubs invested a combined €114 million into their elite schooling.

It was the German FA's turn to improve their own infrastructure again. The *Stützpunkt* education for eleven- and twelve-year-olds was taken out of the hands of the federal associations and centralised: the national network was increased to 366 locations; 600,000 talents could now be seen at least once by the 1,300 FA coaches each year. The annual budget was raised to €14 million. Weise: 'A million more or less – suddenly it wasn't a problem any more.' 'Youth development must be the focal point of our work,' said the new DFB president Mayer-Vorfelder, 'everything needs to be done in order for us to have a team that can challenge the world's great [sides] in 2006.'

The Swabian sometimes said clumsy, disconcerting things about the dearth of indigenous talent in the Bundesliga. His reference to only two '*Germanen*' (Germanics) on the pitch in a game between Bayern and Energie Cottbus particularly jarred. Those sorts of sentiments belonged to the 1930s and 1940s. But, to his credit, 'MV' also clearly grasped the opportunity provided by the reforms to the antiquated citizenship rules under Chancellor Gerhard Schröder after his election in 1998.

A new citizenship law in 2000 dispensed with the requirement to prove a German bloodline, a restrictive regulation dating back to the age of Imperial Germany that had left hundreds of thousands of immigrants, their children and grandchildren without a right to acquire German nationality, even after decades of living and working in the country. Schröder's Social Democratic government (and his coalition partners, the Greens) enabled the offspring of foreigners who had resided for eight years to become naturalised immediately and also made it easier to have dual citizenship. A whole new population stratum could be mined by German FA talent scouts. 'We have to make maximum use of the chances afforded by dual citizenship,' Mayer-Vorfelder said in late 2001. That didn't translate into a specific programme, Schott says, but the DFB took more care to harness immigrant talents and to convince them to wear white and black.

They had lost a lot good players to Turkey before, like the trio of German-born players Yildiray Bastürk, Ilhan Mansiz and Ümit Davala, who finished third in the 2002 World Cup in Şenol Güneş' squad. The Turkish FA has its own dedicated office in Germany tasked with identifying suitable players among the three million Turks and Germans with a Turkish background. 'The German FA didn't really bother much about these guys before,' said Erdal Keser, the former Borussia Dortmund player in charge of scouting for the Turkish FA in Europe.

Meanwhile, the German FA introduced a special licence for youth coaches in 2003 to ensure a uniform level of competence. A year later, a nationwide U19 Bundesliga, split into three geographical tranches, came into being. The 'B-Junioren' (U17) got their own national league in 2007. 'People don't really talk about it that much but I believe the introduction of the junior Bundesligas was a vital part of the reform process,' says Ralf Rangnick, a former youth coach at VfB Stuttgart who went on to become one of the country's most respected managers. 'Pitting the best of the best nationwide against each made it possible to compare players and increase the quality. It also, indirectly, forced clubs into spending more money on youth coaches.'

Weise retired in 2001, aged sixty-seven. 'I didn't want to hear any whispers in the hallways: "What is that old man still doing here?"' His work was done. 'When I saw the Löw team triumph at the World Cup in the summer of the 2014, I thought now and again: oh man, oh man, oh man! You have had a small in part in that, you've worked on that. The football we are playing today is based on those ideas. At least ten players who are involved in the national team today we would have never found otherwise. Think of Toni Kroos. He hails from a small place in Mecklenburg-Vorpommern. No one would have looked at him.'

'These were the foundation stones, these were the beginnings. Everything else followed from that, in a process of continued optimisation,' says Schott, who was appointed German FA director for youth development in 2012. 'But I'm not fond of those who say that everything was revolutionised [after 1998]. The wheel didn't have to be reinvented. The wheel was there already, there was youth development in Germany, obviously. The wheel was just turned further, bit by bit. There were people with smart ideas before, there will always be smart people with good ideas. But the key is for them to be in a position to actually implement their ideas. For that, you need to have history on your side; the opportunity to develop things and see them through: 1998, 2000 and 2006 were such historical moments.'

ICE BARREL CHALLENGE

'The most misunderstood game of all' (Oliver Bierhoff)

Two hours south of Rio by plane and it's all gone: the heat, the noise, the colour. Porto Alegre, the 'happy port', is anything but in the Brazilian winter. The city just seems to lie there, silently, grimly, waiting for the greyness to lift. Architecturally, it resembles what you might imagine the capital of Uzbekistan to look like. Steel, glass, strange shapes, shopkeepers in granite-clad stores selling things that no one needs. Even the people don't look Brazilian, in their baggy leather jackets, their faces angular and pale.

The inhabitants of this state, the Rio Grande do Sul, are referred to as gauchos, like the horsemen who raise cattle in the pampas of Brazil and neighbouring Uruguay and Argentina. Local footballers are believed to fight harder and run more than their northern compatriots. That theory is undermined, just a little, by Ronaldinho (full name: Ronaldo de Assis Moreira), the city's most famous son.

Temperatures around fifteen degrees centigrade would bring out the gaucho in each of Löw's men, too, the nation hoped, after the stifling heat of Salvador and the biblical downpour in Recife. The real Germany would have a chance to shine against rank outsiders Algeria in the Estádio Beira-Rio, a plastic ruff collar of a stadium next to the Guaíba river.

Historically, Germany owed Algeria a defeat. The 'Fennecs' would find special motivation in the injustice of Gijón. But Manuel Neuer was unwilling to atone for the past crimes of others. 'We know North African teams,' said the keeper, 'They are very agile, often have the lungs of horses, run up and down and are good on the ball as well. Defensively, they have their weaknesses. And they're not the only ones who can counter-attack and strike with cold precision. We can do that as well.'

Löw professed himself 'irritated' by the constant 'Gijón' reminders. 'Hardly anyone from our squad was even born then,' he argued. Only reserve keeper Roman Weidenfeller and Miroslav Klose were alive at the time, albeit they were too young to have witnessed what happened in the Estadio El Molinón.

In fact, there had been two further outrages in Gijón that same month. The first, lesser known one, came on 15 June 1982, when West Germany, the reigning European champions, opened their World Cup campaign against the North Africans. The arrogance of Jupp Derwall's team was limitless. Goalkeeper Toni Schumacher promised that his side would score 'four to eight goals just to warm up'.

Derwall, a jovial man, had joked that he would take 'the first train back home' if his side lost and admitted that there was no point in showing footage of the opposition to his men: 'They would have laughed at me.' The Algerian coaches, Mahieddine Khalef and Rachid Mekhloufi, couldn't fail to notice their opponent's overconfidence. 'One German player scoffed that he could play with a cigar in his mouth,' Khalef remembered years later.

Derwall had given his men maximum leeway during the pre-tournament training camp. There were tales of late-night card sessions, plenty of alcohol and non-sporting nocturnal exercise. 'It wasn't rare for [tens of thousands of Deutsche Marks to be at stake in poker games,' Schumacher wrote in his autobiography a few years later. 'Others had screwed all the night and then crawled into training like wet dish-rags in the morning.'

The lax attitude precipitated a fall. Algeria won 2-1, courtesy of goals by Rabah Madjer and Lakhdar Belloumi, a sensational upset to rank alongside North Korea's 1-0 win over Italy in 1966 and England's defeat by the USA in 1950 by the same scoreline. One German TV commentator handed Derwall a mock-up of a giant train ticket at the final whistle; *Süddeutsche Zeitung* compared the debacle to the 'sinking of the *Titanic*'.

That was the first disgrace, the Austria fix the second. The third one had the potential to be the most serious of all, although the truth remains unclear. In 2011, it emerged that three Algerian squad members of the 1982 team had children born with disabilities. Suspicions were raised by the team about the coincidence and supplements administered by the Russian doctor working with them at the time. A formal investigation had failed to find conclusive evidence, and Belloumi told the *Guardian* that all allegations of doping were 'completely false, totally untrue'.

Nevertheless, the match in Porto Alegre offered Algeria the unexpected chance to right a thirty-two-year-old wrong. Germany's failings in 1982 worked against Halilhodžić's men now, however. Klinsmann's and Löw's teams, unlike those before them, had consciously replaced the old sense of entitlement with one of humility and professionalism. The dossiers prepared by chief scout Siegenthaler never failed to ram home the message that lesser teams had to be taken seriously, and specific tactical measures by the coaching staff reflected that earnestness. It was probably no mere coincidence that the new, post-2004 Germany had never lost a knock-out game against outsiders. Elimination had only ever come at the hands of arch-rivals Italy and the all-conquering Spain. And both these sides had already gone home. 'That was important for us, psychologically,' says Mertesacker. 'We felt: wow, we really have a chance here, we are the team of the tournament.'

But first they needed to show it. 'Algeria are a difficult team of high quality,' Löw warned. 'Our keywords are concentration and focus. These knock-out games have a special magic.' The manager also demanded 'great art' from his side after the 'light and shade' of the group stage: 'We know that we can play a lot better.'

Lukas Podolski was unavailable with a knee injury, and Mario Götze started in his place. In defence, Löw also made a change, but it wasn't the reinstatement of Lahm at right-back that so many were demanding. Flu-stricken Mats Hummels, a late withdrawal, had to be replaced by Shkodran Mustafi. He lined up on the right. Boateng moved inside again. As far as the 'number six' question was concerned, Khedira lost out to Schweinsteiger in the centre once more. Löw stuck with his Bayern midfield of Schweini, Lahm and Kroos, in anticipation of opposition that would camp deep in its own half and force Germany to play a slower tempo with plenty of possession.

The pattern was set early on. The *Nationalmannschaft* probed for an opening, without really settling into their own game. Sharp pressing in midfield by the Algerians disrupted the flow of the passes. Every time Algeria won the ball they looked to release their fast strikers, launching it long into the vast space behind the high German line. Raindrops the size of five-pence pieces quickened the pitch, encouraging that strategy.

In the ninth minute, the entire spectacle was played out in microcosm. Islam Slimani ran alone on to a long ball down the left channel. Manuel Neuer dashed out of his box to meet him. For a moment time stood still as they matched each other stride for stride along the touchline. A last-ditch tackle from the keeper put the ball out for a corner. The crowd caught its breath.

Twenty more times over the next 120 minutes Germany's number one would leave his goal to mop up behind his defence, every single incident a potential red card, a game decider. Neuer, the sweeper-keeper, was making sure two dozen counter-attacks by the Algerians never culminated in shooting chances, but his was a high-wire act almost too nerve-racking to watch. 'Harakiri', TV pundit Oliver Kahn sneered on the touchline. He had never willingly rushed out of his box in his day.

Although Germany created serviceable chances of their own, through Lahm, Schweinsteiger and Müller, sloppy passing in the congested final third and the Algerians' super-quick counters made this a much more restless, turbulent affair than anticipated. Löw's men couldn't get a grip on the increasingly disjointed game. Anxiety took hold instead. Disquiet led to agitation, agitation led to further disquiet.

In German, confidence and its opposite, self-consciousness, are the same word: *Selbstbewusstsein*. We don't see the contradiction – to be aware of yourself is to be confident. The Algerians chipped away at the national team's self-assurance by depriving them of their footballing identity: domination by passing. Germany had more possession and better individuals by far but their opponents dictated the game, by striking terror into their hearts with asymmetrical tactics, small-scale, guerrilla-type forays into the German hinterland. The Beira-Rio was witnessing an ambush. Löw's men were lured into cul-de-sacs and beaten up at the other, exposed end.

The confusion in the white and black ranks was reminiscent of the 2-2 draw with Ghana but with one big difference. This time a defeat would prove fatal. Fatal for the team's World Cup campaign, fatal for Löw's tenure. Germany had never been beaten in the last sixteen at the World Cup since the current format was adopted in 1986. Exiting the tournament at this stage, against Algeria, was unacceptable. They stared humiliation in the face. 'Yes, you start thinking [about going out] and there were moments when we looked at each other,' says Mertesacker. 'We didn't have the lightness of touch, nor the security.' 'Phew. And breathe,' the official German FA Twitter feed exhaled at half-time.

André Schürrle was introduced for the disappointing Götze on the right. Initially, however, the second half brought more of the same. Neuer, who would end up running five and a half kilometres during the game as Germany's attacks broke down and Algeria enjoyed the space suddenly opening up in front of them. But, slowly, Germany's passing became crisper, at the same rate as Halilhodžić's men tired. Müller, Schürrle and Lahm spurned good opportunities to take the lead. 'I thought: that's impossible. We're not scoring,' says Lahm. 'We were always getting the final ball wrong, the final move. They were so densely packed in their own half that we had no answers.'

With twenty minutes to go, Germany got their lucky break. Or perhaps that should be a lucky strain. Mustafi, playing at full-back, had to come off with a hamstring tear. He had been ineffectual going forward and shaky defensively. Millions of armchair *Bundestrainer* rejoiced as Löw ordered Lahm back to his customary position in defence. Khedira came on to resume his 2010 and 2012 partnership with Schweinsteiger at the centre.

Lahm's quality told immediately. Only a quarter of all German attacks had come from the right side before the break but that figure jumped to 44 per cent in the second half, as the captain combined well with the hard-running Müller. The recalibrated Germany found its balance on the pitch, and with that came serenity. Their combination game recovered. 'Sometimes when you pass the ball a lot it looks like it's ineffective but the Algerians had to run a lot,' Toni Kroos said. 'And in the end, they were spent. Every three minutes, another one of them was on the floor with cramp.'

But the end wasn't the end, unfortunately. Algeria dragged the game into extra-time. That was an important staging post for the Fennec but Germany had managed to chase the spectre of failure away. They had stopped worrying about losing or about the dramatic contest going to penalties. The thirty minutes of extra-time were a gift; all the run-up they needed to finish off opponents who were already on their backs. 'It helped us to find our own game again,' said Mertesacker.

And so it came to pass two minutes after kick-off. Müller held off a challenge from Sofiane Feghouli to break through on the left-hand side and drill the ball low and hard across the box. Schürrle had timed his run into the goalmouth well to be onside but he was a little ahead of the slightly defected cross by the time it fizzed towards him. The Chelsea player improvised. He pushed out his left foot and back-heeled the ball behind his body on a half-volley into Raïs M'Bolhi's goal. The most beautiful finish to banish all ugly scenarios.

Mesut Özil, who had had an extremely quiet game, put Germany's progress to the quarter-finals beyond doubt with an angled shot – from a Schürrle rebound – at the death. There was still time for Abdelmoumene Djabou to beat Neuer with a volley from a Feghouli cross. Lahm, of all players, had been caught out of position. But that was it.

The predominantly Brazilian crowd booed and whistled. They had wanted Germany, a team that threatened their own side, to lose. They had also wanted the underdog to win. Neutrals always do. On top of that, they felt a little cheated. The game's predictable denouement didn't seem appropriate for one of the World Cup's most open, riveting matches. The Germans had spoilt the party but it was they who left the ground looking like losers, staring blankly into the middle distance while the Algerians enjoyed public accolades for their spirited resistance.

Algeria's goalkeeper was named FIFA's Man of the Match by Twitter users. The international audience had taken to his courageous efforts during the match, and the German goalkeeping coach Andreas Köpke was full of admiration as well. 'You have to say he was excellent,' Köpke said, standing between concrete pillars in the unfinished Beira-Rio mixed zone. The vote-winner himself didn't look at all happy, however, and that wasn't entirely due to the somewhat ugly trophy in his hands. 'We are very disappointed,' said M'Bolhi on the press conference podium. 'We had a chance to win today.'

Neuer, the match-winner in German eyes, was at the same time wandering through the bowels of the stadium, nonplussed. Of his all-or-nothing last-man antics he said with a shrug: 'The pitch lent itself to that today, it was very wet out there.' A smile broke out only when he talked about having overcome his shoulder injury. 'You could see that today I could throw out the ball properly again, for the first time,' he said, contently.

His pinpoint throws were not the whole story, though. *Süddeutsche Zeitung* wrote that his participation amounted to an almost unfair advantage: 'Germany had effectively twelve players on the pitch, since Neuer was both a keeper and outfield player.' He had saved Germany in a handful of 'dangerous situations', Löw said, 'he played like a libero'. Only Franz Beckenbauer, joked Köpke, had swept up better for the national team. Benedikt Höwedes, his former team-mate at Schalke 04, revealed that Neuer had often shone in training matches with his feet. 'He's so quick, I couldn't have caught up with him,' said Schweinsteiger substitute Christoph Kramer, admiringly. ('Probably third division,' the keeper once replied when someone asked him what level he could have played without gloves.)

The game's hero played down the daredevil nature of his own involvement ('I help where I can. Sure, I took a risk here or there but that's part of my game. It was a bit tight today') as well as the worries that arose from his frequent involvement. 'It's a similar story at Bayern. It wasn't a failure of the system, it's a question of trust; automatisms that kick in between me and the defence,' he insisted.

Köpke: 'Yes, there's an element of risk but I never had the feeling that he could misjudge the situation, I don't think he's a red card waiting to happen. I'm always very calm on the bench. He even enjoys playing football and outsmarting a player from time to time. He's the world's most complete keeper, and that's the style we play. That style is important for us.'

But did that importance have to go as far as the team relying solely on Neuer to stand between them and Algeria scoring half a dozen goals from counter-attacks? Lahm thinks the question misunderstands Germany's set-up. 'We know that there's a keeper in goal, one who can play football,' he says. 'We know that he'll be there and that he'll do his thing. That lets you play a more attacking game. If the others launch it long, Manu is there. I didn't have the feeling that they had a hundred chances and that nothing was going for us.' Neuer had 'the eye for dangerous situations and the ability to defuse them', said Mertesacker. 'That's why he's world-famous, that's why we need him.'

Bierhoff: 'Neuer was outstanding. But he had played like that before, it wasn't anything new. The only difference was the number of opportunities he had to show his class in that game.'

That much was indisputable. But long-term observers of the national team weren't sure all the praise for the man from Gelsenkirchen-Buer wasn't in fact a back-handed compliment to Löw's team. The era of Germany defining itself as as *Torhüterland* (goalkeeping country), because only their shot-stoppers could be considered world class, was supposed to have been over a while ago.

There were bigger, more troublesome questions on the night. Why had the team lost their composure so badly? Why had they so nearly buckled in a game in which there was no room for error? Should they really be lauded for backing themselves into a corner against Algeria, then valiantly fighting their way out?

Löw certainly thought so. 'You can't play fantastic football in all games,' he said curtly. 'Am I supposed to be angry that we're in the next round? You have to take a deep breath after such a game. It was a victory of willpower in the end, you have to battle through these types of matches.' Job done, move along now, nothing to see.

That might have been the end of a puzzling evening, but for Boris Büchler. Büchler was the ZDF touchline reporter for the game. He had put in requests for Thomas Müller and Sami Khedira as second 'flash' interviewees (after Neuer); both were undergoing doping tests, however. In their place, a sweaty, weary Per Mertesacker appeared in front of the advertising board. Büchler took a hard line.

*

'Congratulations on reaching the quarter-finals. What made the game of the national team so cumbersome and vulnerable today?'

'I don't care [shakes his head angrily]. We're through to the last eight. That's what matters.'

'But that can't be the level [of performance] you expected. You'll have to improve for the quarter-finals, that should be obvious to you.'

'What do you want from me now? What do you want, so soon after the game? [shrugs shoulders violently]. I don't understand.'

'I'm congratulating you, firstly, but I'm asking why it didn't go as expected at the back and in the transition game. That's all.'

'Do you believe [Algeria] are a bunch of clowns here, in the last sixteen? [shrugs] They have made it really difficult for us, over a hundred and twenty minutes and we fought until the end. We were convincing [in the end], especially in extra-time. It was end to end, we showed courage. We conceded chances but nevertheless, you have to keep a clean sheet for a long time. We managed that. And on top of that, we won deservedly in the end. Everything else . . . I will lie down in an ice barrel for three days now. Then we analyse the game, then we'll see.'

'A *tour de force*, you powered through. Do you think that the wow effect will come eventually, like at the World Cup 2010, so that there's better football, too?'

'[Shrugs] What do you want? Do you want a successful World Cup or do you want us to get eliminated again, playing beautiful stuff? I don't understand all these questions. We are through, we are incredibly happy and now we're preparing for France.'

Within minutes, the clip of the outburst was setting social media alight. People tend not to like football commentators and reporters, especially those on public broadcasting channels; Mertesacker was showered with praise for standing up to the irreverent line of inquiry. There was a strong novelty factor at work as well. Mertesacker's generation of national players didn't say controversial things, and they certainly didn't fall out with their interlocutors live on camera. They were, a cliché had it, perfect sons-in-law.

Even by the standards of the class of Löw, Mertesacker, the Hannover-born son of a bank manager, was an incredibly articulate, genial guy, a new breed of football professional. He was still a spotty youngster living with his parents and undertaking '*Zivildienst*', community service, in lieu of mandatory national service, when Klinsmann first called him up in 2004. Nobody was forced to bear arms in the *Bundeswehr* (national army) but those who wanted to serve their country in different ways had to explain their reasons in a letter to the Ministry of Defence. Mertesacker wrote that he was a pacifist and also mentioned that his height – 1.98 metres – made it impossible for him to fit into tanks or submarines. The government accepted his plea. On his own volition, he worked eighteen months with handicapped people in a secure mental hospital. 'That puts everything into perspective,' he said.

Bild had mocked him and Christoph Metzelder as 'Mr Snore and Mr Slow' during Euro 2008. Mertesacker was never the quickest of players. He lost his place to Mats Hummels in 2012 but never made a fuss. The F in 'BFG', his Arsenal nickname, doesn't stand for 'friendly' – 'We have a Big Fucking German,' the chant at the Emirates goes – but Mertesacker was the proverbial gentle giant and a sincere team player. 'He was much more important for the team than most people realise,' says a member of the staff. 'If he felt good, those around him felt good.'

So if he had lost his cool it meant Büchler must have touched a nerve. The reporter later revealed that the centre-back had kicked an advertising hoarding in frustration before the interview had even started. After their on-screen confrontation, the defender turned to shout at a DFB press officer: 'Incredible! How dare that guy?'

A shower and change of clothes later, Mertesacker had calmed down but he was still unwilling to address Germany's failings. 'I'm not going to look at this game and tell you what we need and who we need,' he told me after the match. 'The decisive factor was how we fought for each other, how we stood up for each other. All those who complained about us failing with beautiful football now start complaining that we didn't play well. I don't care about all of that. All games [in the knock-out round] have been tight. We're through.' Pressed on the game's open nature, a tired 'It's not what we wanted' was all he could muster.

'I understand that the media focus on the negative things,' he says, a few months hence. 'But as a player, you experience such a game very differently. You feel: the opposition are growing in confidence, they're surpassing themselves, and you have problems. But you come back, due to your maturity and class, due to superior fitness, too. It was a bit of that Bayern mentality. We knew: come what may we'll win this thing! At the end you're incredibly proud of having progressed and given your all for Germany. But others feel you've done everything wrong. Worlds collide there. I think there's no harm in making that point publicly.'

In a joint interview with Büchler for *Die Zeit* in November 2014, Mertesacker revealed that his strong reaction was not entirely a product of raw emotion but partly calculated. 'I knew myself that not everything had gone well in that game. But I wanted to protect the positives for us from the people outside. Criticism is okay but, as a player, you think about having to go again in three, four days. You can't let anybody talk you into feeling weak at that moment.'

His team-mates understood where he was coming from. On the flight back to their base camp, they showed him clips of his interview on their mobile phones. 'What do you want? Ice barrel! Clowns! Super interview, Per. You have made history,' they repeated gleefully. It was great fun, but serious, too. They felt he had spoken up for them. 'They won't get us down. We are one team, we want to go further, that's all that matters,' they told Mertesacker, as he recalls.

You'd think that a TV interview is pretty far down the list of things that can positively influence a team's tournament campaign. But in this case you'd be wrong. 'Per's interview was a breakthrough, as far as the perception of the team was concerned,' claims Bierhoff. 'It pointed to the way ahead. People realised these guys were serious, that they gave their heart, their passion, and that how they [the media] dealt with it was wrong.' The Mertesacker–Büchler exchange was included in *Die Mannschaft*, the official World Cup documentary by the German FA. In cinema screenings the scene was greeted with applause.

A collision of worlds. The Algeria game marked the fault line between sky-high expectations and the much less sparkling realities on the pitch. *Die Welt* sensed that Germany's campaign had just witnessed a momentous occasion, that it had reached a turning point. But where that turn would take the team, they didn't know. 'This extra-time win will presumably go down in DFB history later,' the middle market paper wrote, 'either super-elevated, as the initial spark for the World Cup title or demonised, as a symbol of pre-announced failure, the writing on the wall for the end of Löw's era.'

'The external reaction, but also the internal one, to a point, made me wonder,' says Bierhoff. 'We knew in preparation that it would be a tough game, the Belgians later told me that Algeria were the hardest opponents they had faced. You have to have that kind of game in any tournament. It doesn't work otherwise. Basically, it was a good sign. There was drama, yes. But there was a lot of drama in the second round. There was an assumption – maybe a presumption – that the big teams would just turn up and win but it was up and down, end to end. Everyone thought the games would be slower, more cautious in the heat of Brazil. But the matches were much more eventful than expected, no team truly dominated. I was surprised by the perception and by the assessment. It's as if the German national team has to do differently from all the others.'

Bierhoff suggests there's something succinctly German in that disposition, an ingrained unwillingness to accept imperfect performance, irrespective of extraneous circumstances. 'There's an economic crisis everywhere – but we don't have one. The banks going bust? Not here, that mustn't be. As a strong nation, as a strong team, you can counterbalance and compensate, but there are reasons for these problems, reasons you cannot always escape.'

But what about the problems that were decidedly of their own making? For the fourth game running the limitations of Löw's full-backless formation had been plain for all to see. Sticking with Lahm in the centre was one thing, not playing any natural wide defenders to provide an attacking outlet was quite another. It was a mystery why Löw didn't give Erik Durm or Kevin Großkreutz a chance; both had shown for Borussia Dortmund in the Champions League that they were up to the task. Schweinsteiger was dead on his feet after 110 minutes. His partner-cum-rival Khedira wasn't at all happy about being relegated to the bench again. 'Ask Mehmet,' Khedira had scoffed at reporters in the mixed zone, and left without another word. Mehmet Scholl, the former Bayern midfielder turned TV pundit, had criticised the player on air for his thinly disguised dig at Schweinsteiger's role in the USA win.

In attack, Thomas Müller was the only starter who had played reasonably well. Mesut Özil, despite his goal, still looked lost for long spells, unable to get to grips with his more peripheral role after losing the central attacking midfield spot to Toni Kroos. Götze had put in forty-five minutes to no effect. Not a single German reporter wanted to ask him anything after the final whistle.

One or two heads did drop momentarily in the wake of the close shave at Porto Alegre, but the general mood inside Campo Bahia was more positive than that of the German public. The players hadn't forgotten how the nation had feared the worst during the South Tyrol training camp. 'There was no euphoria whatsoever [before the World Cup], that helped us,' says Mertesacker. 'We said: "Let's start with small steps, let's think small," let's get past the group stage first. Ghana and Algeria were the key games. We were shaken up, but the team were truly alive. We had to cope with things we hadn't anticipated, against opponents we had perhaps underestimated a little. That was a big test of character for everyone individually, and for the team. Against Ghana, we were behind; Algeria had one counter-attacking chance after another. But we didn't capitulate. We found our way back on to the right path at the right moment.'

That's how it looked from the ground. Higher up inside the stadium, and at home in front of the television screens, the troubling extent to which the *Nationalmannschaft* had veered off course in the first half left little room for praise of the team's self-righting mechanism. Löw, like so many modern football managers, envisaged a football that minimised the role of luck, a mastery of style that tamed the game's countless vagaries through the means of positional fidelity and ball circulation. Three days before the quarter-final against Didier Deschamps' rejuvenated, impressively clinical France, Löw's Germany had looked further away than ever from achieving that sophisticated aim.

Schürrle, who had seen how far short the team had fallen of Löw's ideals from his vantage point on the bench in the first half, knew there was no point in sugar-coating the lesson of the trip south. 'If we play like that against the French,' he said, 'we're going out.'

MORE IS MORE

Mitzvah goreret mitzvah, 'One good deed begets another' it says in the Talmud (Ethics of Fathers). It is often understood as an ancient version of the 'pay it forward' principle, the idea that kindness is self-proliferating. The original meaning is more complex. The good deed of a 'mitzvah' is one specifically decreed by one of the 613 divine commandments. The fulfilment of one commandment leads to the fulfilment of the next one, says the Talmud. *Mitzvah goreret mitzvah* is an insight into the logic of religious submission. The moment you accept a specific demand on your behaviour imposed by a belief system, it's very hard to explain to yourself why you should not accept another one.

Even though nobody descended Großer Feldberg – the tallest mountain in the Taunus range, thirty minutes north-west of the German FA HQ in Frankfurt – with a set of stone tablets at the turn of the century, the leaders of German football, of club and country, came to place their faith in the law. The law of larger numbers. Once they accepted that more coaching for more talents equalled more skilled football players, the next steps were obvious. All the system demanded was steady increments of the few variables involved – in quantitive and qualitative terms – to produce even more and even better professionals.

*

Getting to that point took a while, however. 'It was a fight,' says Ulf Schott. 'Firstly, it was a battle to get the clubs to overhaul their youth development. Secondly, it was an ongoing battle to convince them of the need to keep at it. You couldn't expect any positive results after two or three years, as youngsters who had entered the system as ten-year-olds were still far too young to get anywhere near the Bundesliga teams. Nor was each and every club convinced all the effort was necessary. You were in constant discussions.'

Those reservations encroached on the work that was being done to put the reforms into practice. The standard of footballing education at the academies varied in those early years. 'We had set the initial bar at 1.40 metres, and everyone jumped over it,' says Schott. 'But some clubs really should have been aiming to clear 1.90 or maybe even two metres. What we needed was a mirror that we could hold up to the clubs and show them where they could be doing better. An objective benchmark.' The Belgium company Double Pass was chosen to devise a certification regime. They had developed similar models for the development of talent in basketball and ice hockey.

Today, Double Pass (via its subsidiary Foot Pass) judges the clubs's performance centres on 250 criteria, ranging from infrastructure (minimum requirement of four training pitches, including one made of Astro Turf) to personnel (at least one sporting director with a UEFA A-level licence, a minimum of two coaches with a UEFA Pro licence, at least one A-level coach, one goalkeeping coach, two physiotherapists), performance diagnostics and the adoption of a uniform philosophy or blueprint throughout the club. Their ratings system follows that of Michelin – three stars signify educational excellence.

To call the regulations detailed would be an understatement. Bayern Munich's former youth director Werner Kern, the man who developed the talents of Bastian Schweinsteiger, Toni Kroos, Philipp Lahm and countless others, once complained that Double Pass had marked his club down because their youth training pitches at Säbener Strasse weren't clearly numbered.

In the initial ratings period, 2007–9, seven Bundesliga clubs were awarded three stars by Foot Pass, the top mark. By 2011, eleven top-flight clubs were rated excellent, and in the latest round of testing (2014), fifteen out of eighteen Bundesliga clubs were awarded three stars. A bonus star is available for performance centres which produce a high number of first team players.

The competition for stars is encouraged by the financial rewards that are linked to it. The German FA redistributes a part of the annual payments from UEFA's Champions League solidarity fund to the thirty-six professional clubs. Three stars are worth €400,000. Centres without any stars get €100,000. Champions League participants don't receive any funds.

The money from the German FA can only go some way to finance youth development at the clubs, however. Running costs range between €2.5 and €5 million annually. By the end of 2014–15, the thirty-six top-flight teams had spent well over €1 billion on fostering young talent since 2001. About 5,200 young players were being developed in fifty-four performance centres that season, at a cost of approximately €125 million. Academies have sprung up in the third and even fourth tiers of the football pyramid as well.

Nobody would invest this much if there wasn't a clear economic upside, as appealing as doing something solely for the greater good of German football might be. The breakthrough, in that respect, didn't come until the 2010 World Cup in South Africa, says Schott. Löw's young team didn't win the competition but they played a brand of exciting attacking football that hadn't been associated with the national team since the 1970s. Schott: 'Everybody could see a new generation of players had arrived, the first generation of *Leistungszentrum* (academy) boys, players who had undergone schooling in the performance centres for eight, ten years. They could do things that previous national team players simply couldn't do, and Löw was able to have them play in a way his predecessors weren't able to. That's when the public became aware that the reforms were beginning to bear fruit. That's when the clubs realised they were adding value.'

In 2006, Bundesliga clubs with rebuilt, modernised stadiums for the World Cup had been the first big winners of the renaissance. Now, those who produced great kids in their academies benefitted, too. They could sell them on expensively or use them to bolster their squads.

'There was a definite jump in quality in youth development that improved the football being played in the Bundesliga,' says the former Bayern Munich president Uli Hoeness. 'On top of that, I also believe that the 2006 World Cup completely changed football's standing in society. There were new or modified stadiums that were comfortable, clean and sheltered you from the rain, there were good sight lines and the architects made sure the stands were protected from the wind, which made them more appealing to women in particular. There were new VIP lounges and football addressed issues in society. The stadiums and infrastructure, coupled with the positive developments on the pitch, changed the crowds' behaviour. They now came two hours before the game and stayed for an hour after it. You were now able to spend time in a stadium with friends and family, and enjoy yourself.' A virtuous cycle was set in motion. 'More comfort and a better experience in the stadium led to higher revenues for the clubs and football's elevated social status resulted in better TV deals. Fans bought more shirts, income from merchandising increased, corporations caught on to the fact that more people were following football and were thus prepared to pay more for shirt sponsorship and advertising boards. At the same time, other football markets like Italy collapsed and left a gap that German football exploited with relish.' Better grounds, better German players and more money to be invested all came together in a perfect storm.

*

There was, however, as Schott is keen to point out, no comprehensive master plan for the technical education of Özil, Götze et al. 'Some people felt that we should provide a full, binding curriculum of lessons to be taught at the academies. Others said the coaches should be given free rein to allow for individualism and prevent everyone doing exactly the same thing. Those were the two extreme positions. We met in the middle. We came up with a framework of basic objectives that should be met, without being dogmatic. I don't think that was very important, though. The biggest, most decisive effect resulted from the increase of full-time professional youth coaches. In 2000, we had about a hundred, FA and clubs combined. Today, there are four hundred – four hundred licensed coaches who do nothing else but to think about coaching youngsters football every single day. We provide them with platforms for regular meetings, for the exchange of ideas. As they get better and improve, so does their training and the players they develop.'

Having more qualified coaches directly translates into more time spent on the training pitch for the 800 most talented youngsters that get into the club academies each year. However, this is only 0.5 per cent of the 196,000 teenaged boys who play football each week. There are a lot of skilled players who don't make the cut. Fourteen thousand of those therefore receive weekly lessons at the FA's 366 *Stützpunkte*, where they are trained by experts and watched by scouts. The annual cost of the DFB's network has ballooned to €21 million.

'The football that is being played today has nothing to do with different training plans for a "more modern football",' Schott reiterates. 'It's simply due to talented players at eighteen, nineteen or twenty having enjoyed between 50 and 100 per cent more training sessions in their lives than those who came into the league at the same age fifteen years ago. Elite youngsters trained three, at most four times a week. Now it's six to nine times a week, with full-time professionals who don't just happen to know football but can also teach it.'

Hannes Winzer was one of them. The former team-mate of Per Mertesacker in the Hannover 96 youth team ('I was the better footballer then,' he laughs) experienced *Stützpunkt* training as a fifteen-year-old and then moved on to become an A-licence coach himself, after not quite making it as professional footballer. 'I was at TSV Havelse, a club from outside Hannover and, every Monday, I received some extra technical training at the German FA centre,' he says. 'That was good but at fifteen it's really too late to make a real difference. You have to do that with nine-, ten-, eleven-year-olds. When I came back eight years later, to teach at a *Stützpunkt* myself, you could see how far things had progressed. The quality of the coaches in particular had improved markedly.'

'Investing in personnel and manpower is important,' says FSV Mainz 05's youth director Volker Kersting. 'But more important is investing in heads, in concepts and philosophies. Twenty years ago, the professional team and the youth teams were run as completely separate entities. If somebody made it through the ranks, it was a bonus. Since 2000, the boards have become aware of the need for a uniform footballing philosophy from the top down. Today, we are preparing youngsters very much in line with what's demanded of them in the first team. Our first team coaches don't have to be brave to play these guys; they know that they will come ready for the kind of football we're playing. And as a consequence, more players than ever make the leap.'

Winzer: 'The level of youngsters coming through is incredibly high now, they're basically perfectly developed. That wasn't the case at all when I was their age. I had never seen a light barrier [for measuring sprint time] before training with Ralf Rangnick's first team at Hannover. It was the same as far as tactics were concerned. I had been essentially untouched by that until I was nineteen and was taught about them by Rangnick. My eyes were opened, I began to see football and the underlying structures of the game in a new light. The idea that tactics can help you hide your flaws and bring out your strengths . . . it only dawned on me then how basic and incomplete my own footballing education had been up until that point. And fitness-wise . . . I was given a gym membership. Go and bulk up. Today, you have fifteen-year-olds doing systematic exercises to develop acceleration power.'

At Mainz, training sessions are prescribed for each year; they follow a programme that can be broken down to the specific priorities of any given week during the season. This production line only functions, of course, if everyone working on the system knows what the finished article is supposed to look like. The club has to define the strategic direction and then find first team managers who are suitable for it; not hire managers who define strategy for them. Otherwise, the entire youth department would have wasted their time producing components that don't fit the new boss's design (and have to be offloaded to some other club willing to pay for them).

Mainz, one of the smallest clubs in the top flight, can't afford such inefficiency. Their entire first team budget was a mere €24 million in 2014. 'If you have a lot of money, you can do things differently: you can simply concentrate on buying the best players. That's also a philosophy,' Kersting says, stony-faced.

The biggest, most eye-catching day-to-day change on practice pitches Kersting can attest to is the prevalence of individualised drills: 'Footballers spend nearly as much time on the ball by themselves now as playing with the team.'

Affording players that much specific attention was made possible by closer cooperation between academies and local schools. The licensing system required the newly built Bundesliga academies to join forces with schools which could tailor their curriculum to the needs of budding football professionals. Synchronising the schools' hours with that of the club reduced stress levels for kids, allowed them to train during the day and enabled them to stay in education for longer. Supervised homework hours and individualised exam schedules were part of the package.

Lahm: 'I'm part of the first generation who grew up in the performance centres. That's where it started: everything became a lot more professional. I remember going to Bayern every Tuesday and Thursday after school, at 2 p.m. Training, lunch, then there was ninety minutes of studying with teachers, then another training session. You had to get all your schoolwork sorted out, they were checking your grades.'

'But after a couple of years of the new system being in place, we found that there was still a lot of room for improvement at many clubs,' recalls Schott. 'We had the choice of applying more pressure or coming up with new incentives. We chose the latter.' A list of eighteen criteria that defined the desired levels of cooperation with schools was drawn up. Schott: 'Schools had to be flexible, there had to be a detailed plan for football kids, a binding contract between the schools and the regional FA, other regional clubs and the Bundesliga club itself.' Clubs and schools which fulfilled these requirements were certified '*Eliteschule des Fußballs*', elite school of football, as a reward.

Many of these elite schools are in fact made up of two or three different types of secondary schools in the same vicinity. *Hauptschule* (years five through to nine or ten), offers lower secondary education. At a *Gymnasium*, the German version of high school (years five through to twelve or thirteen), children receive advanced secondary education, with a view to attaining *Abitur* (A levels), the requirement for attending university. *Realschule* (years five through nine or ten) ranks somewhere in the middle. (There are also some hybrid forms and schools geared towards vocational education.) Talented footballers are being educated in line with their intellectual capabilities, at the type of school that serves them best. There are no special dispensations when it comes to the required grades.

You would expect kids of widely diverging educational achievements among the most talented footballers in a nation of eighty million people, but studies have shown the spectrum to be surprisingly narrow. Research from the University of Bremen found that the rate of

Gymnasium students in the academies (55 to 60 per cent) was significantly higher than in the general population (50 per cent). If you dig further down to the players who get called up to the FA's youth national teams, the percentage of *Gymnasium* pupils jumps to 70 per cent. At some Bundesliga clubs, Kersting estimates, as many as 85 per cent of academy students are doing their *Abitur*. 'It used to be completely the other way around. You'd maybe have 15 per cent of *Abitur* students in the youth teams.'

German football has, it seems, become thoroughly middle class.

'There are a few possible explanations for this trend and none of them is scientifically proven yet,' says Schott. 'It could be that high intellectual performance is needed to make it as a footballer today. Or, if you want to put it more generally, kids who can sacrifice and organise themselves and their time well tend to thrive. If they can do that on the pitch, they can do it at school as well – and vice versa. You need to set yourself targets and prioritise them, then make sure you achieve them.' Youth football, he says, is like an extended version of the Stanford 'marshmallow' experiment, a giant exercise in delayed gratification. At Stanford, children were given a marshmallow and rewarded for not eating it by receiving a second one a few minutes later. Those who were able to defer instant pleasure were later found to have higher incomes and were less likely to develop addictions. In short: they were more successful.

Kersting: 'I always say that the brain is the most important thing a footballer possesses. What doesn't happen upstairs can't happen down below at the feet either. You can be technically perfect on the ball but that in itself won't do at the highest level. You'll have to go and play Futsal indoors or free-style football instead.'

Football has become a mind game. Twenty years ago, when players made it as a pro at twenty-two, twenty-three – 'that was considered young then' (Kersting) – they might have known a couple of tactical systems. 'Today, you have to be able to switch formation and systems four or five times during a game – whether you are sixteen or an established first team player,' says Kersting, who has overseen the development of world champions Erik Durm and André Schürrle at his academy. Both took A levels at Integrierte Gesamtschule Mainz-Bretzenheim, one of two partner schools of Mainz 05.

As the game has become more physical, so the mental demands on young players have grown even more, exponentially. They need to be able to function at a drop of a hat in a variety of positions, understand the requirements those changes entail and have the patience to have their mistakes explained to them in countless sessions with video analysts. 'We start as early as fourteen,' says Kersting. 'We present clips for the whole team as well as individual scenes. Sometimes, they're juxtaposed with footage of one of the world's best players, to show what a solution looks like in that situation. It's a huge effort, but it makes a big positive difference for the player's learning.' As the job profile has evolved, so have the applicants. 'We have a completely different type of footballer now,' he says. A smarter type.

Lahm: 'In the old days, you would get the line-up from your manager and be told what your role was and who you'd play against. Maybe also how you were supposed to move across the pitch as a team. Today, it's much more concrete, much more detailed. You get shown solutions for specific problems on the pitch. There's much more focus on the attacking game. You practice it more and you talk about it more. Football is very dynamic, so it's hard to plan for specific moves, but a good coach will show you where the vacant spaces are and what you have to do to get into them. That's become standard. Players don't just take it on board – they expect it now.'

Most Bundesliga academies have formulated detailed guidelines for tactical behaviour that are binding for all age groups. The level of sophistication is quite remarkable. A short presentation of the playing concept that one particular club sends out confidentially to prospective academy students aged fifteen and younger shows the ideal positioning against a 4-1-4-1 system, a detailed breakdown of various phases of an attacking move and explains the transition from 'order' to 'spatial pressure' to 'ball pressure' in defence.

Twenty-one of the twenty-three 2014 World Cup squad members were products of the academy system. (Goalkeeper Roman Weidenfeller and Miroslav Klose were already professionals when the reforms were introduced.) Six of those received their first elite training at an FA regional centre. Thirteen went to a '*Eliteschule des Fußballs*', and as many graduated with *Abitur* or equivalent qualifications.

Natural selection in an ever more complex, intellectually challenging environment has surely played a key role, but the FA's move to synchronise academic and athletic education through the elite schools has accelerated the process of what might be called dressing-room gentrification. Clever footballers can get even sharper by staying in education for longer. Middle-class parents who would have been reluctant to let their teenaged sons embark on a football career in light of the minuscule chances of success in the past can now breathe a bit easier. Their kids no longer have to sacrifice the chance to go to university in pursuit of their dream. Furthermore, it makes good economic sense to aim for advanced secondary qualifications, even if you are already firmly on course to becoming a professional. The traditional route – leaving school at sixteen to start an apprenticeship, like Miroslav Klose, who trained to be a carpenter – is no longer viable because vocational courses are not flexible enough to accommodate the complex time and travel demands of academy players. You are almost forced to stay in school – unless you want to risk having neither educational nor vocational qualifications after the academy. And kids who don't make the final cut, football-wise, at eighteen or nineteen, are still likely to find part-time employment in the fifth division. The wages there are modest, but they can at least pay for their university education. 'It's not a question of football or school for us – school always comes first,' says Kersting.

Being very good and very smart is mandatory, but it's still not quite enough to make the big time. Having 'a well-rounded personality' (Schott) or 'maturity', as Kersting prefers to call it, is seen as a crucial quality in its own right. 'Maturity can come at different times for these kids, so we have to help them by setting behavioural rules, conducting mental training and sessions with psychologists,' he says. 'You cannot always influence these matters [as a club] but you have to try as much as possible.'

Academy students live different lives from their peers, with different pressure. Schott: 'Because football is relatively more important to them than other things, their confidence is also much more dependent on it. Getting closer to the dream means you worry more. That's why we have to counter-balance it, by making sure they understand the value of family, friends and education. We don't want them to concentrate solely on football. They get educational and psychological help from us.'

'The players who get into the Bundesliga today have benefitted from outstanding education,' said Ernst Tanner, a former youth director at 1860 Munich and Hoffenheim who now works in the same role at RB Salzburg in Austria. 'They are technically and tactically on an extremely high level; some of the games they will have played as teenagers would have been tactically and technically better than the seniors in the second or third division at the same time. And they tend to be well developed as personalities. The clubs are the main source of the boom in talents.'

Hoeness is proud of his club, Bayern Munich's, achievements in that field; achievements that predate the German FA's reforms by a few decades. The record title holders are loathed by one half of Germany as the league's rich overlords who bully all their rivals into submission. The other half, all Bayern fans, love them for it. But it's often forgotten that the Reds' empire was built on the back of a strong youth department that harnessed the talents of Franz Beckenbauer, Sepp Maier and Hans-Georg Schwarzenbeck, the nucleus of the team that would win three European Cups in the mid-seventies.

Hoeness: 'We haven't just developed young players who left their mark on their generation. We have also developed personalities. Almost every important footballer in front of a German TV camera today hails from FC Bayern: Franz Beckenbauer, Udo Lattek, Jupp Heynckes, Oliver Kahn, Mehmet Scholl, Stefan Effenberg, Thomas Strunz, Thomas Helmer, Lothar Matthäus. FC Bayern is a bit more than a normal football club. It seems to have become an important part of society.'

The club's fortunes and that of the national team have often gone hand in hand. Five regular starters, the spine of Löw's team in Brazil, were Säbener Strasse academy graduates: Schweinsteiger, Müller, Lahm and Kroos, as well as Dortmund's Mats Hummels. German teams have had superbly talented players before but probably never such a well-adjusted, professional group. 'It's apparent that our players have also been educated in real life,' says Hoeness. 'They can express themselves, they can put a point across, they have an opinion. They are not oafish footballers. They've been brought up to be good boys. Here at the club, too.'

Before Euro 2012, Lahm spoke out against human rights violations in Ukraine and its undemocratic government. Schweinsteiger and his Bayern team-mate Holger Badstuber, who missed the World Cup in Brazil through injury, handed out clothing worth €20,000 at a centre for political refugees in Munich in October 2014, at a time when calls for a curb on immigrants from war-torn countries had become louder still.

Almost all the young German players at Bayern were living in Munich's centre, in apartments, whereas previous stars had sought the privacy of a villa in Grünwald, a green but dull enclave of the rich in a southern suburb.

The academy boys have changed the culture of the club. In the nineties and noughties, Bayern were a a collection of big, brash personalities, quite keen for their players to make the headlines. Lahm and Schweinsteiger were quieter leaders, setting the tone through their adaptability on the pitch and their dependability.

Schweinsteiger's teenage days were certainly not without the odd misstep. He was once caught late at night in the Säbener Strasse jacuzzi with a girl; she was his cousin and wanted to see the facilities, he told the incredulous club. Hoeness took offence at the young midfielder making a great show of kissing a girlfriend's charm bracelet after goals and repeatedly warned that he needed to be more critical of his own performances. 'He has too many people blowing icing sugar up his arse,' the architect of Bayern's recent return to the circle of European super-clubs thundered.

These were but minor indiscretions in an otherwise exemplary career, however. TV pundits and former players could fret all they liked about 'the lack of big characters' after the retirement of Oliver Kahn, the last remnant of more vocal, extrovert times. The takeover of Bayern and then the national team by Schweini–Lahm signalled the irrevocable triumph of the performance centre kids.

Bayern's press officer Markus Hörwick has revealed that the latest products of Germany's youth system do not require media training any more. They arrive as fully-fledged pros, aware of their duties and the pitfalls of the mixed zone.

Nevertheless, the club is adamant that they remain exposed to the real world. Most training sessions are public and can attract up to 3,000 people. Every year before Christmas, every single player is sent out to spend an evening with one fan club. 'I don't think they do that at Manchester United or Real Madrid,' says Müller. 'We are a global club but we don't forget our roots.'

As long as he can remember 'Bayern have defined themselves as winners, as being No. 1,' he adds. Lahm joined them at eleven from his local team FT Gern, an outfit situated not far from the Olympic Stadium. He was systematically versed in the club's '*mia san mia*' (Bavarian dialect which translates as 'we are who we are') ideology, an unshakeable belief in their own greatness and almost impossible ambition: second best is a disgrace. 'You get told at a very young age that only winning is acceptable,' explains Lahm, 'but also that playing for Bayern comes with a lot of responsibility. You are representing the club and have to behave accordingly.'

Every Bayern team, from the seniors down to the U9s, has stronger players than any domestic rival. Winning isn't just mandatory but statistically quite likely. The Bayern players know that and so do their opponents. That aura of invincibility alone is worth a few points.

The German junior national teams, by contrast, were perennial losers. Even in the glory days of the seventies and eighties they only won three trophies, and none whatsoever after 1984. A multitude of sins were responsible for the DFB's youngsters repeated failings. The bottom line? There were not enough good players, but also a self-defeating mentality had set in. Because they weren't expected to win, nobody really cared. There was no pressure to win. So they didn't win. And even fewer people cared. All that mattered were the seniors.

On top of that, even progress to the U21s didn't guarantee a Bundesliga career, as the top clubs were reluctant to call on the services of youngsters. Youth internationals were just as likely – if not more likely – to get lost, career-wise, as to make the transition to full-time pro. So why bother?

Teenagers possessed by demons of sloth. The German FA called for an exorcist and found one in sporting director Matthias Sammer, 1996 Golden Ball winner, member of the last successful *Nationalmannschaft* (Euro 96), 2002 Bundesliga winner as coach of Borussia Dortmund, high-priest of 'can do'.

The April 2006 appointment of the former midfielder, who'd started his career at Dynamo Dresden in the GDR under his father Klaus Sammer, had been a blow for national manager Klinsmann. Klinsmann and Bierhoff had favoured Bernhard Peters, the former hockey national coach, for the position. The hiring of the grimly determined Sammer was seen as a reactionary choice, evidence of the German FA undermining the reformist drive of Klinsmann and Bierhoff. Unlike the duo in charge, Sammer didn't speak of 'energy fields' but about the need to win individual battles on the pitch and wanting it more than your opponent. His syntax was needlessly complicated, stacks of half-sentences that could, but didn't have to, relate to each other, layers of words obscuring simple messages that sounded worryingly like the old 'German virtues' lectures.

But away from the microphones Sammer was far from the human handbrake on modernity he appeared. He tackled his task of overhauling the youth teams with typical determination. Every youth national team was given its own support staff that included a sport psychologist. Underperforming coaches who owed their positions to past deeds as players were ruthlessly purged. Sammer also brought in an external expert, Marcel Lucassen, a former football player turned physiotherapist and youth coach, to come up with more detailed guidelines for the technical sessions at the regional centres and in the national teams. As Sammer told *Die Zeit* in 2012, they broke football down into its constituent parts: the small movements, the right positioning, the concentration needed to control and play a ball properly. Instructional DVDs were sent out to all the German FA coaches, advising them on the need to look at the microscopic details, like players holding both arms in the same position when balancing a ball. 'Strife inside the body equals strife with the ball,' Lucassen said.

In 2009, the ramped-up pressure on youth teams to deliver and advancements in training at club and national level bore fruit, spectacularly. In May, the U17 team of Marco Pezzaiuoli, a Sammer appointee, won their first ever competition, the European championship on home soil. Marc-André ter Stegen (now at Barcelona), Shkodran Mustafi and Mario Götze were in the line-up for the 1-0 win over the Netherlands in Magdeburg.

A month later, the U21s destroyed Stuart Pearce's England 4-0 at the Euro finals in Malmö. Manager Horst Hrubesch, the hero of the 1980 Euro final and goalscorer in the far less heroic 1-0 shame of Gijon, had replaced Dieter Eilts shortly before the tournament at Sammer's behest. Six World Cup 2014 regulars – Manuel Neuer, Benedikt Höwedes, Jérôme Boateng, Mats Hummels, Sami Khedira and Mesut Özil – broke a long trophy-less spell going back thirty years. (All bar Hummels were already first team mainstays in their clubs at the time but there was no question that they should be promoted straight to the seniors. You had to pay your dues first.)

The triumph in Sweden completed a hat-trick, since the U19s had also come back from the Euros in the Czech Republic with the cup in 2008. Horst Hrubesch had led them to a 3-1 win over Italy; Ron-Robert Zieler was in goal, the two Bender brothers in midfield.

FA president Theodor Zwanziger specifically thanked Sammer as one of 'the many fathers of success' on that 'great day for German football' in the Swedish capital. His victory toast in a fashionable restaurant was interrupted by players chanting 'Theo, get your cash out,' a playful reminder to him of the the DFB's promise to pay €12,000 to each squad member for the win.

Joachim Löw, who'd observed the mauling of England from the stands, praised the playmaking 'genius' of Mesut Özil but also admitted that the U21s win had given him 'food for thought'. It had come, he had noted with some surprise, 'largely without any strikers'. Classic centre-forward types would remain a glaring gap in the football factory's modern assortment.

The year 2009 opened the country's eyes to the stirrings of future greatness. Germany had talent, and they now had the X-factor, too. 'Being gifted alone doesn't get you a Euro youth title,' wrote *Frankfurter Rundschau*. 'The German FA have won the three trophies because Sammer's fierce staunchness has become [part of the] programme.' *Der Stern* didn't feel the need to sit on the fence either. 'If the team continue to develop in that way, we've seen the core of the side who will win the 2014 World Cup in Brazil here,' their Malmö correspondent predicted.

The German FA were initially worried that the clubs would fill their academies with foreign teenagers. They therefore imposed a minimum quota of twelve Germans in any class of twenty. In practice, their fears have proved unfounded. 'Ninety-five per cent of all academy players are eligible to play for Germany,' says Schott. It's telling that Bayern Munich, the country's wealthiest and most successful club, stopped scouting for youngsters in South America altogether in 2011, opting to concentrate on the talent coming through on their own doorstep, in Bavaria, instead.

Two-thirds of all Bundesliga professionals were German in 2013–14, and more of them than ever before were native youngsters. Sixteen per cent of U21 players were on the pitch that season. In 2000–01 that figure was 8 per cent.

The market for footballers is not too different from others; the rules of supply and demand apply. The Bundesliga quickly cottoned on to the fact that churning out a steady number of players (and coaches) through their *Leistungszentren* kept transfer fees and wages in check. There is simply no need to ship in footballers wholesale if the indigenous workforce is both numerous and qualified enough to do the job.

In 2011, a DFL report on the ten-year-anniversary of the academy system found that more than half of all Bundesliga players (52 per cent) had come through the clubs' own youth systems. (Other, less easily quantifiable benefits are the fostering of a strong club identity among players, staff and supporters, and the internal dissemination of know-how.) According to the DFL's CEO Christian Seifert – the DFL is the umbrella organisation of Bundesliga 1 and 2 clubs – the thirty-six elite clubs spent only an average of 36.8 per cent of their €2.45 billion turnover in 2013–14 on wages. 'The average in Europe is 65 per cent,' he says.

*

In hindsight, it seems fairly puzzling that the clubs hadn't devoted themselves to systematic in-house player development much earlier. Germany, with its strong emphasis on such vocational training, has long imposed official standards and regulations on many job-seekers, from trainee plumbers to car mechanics. Professional qualifications are not optional but a must. Why should football have been any different?

In addition, the club ownership model lends itself to sustainability. A few historic exceptions apart, clubs are majority owned by their members, who elect the board. They cannot – and don't want to – depend on the generosity of wealthy owners, whether they're local luminaries or Russian oligarchs, when it comes to improving the quality of the club's squad.

Such organic growth takes time and good decisions. Neutrals are understandably more thrilled by the far more rapid change in a club's fortunes afforded by the turbo-capitalist Premier League, where minnows can become part of European elite overnight (and big, traditional clubs can, conversely, die a rapid death as a result of irresponsible overspending). But after years of playing third or fourth fiddle in Europe, Bundesliga clubs have recently begun to show that international success and financial self-reliance do not have to be mutually exclusive. In European competitions, only Spanish clubs have collectively done better in UEFA competitions in the five seasons from 2010–11 to 2014–15.

'I wonder what the Bundesliga would do if it had as much money as the Premier League,' says Seifert. 'Would we still be world champions or try to have a global All-Star league instead?' The twenty best teams in England turned over approximately €4.1 billion in 2013–14, based on March 2015 exchange rates – that's 167 per cent more than the eighteen elite German clubs. The inference from Seifert's question is that (relative) shortage of money breeds innovation, whereas excess wealth breeds complacency.

*

If you follow the path of the commandments, the 613 *mitzvot*, there is no endgame, no ultimate state of total submission or highest enlightenment to be arrived at. No one can actually fulfil all 613 commands because some of them pertain to eventualities that might never arise or to a past that's no longer applicable, like making animal sacrifices at the temple in Jerusalem. The best you can do is the minimum of what you must do: stay the course and keep going.

Almost every single person interviewed for this book on the developments of the past fifteen years prefaced his thoughts and recollections with the warning that it shouldn't be considered a story with a happy ending but an ongoing one. 'Football is always changing, and we have to make sure to change with it,' says Kersting.

For five years, Bierhoff says, he 'got it in the neck' for suggesting the German FA build its own performance centre/academy for the coaching of the national teams and the development of players. But at the FA headquarters in Frankfurt they have at last bought into his vision. After the World Cup in Brazil, DFB president Wolfgang Niersbach announced that the €89 million project will go ahead, with Bierhoff at the helm until 2020, at least.

'The [DFB] academy can become the second flagship after the national team,' Bierhoff says. 'After the 1990 World Cup win, Franz Beckenbauer said we'd be unbeatable for years to come. Then we woke up in 2000 after patting ourselves on the back for ten years. We mustn't make the same mistake again. We don't want to wake up in 2024 – when the Euros will hopefully be staged in Germany – and say: "We missed the boat and rested on our laurels." By developing players and coaches and utilising centralised knowledge we can get ahead of others.'

Will a more centralised process lead to more homogenous products? Recently, the German syllabus has produced 'more players who are like midfielders', as Lahm says, but that doesn't mean that future academy graduates will all look and play exactly the same way in the future. 'You won't win anything with ten Messis,' says HSV sporting director Bernhard Peters. 'I'm not worried at all that tall strikers and burly defenders will disappear, not at all,' concurs Kersting. Some specialists' qualities, he explains, will remain so useful that their 'deficits' will be outweighed by them.

While there's widespread agreement that young German players are better educated in every sense of the word than ever before, the development process remains fraught with uncertainties. Statistical data from the German FA shows that for every 5,800 players who begin their coaching in the FA regional centres or club academies as U12s, only twenty-one make it into the Bundesliga later on: less than 3 per cent. Individual progress proves notoriously hard to predict.

'It's still the same as it was when I played,' says Winzer. 'Much-hyped fifteen-year-olds somehow fall by the wayside. Others come out of nowhere, from smaller clubs, and surprise everyone late in the game. It could be that they had more responsibility as the star of their team, taking all free-kicks, dictating the game, as opposed to earlier developers who play with team-mates of similar quality and don't stand out as much.'

'Predicting talent is very complicated and riddled with problems like the relative age effect, the lack of objective benchmarks for adult performance later on and the inherent difficulty in measuring factors like game intelligence or cognitive reaction,' says Oliver Höner. The professor of sports science at the University of Tübingen has been researching the success rate of talent development on behalf of the German FA since 2008 with the help of data that's being collected nationwide every six months by twenty-nine coordinators at the 366 DFB regional competence centres. Fourteen thousand youngsters are being tested for their 'motor performance' in six disciplines: twenty-metre sprints, agility, dribbling, ball control, shooting and ball juggling.

Thus, youth coaches and players are provided with objective feedback. Talents can be measured against a national average (for their age), and regional centres can compare their results with each other.

In a 2013 study, Höner ascertained that U12 players produced better results, year on year, on average as coaching at the DFB competence centres improved. The bigger part of his research, however, looked back at the historic test results of players who were later called up for a national youth team or joined a Bundesliga youth academy. Höner: 'We found that U12 players whose results were ranked in the top 30 per cent were seven times more likely to be called up for youth national teams three years later on than those ranked in the worst 30 per cent.'

Raw data will never outweigh the subjective opinion of coaches, Höner adds, and the small absolute number of U12 talents who make it to the very top (3.3 per cent get at least as far as representing their regional associations) make it impossible to predict whether any given individual player will succeed. There are too many other personal, constantly changing factors – like body and personality development, and family environment – involved. But the scientifically proven prognostic power of group probabilities can help the FA and clubs fine-tune their development programme going forward.

Höner's data show that early top-ranked youngsters continue to outperform their less gifted peers consistently, on average, but not in every case. In the future could one discuss concentrating on fewer, more talented youngsters at the expense of those in the bottom third of the tests? The flip-side to early selection is the loss of late developers, of course. As more data accumulates over the course of the next years, the study of motor diagnostics could be extended to look at group probabilities of youth players in relation to later success in adult life. And in addition to a parkour of cones and electronic stop-clocks, teenage prospects are soon likely to be faced with questions about their childhood and feelings, *Bladerunner*-style – minus the tortoise in the desert.

'The next step of TID [talent identification and development] might move beyond motor diagnostics, towards psychological and cognitive tests,' says Höner. An internet questionnaire-based study of his proved that U12 youngsters chosen to represent their regional association performed better in a psychology assessment of personality characteristics assigned to motivation, volition, self-referential cognition, and emotion than their non-chosen peers at the DFB competence centres.

'At the moment we are not yet at the point where personality characteristics should be used for the purpose of talent identification,' he cautions. There are no data for the development of these values after the age of twelve and therefore no way to predict future success based on these results. 'But such personality data could be used to support the individual players' sport psychological coaching and training,' says Höner.

As the process becomes more and more streamlined, technocratic and efficient, there will be those who will lament the talent autobahn paving over the old, twisted, much more obscure route to the top occasionally travelled by late-bloomers like Klose or overnight sensations like Borussia Mönchengladbach's André Hahn, a German international who was still living on rice and frozen pizza as an amateur player for fourth division FC Oberneuland when he was nineteen.

The idea of football as a school of training ground hard-knocks is also disappearing. Listening to Lahm turn his thoughts back to the national team's '*Urknall*', the big bang of 2004, you can detect one or two doubts as to whether the modern production line isn't perhaps working too well already, hot-housing youthful prospects in ideal, clinically sterile conditions, mollycoddling them: 'Sometimes I feel that the academy players want to do everything with technique, with passing, instead of perhaps winning a tackle or getting a bit physical. Maybe that robustness is missing a little bit. It's positive that young players are given a chance immediately, that they're integrated into the team instead of being bullied. But I'm also happy that I'm old enough to have experienced the time before, when it took a long time for you to get any respect at all. It was a good way to learn that things didn't come on a silver platter, that you had to work hard. Sometimes that's missing a bit today. That sense of "I have to perform and earn the right to be here." I remember having to go into the middle during five against two games for no reason whatsoever. You had to fight your way out of it. That wasn't so bad. I think it wouldn't really hurt a young player doing the same thing today.'

GRILL SHACK

'That's when you realise what a fascinating organism a cactus is.'

Why can't we be more like the Austrians? It's not something Germans contemplate that often, if we're being honest. But Oliver Bierhoff caught himself pondering that very question after the strenuous last sixteen win in Porto Alegre. An Austrian radio reporter had accosted him at the very end of the mixed zone, with a jovial request to say a few words for his listeners. 'Herr Bierhoff, Herr Bierhoff. Can you please say: "Good morning, Austria"?'

Bierhoff looked at the man with incredulity. He had just spent a good half an hour talking up the 2-1 win in front of the German press corps, explaining why this had been a minor triumph, not a near-disaster. A White House press officer couldn't have have done a slicker PR job but the mood inside the Beira-Rio was still more 'national crisis' than 'hurrah: quarter-finals'. The Austrian journalist was either totally oblivious to all of that or simply didn't care. Bierhoff was trying to work out the angles, you could see it in his face. Then, ever the pro, he simply did as he was told. 'Good morning, Austria. This is Oliver Bierhoff. Thanks for rooting for us!'

The reporter stopped recording, thanked him profusely and then helpfully proceeded to put everything – this wretched, lucky, deserved, flattering, frightening, demoralising, encouraging game – into its proper context. 'I don't understand what they all want,' he laughed. 'We, as Austrians, would just be happy to have made it into the quarter-finals.' Bierhoff cracked a big smile. 'You are so right,' he said. Then he left for the team bus, his mood lighter.

'It's a German phenomenon: sometimes the basic joy is missing,' Bierhoff told the media at Campo Bahia a couple of days later. What he meant was that his pernickety countrymen were, typically, too busy fussing over the flaws of a below-par win to delight in the successful result and enjoy the moment.

'We've achieved a lot. I think that should be recognised more,' a rather tipsy Per Mertesacker had said after the defeat in the Euro 2008 final in Vienna, post-match bottle of Becks in hand. Jan-Christian Müller, the *Frankfurter Rundschau* journalist talking to him in the mixed zone, was sympathetic to the young defender's complaint but informed him matter-of-factly 'the German doesn't think that way'. The two men looked at each other for a few seconds. What else was there to say?

A first final appearance in that competition since the Wembley success in 1996 would have been cause for celebration in many countries – and the *Nationalmannschaft*, upon their return, were indeed received by half a million jubilant fans at Berlin's Brandenburg Gate determined to party through another magical summer.

But the wider echo, in newspapers, pubs and bars wasn't nearly as positive. Löw's Germany had gone to Austria/Switzerland as one of the favourites to win the competition but they had been outclassed by Spain in the final and only made it to Vienna courtesy of a pretty chaotic, defensively unsound 3-2 win over Turkey in the semi-final. It didn't feel like a success.

Germany, after spending a few years as Austrians, in the international football scheme of things, had become themselves again: mature enough to deal with defeat on an emotional level but rationally unable to forgive their representatives an imperfect – in other words incompetent – performance when it counted.

In the days before the France game, the dispatches from Santo André anticipated the impending end of Löw's reign. *Les Bleus* were resurgent under Didier Deschamps, but a quarter-final was still just that. The national team's failure to progress further would have made Löw's position at the FA untenable, that was beyond dispute. Perhaps he was no longer worried either way, having decided to call it a day whatever the outcome in Brazil. The *Bundestrainer* cut a remote, introvert figure at the tournament, much less approachable to the (print) media than in previous campaigns.

The old Löw was criticised for shirking tough choices and accommodating players too much. The new, Brazilian, Löw appeared stubborn, fixated on showing millions of experts back home and abroad that his way – no full-backs, Lahm in midfield – was the best way forward. In tactical terms, you could argue that he was merely playing safe, abandoning his lofty principles regarding the beautiful game, just as his many detractors had demanded for a couple of years.

But football supporters and people in general are deeply suspicious of change, and the natural reaction had been to blame Germany's failure to play to their strengths on Lahm's new(ish) central position, and, by extension, on Löw's puzzling intransigence. (Conversely, managers who lose with a tried and trusted formula are routinely admonished for lacking a plan B or being too inflexible tactically. It's how the human mind works.) The way the *Nationalmannschaft* had regained control of the Algeria tie after the captain had moved back to his more natural role wide out in defence had, in the eyes of many, only shown up the folly of Löw's grand plan more clearly. After the 4-4 draw against Sweden and the 1-2 defeat to Italy at Euro 2012, it had been another game that proved that the coach simply couldn't be trusted to get the most out of the array of talent at his disposal.

Even his supporters in the media realised that the public's discernible lack of trust in his judgement created a new type of dilemma. Löw was stuck between following a strategy that looked discredited and caving in to pressure and being seen as weak.

'Do you know what leadership means, Lord Snow?' master-at-arms of the Night's Watch Alliser Thorne asks in the TV blockbuster *Game of Thrones*. 'It means that the person in charge gets second-guessed by every clever little shit with a mouth. What if he starts second-guessing himself? That's the end; for him, for the clever little shits, for everyone.'

Unlike Thorne, Löw didn't have to contend with an army of murderous Wildlings at Fortress Maracanã on 4 July, just the French. The criticism wasn't coming from his deputy or anyone inside the camp either, but Löw could probably relate to the fundamental problem Thorne had expressed so eloquently. Everyone wants their leader to second-guess himself. But nobody wants a leader who actually *does* second-guess himself.

Löw didn't seem to willing to buckle. 'I free myself of criticism,' he said. On the day before the trip to Rio, *Die Zeit* ran an interview in which he reiterated his position. 'I have made my decision in relation to Philipp Lahm's role,' he said, 'and I stand by it, until the end.' The actual interview had taken place before the near-fatal tête-à-tête with Algeria, but it was authorised by the German FA on the morning after it. One had to assume that it still accurately reflected Löw's thinking.

Damned if you do, damned if you don't. The same went for a team which had won exactly in the sort of 'dirty', ugly way of which nobody had thought them capable, only to get shot at for not 'playing like ballerinas', as Thomas Müller put it, a little bit irritated. 'The Algeria game was described as the end of world but if the Italians win like that, everybody says: what clever guys. If we win showing a lot of willpower, you feel as if you have to apologise.' His team weren't playing for the right 'headlines', Müller added. 'I don't want to win the

World Cup, only to have to stand there afterwards and say sorry for winning by only one goal.'

Bierhoff rightly suggested that tournament games were prone to overinterpretation. 'It's the normal mechanism: good games tend to get overrated, and after less good games it's panic stations.' He was also right to point out that Germany reaching the quarter-finals for a fifth successive time showed admirable consistency, which other countries of similar stature would have been proud of. But all that didn't make a possible defeat by the French any more palatable. 'It was my biggest worry that we wouldn't be able to do it,' he confesses a few months later.

Out of all overrated games at football tournaments, the final aside, World Cup quarter-finals come with the biggest hype attached to them, because of the way the tournament is structured. The round of the last eight is the T-junction, separating the truly decent sides from the lucky and the also-rans. Losers go home with little more than the sense that they weren't up to the job against the first decent opposition they faced.

Quarter-final winners, on the other hand, can consider themselves genuine contenders as one of the last four teams. And, what's more, they're guaranteed to make it to the end of the campaign, albeit as contestants of the third-place spot if they lose the semi-finals. Either way, they can go home in the knowledge that they've had a respectable competition. Losing a semi-final, in all likelihood against the hosts Brazil, was a scenario that looked just about forgivable.

'No decision is set in stone,' Löw said at the pre-match conference in Rio when asked about the all-important 'Lahm' question. 'It'll be easy to see where he will play,' the *Bundestrainer* added, mischievously.

A little later, the team were informed that there would indeed be a reshuffle. Klose played as central striker, Khedira was back in midfield and Lahm . . . in his traditional position on the right side of defence again. Boateng would move into the centre as a result, Mertesacker was out of the line-up.

'I didn't sleep the whole night,' the Arsenal defender revealed after the final whistle the next day. The Algerian counter-attacks had made it tricky for the tall, not especially pacy centre-back, but Löw's decision was less a reflection on him than on the need to bolster Germany's attacking game on the flanks. 'I wanted a new impulse,' the *Bundestrainer* explained later. Pre-match analysis by the scouts had revealed that the French full-backs were very narrow and didn't enjoy much protection from players in front of them. That left the Germans with a clear forty-metre run-up on both sides. But their midfielders couldn't make progress alone. At least one of the wide defenders needed to support the attack.

Lahm was picked to do just that, behind Thomas Müller on the right. The captain had spent all year making a case for his deployment in midfield, but relented after a couple of heart-to-heart talks with Löw in Campo Bahia. 'I play where the manager wants me to,' he says, as if it wasn't a big deal.

Mertesacker, in the meantime, dealt with the disappointment of his demotion the same way he had done at Euro 2012, the first tournament of his career in which he hadn't been a starter for the *Nationalmannschaft*. 'I made a vow to give it my all on the bench, to support the team from the sidelines,' he says.

There's only so much you can do off the pitch, of course, but the unbearably hot midday kick-off at the spiritual home of football did give him a chance to get involved in some way. Mertesacker, it emerged after a few, sweltering minutes, had taken on the job of chief water-carrier, jumping off the bench, throwing bottles to his thirsty team-mates like an elongated Mr Game & Watch, the character from 1980s Nintendo games.

'It was amazing to see how he gave it all for the team,' says Lahm. 'Sensational' was the word the London-based defender himself used to describe his ninety minutes on the touchline where he had encountered a very different attitude among the substitutes a couple of years earlier. Everyone was pulling in the same direction. 'We are happy and thrilled,' Mertesacker said after Germany's 1-0 win. 'What I experienced today was fantastic. I wouldn't have wanted to miss it. You don't just win the World Cup playing, you win it on the bench, as well. Everyone is involved, everyone is ready. You have to give in sometimes; be happy for those who play and make them feel good. We should keep this extraordinary thing going.'

The game itself wasn't quite so extraordinary; more of a let-down from the neutral's point of view. Germany started well, though, putting immediate pressure on *Les Bleus* by making the pitch 'big'. Özil on the left and Müller were probing away at high tempo; Klose came deep to make it a four-man attack alongside Kroos.

Defensively, the *Nationalmannschaft* persisted with a high line. France nearly caught them out twice within ten minutes. Karim Benzema dragged a side-footed volley wide of Neuer's right post. Mamadou Sakho, with too much time on the ball, lofted a pass over the back four to spring the offside trap. Boateng couldn't catch up with Antoine Griezmann, but his low cross was cut out by a last-ditch intervention from Hummels. Benzema would have had a tap-in.

A few moments later, Germany were ahead. Kroos, going nowhere midway in the opposition half, was brought down by Paul Pogba. The Germany playmaker swung in the free-kick from the left. It arrived centrally, between the penalty spot and Hugo Lloris's six-yard line, right in front of of Hummels. The Dortmund defender had wrestled Raphaël Varane out of the way to head the ball in off the crossbar with the back of his head. The finish recalled Uwe Seeler's speciality (not least his equaliser against England in Mexico in 1970). France, for the first time in Brazil, found themselves behind in a game.

*

It was Hummels' second goal of the competition, his second header from a dead-ball situation. A classic German goal, recalling a long forgotten aerial prowess, by a very modern player. Tall, dark and handsome, Hummels looked more like the leading man in a Mexican telenovela than a defender from the land that had spawned tackling machines called 'Katsche' Schwarzenbeck, Karl-Heinz Förster and Jürgen Kohler.

The Borussia Dortmund centre-back perfectly epitomised all the promise and the problems of the Löw generation. His unhurried poise on the ball and finely crafted passes into the opposition half lent him an air of sophistication, even in his generation of academy taught, technically proficient kids. But Hummels also had the unfortunate habit of trying to make everything look extremely effortless all the time, to the point where he sometimes misjudged the seriousness of the situation. '*Bruder Leichtfuß*', brother lightfoot, they used to call players who took things a little too easy in Germany. These types tended not to go very far in a footballing culture that couldn't abide mistakes.

Hummels had broken into the national team as a twenty-one-year-old, on the back of two fantastic, title-winning seasons with Borussia Dortmund. He was the shooting star of Euro 2012 until Germany got knocked out by Italy in the semi-final in Warsaw. The first of Mario Balotelli's two goals was the result of a cross from Antonio Cassano. Hummels had been close to Cassano, very close in fact, but still had failed to cut out the centre.

Joachim Löw obliquely pointed the finger at Hummels for the opener. The player felt hard done by, not for the first time. Löw had publicly reprimanded him for playing too many long balls out from the back prior to the tournament, and there was more than a suspicion that the conflict averse coach had not taken kindly to the player's very confident demeanour either.

Hummels frequently clashed with his club coach Jürgen Klopp but his was always the first name on the team sheet because, in Dortmund's young side, the kind of 'positive' arrogance he projected was seen as beneficial. One BVB insider told the story of a black and yellow regular shaking with nerves inside the Bernabéu changing room ahead of the Champions League second leg semi-final against Real Madrid. Hummels calmly got up and said: 'I don't know what the issue is. We will go out there and hammer them.' (Dortmund lost 2-0 as it happens but still made it to the final at Wembley.) His strong-mindedness might have made him a pain in the arse for coaches, but on balance they appreciated his unwavering self-belief.

Having a way with words came naturally to him. Hummels' mother, Ulla Holthoff, was the first woman to commentate on Bundesliga games on *ZDF Sportstudio* in the early nineties, at a time when sexism was rampant in German football. Otto Rehhagel once asked her whether she understood the offside rule in a phone call ahead of an interview. 'We've met before,' Holthoff explained. 'Ah, yes? Well, if you were pretty I'm sure I would have remembered you,' said the Werder Bremen coach. 'I can't help your taste,' Holthoff replied.

She had also been a a very good water-polo player but had never been called up to the German national team after writing an article criticising the association. Holthoff later moved to commercial broadcaster DSF, where she conceived the hugely influential *Doppelpass* talk show, as well as *La Ola*, a highlights programme that showed the goals from Europe's top leagues. 'The mother of modern football,' *Stuttgarter Zeitung* called her.

Hermann Hummels, his father, worked as a youth coach at Bayern, where young Mats played alongside Thomas Müller. His U14 coach Heiko Vogel recalled playing him as a striker – 'he knew where the goal was' – but also the teenager's penchant for 'long debates'. He was a player who demanded explanations for everything the manager did. And he was the one player who got away, too, as far as the Bavarians were concerned. They sold him to Dortmund for €5 million in 2008, only to see him thrive at the Signal Iduna Park and become a dressing-room leader for the Westphalians. They tried to exercise a buy-back clause for €8 million in 2011 but Hummels refused to go back. Bayern weren't used to getting turned down.

The Dortmund bloc of Hummels, İlkay Gündoğan, Marcel Schmelzer and Mario Götze (plus BVB-bound Marco Reus) were basking in the warm glow of a domestic double that hinted at a power shift in the league going into Euro 2012. Bayern's Schweinsteiger, Lahm, Neuer, Müller, Badstuber, Kroos, Mario Gómez and Boateng, on the other hand, had just had their dreams of a Champions League win in their own Allianz Arena cruelly destroyed by Chelsea. It made for a fraught camp.

Reds v black and yellows wasn't the only conflict. Younger players were also openly demanding more playing time and criticising the team's performances. 'I don't see us having played outstanding football so far,' Kroos said after the first two matches. Two matches he had sat out. 'I'm not satisfied with the way the tournament has gone so far [for me].' Löw started the midfielder for the first time against Italy, a decision that wasn't received well elsewhere in the team. 'Kroos should not have been rewarded for going on such an ego trip,' one trusted staff member said.

Mertesacker, who had lost his place to Hummels in defence in Poland/ Ukraine after suffering an ankle injury in the spring, didn't make a fuss. The same could not be said when the roles were reversed for the World Cup qualifying campaign. Hummels thought Löw's decision was wrong, and let his opinion be known in front of TV cameras and in the dressing room. He complained about Bayern players getting preferential treatment ('it's easier to get into the national team if you're there,' the defender said), claiming that 'at the German FA, they don't like criticism'. Hummels reckoned, not always without justification, that Löw singled him out as a culprit after goals conceded in friendly matches. His relationship with Mertesacker had broken down almost completely. Things were so bad ahead of one round of matches that a member of the national team's player council had to sit him down and tell him to show more respect to his team-mate.

Remarkably, the German FA and national team managed to keep any internal strife almost wholly hidden from the public. Schweinsteiger surprised everybody when he noted in an interview with *Süddeutsche* in October 2012 that not all substitutes had jumped for joy after Germany's goals at the Euros and unfavourably compared the attitude in the national team with the 'good spirit' at Bayern, but backtracked under questioning from reporters. The true extent of the rifts only became apparent once Germany's internationals started contrasting the much more respectful mood at Campo Bahia with that of the Euros.

'Two thousand and twelve is over,' Hummels had said before the France game. A few weeks earlier, he had all but acknowledged his past misbehaviour. 'I'm not the kind of guy who straight away goes to the back of the queue, where I should have been at the time,' Hummels said about the two years leading up to Brazil. 'Maybe I saw myself in a higher position in the [team's] hierarchy than I really was. It's possible that I came across as a little insubordinate in the beginning.'

Mertesacker believes that his own good form for Arsenal, with whom he won the FA Cup in May 2014, as well those of his rival centre-backs in the preceding months, also changed the dynamic in Brazil. 'The starting point was very different than in 2012. Because the performances had been good during the season. Everyone notices that. Nobody said: "I will play, in any case." Instead, it was "two good centre-backs will be playing at the World Cup, in any case". Your self-confidence notwithstanding, you want to be a bit less categorical [about your own chances], since you know that your team-mates are playing well, too. Everyone took on responsibility for the greater good. Everyone accepted each other as an equal member of the the group. That was absolutely key – and maybe a little different from the Euros.' In addition, Löw's formation, with four centre-backs for the first four games had obviously eased competition at the back but the attitude had changed throughout the squad, says Bierhoff: 'There wasn't the same sense of entitlement.'

'Germany won playing centre-back football,' *Süddeutsche Zeitung* wrote after the France win. What would have been something of an insult a few years back was now a big compliment. There was an uncompromising, avoid errors at all cost hardening of body and mind about the performance. It was all function. Temperatures 'like in a grill shack on the right flank' (Müller) that had the Bayern forward wondering about the the heat-resistant characteristics of desert plants in the Maracanã ('That's when you realise what a fascinating organism a cactus is. How it doesn't wilt . . .') certainly worked in Germany's favour. They could concentrate on protecting their lead and try to hit the French on the counter. 'We stood well,' said Lahm, but that solidity had come at the cost of a lot of hard work. Collectively, Germany had run more than seven kilometres more than their opponents, despite defending the slimmest of margins for seventy-seven minutes. Müller recalled not being able to lift his legs any more at one stage shortly before half-time. 'You don't play a World Cup quarter-final every day,' he said later. 'If you're given the chance to move about a bit, you should take it.'

France were dangerous, however. Mathieu Valbuena had an angled shot saved by Neuer, who scooped the ball up with a strong left wrist, as if he were digging out a difficult forehand at Wimbledon. Hummels – always and again Hummels – blocked the follow-up from Benzema.

In the second half, substitute André Schürrle failed to put the tie to bed after two counter-attacks that faltered without the requisite finish. Deep into time added on, Deschamps' team broke through one last time. Benzema played a clever one-two with Olivier Giroud, stepped past Boateng and took aim from a tight angle with his strong left foot. The ball zipped towards the underside of the bar. Neuer, however, put his right hand up, barely moving the rest of his body. A man in a straw hat hailing a cab on London's Oxford Street on a sunny day with his mother-of-pearl walking stick couldn't have looked less harried than the Germany keeper. 'Oohs' and 'aahs' in the stadium greeted the spectacularly unspectacular save at the death. Neuer, though, wouldn't hear of it. 'If that one goes in, it's a goalkeeping mistake,' he offered drily.

'It was a good game from us, but we had to worry right until the end because we didn't score the second goal,' says Lahm, only partially agreeing with the notion that the match against France had shown the *Nationalmannschaft* at its most composed in Brazil up to that point. Bierhoff: 'We felt we were the better team but the heat brought both sides together. It was so hard to create chances out there, which made us taking the first one all the more crucial. Neuer was sensational. He wasn't involved as much as he had been against Algeria but he maintained his concentration for one, two superb saves when it mattered . . . He was incredible.' What else could you say? 'That kind of goalkeeper can make the difference between getting knocked out and winning the World Cup,' felt Mertesacker, 'it's unbelievably important for a defence to know there's someone behind them who can play football or make an important save on the line,' said Löw. Neuer was the team's insurance policy but he appeared almost a little embarrassed when reporters converged on him after the game. 'Goalkeepers have shown very good performances at this tournament,' he said, as if he had nothing at all to do with those people. 'I'm only in goal because I was the new kid when I joined Schalke aged five. The last one is the idiot. He has to go in. Maybe it's good that I was the idiot,' he shrugged. Technicalities, that's what he was much more interested in discussing. 'Kick-offs at one in the afternoon are in full sunshine, the water from the sprinklers evaporates more quickly. That makes the ball run slower,' he said, and that he'd prepare for the next game wearing warm, long-sleeved clothes again, to sweat even more. A few metres further along Bierhoff was extolling the Germany number one's all-round 'game intelligence': 'He's good at playing cards, he's good at everything he does.'

Neuer had won the day, again. But this time the praise for Germany's last man didn't carry undertones of criticism for Germany's showing on the whole. They had edged a tricky tie in stifling temperatures in a business-like manner, with traces of the old results-focused reliability that opponents used to fear. 'They were more experienced than us,' said Deschamps. Nothing could have sounded sweeter to Löw's ears at that moment.

In Hummels, the man of the match, he had found the player that Hummels himself had always wanted to be: the de facto leader of the defence, calm, measured, alert, dependable. 'The way he fought for the ball was sensational, he was always in the right place,' Löw said. Hummels had won 71 per cent of his duels. Centre-backs very rarely manage a better success rate. 'A giant' was Italian daily *La Gazzetta dello Sport*'s verdict.

Hummels played down his defensive masterclass. 'I was just lucky to be in the right spot,' he said. That day in the Maracanã he became one of the faces of the team, one of three players – Neuer and Müller were the other two – who had fully convinced in Brazil to take Germany within two wins of writing history. The nonchalance had gone from his and his team's game, like a regrettable teenage crush suddenly overcome. Löw had learned to trust his man and vice versa. 'The coach and me needed some time to get used to each other,' Hummels had said before Brazil. 'Now the process is complete.'

The *Bundestrainer* had gambled on his personal future by going back on his line-up changes but the team was 'so stable, so steady', he said, that they no longer needed four centre-backs to eke out a win. Talking about defensive rigour and Germany's pared-down attacks, he didn't sound at all like the Löw Germans had got to know over the last ten years. And he certainly didn't look like him either when he turned up at the post-match press conference wearing, for reasons that could not quite be determined, a white T-shirt instead of his customary dark shirt. The German press corps were shocked to see him looking so casual.

Süddeutsche thought that Löw's unusual choice of attire was intended to send a signal. 'These Germans are no longer interested in aesthetics,' the broadsheet wrote. 'It's not about looking good any more. It's only about functionality now.' A reverse metamorphosis: the debonair, silk-shirted creative director admired for his style, but distrusted as being flighty, had turned into a results manager, gobbling up opponents with scant regard for decorum.

Such a metaphor was probably stretching it a bit. There could be no doubt, however, that Löw's tourist-at-the-Copacabana look did say something about where he was at that moment in time: already back in Santo André, on one of his morning beach runs that German TV captured every day, with the woman from ZDF greeting him with two air kisses and deferentially asking about his feelings.

11 Freunde editor Philipp Köster and others had criticised the blanket coverage as the output of 'the German FA's covert PR department', but maybe the endless array of beautiful, sun-kissed shots had actually come closer to the truth than hundreds of articles trawling through the manager's many predicaments and quandaries. Löw had been happily living in his own bubble in Brazil, oblivious to the doubts and demands back home.

'I'm in a state of deep relaxation,' he had told the world's media on the night before the quarter-final, convinced of his team's progress. It hadn't been bravado. He was no longer concerned with what others thought of him and his selections.

AN ISLAND OF MODERN FOOTBALL

The future was there, so easy to find, every summer, at Sportschule Ruit-Nellingen, less than half an hour's drive south-east of Stuttgart. But who could be bothered to look?

This was the mid-1980s, the halfway point of a prosperous, continuously successful decade that had started with (West) Germany winning the 1980 European Championship and would end with a beaming Lothar Matthäus in Rome's Olympic Stadium, lifting the golden trophy after the national team's third World Cup final in a row.

There was one disappointing result, the first-round exit in the 1984 Euros, after which a grumpy Franz Beckenbauer had warned live on ZDF Sportstudio that German football should no longer be considered the best in the world. But that was just the Kaiser, cleverly managing expectations after he'd been appointed to succeed the good-natured but uninspiring Jupp Derwall (tabloid nickname: 'Chief Silver Hair') as boss of the national squad. Everybody else saw that mishap at the competition in France for what it so clearly was: a glitch, quickly forgotten among all the triumphs and close shaves.

That Germany had the best players, the best mentality, the best tactics, the best league was beyond dispute. 'Maybe the Italian league can challenge the Bundesliga [for top spot],' Ernst Happel, the Austrian

Hamburger SV coach who famously never spoke to his players, told *Playboy* magazine in 1984. Maybe.

The near-total lack of introspection within the game was not simply informed by arrogance. It was also a deliberate psychological ploy. You didn't become a serial winner by asking questions. Questions were dangerous. They might lead to doubts, and doubts might lead to diminished confidence. That was not the German (football) way. Its heroes were doers, not thinkers; men who could take leave of their critical faculties to run, shoot and score as if on autopilot, plugged into one big determination to succeed that existed independently of themselves.

Envious foreigners sneered about the Teutonic 'Panzers', about a methodical, mechanical approach to the beautiful game that verged on the robotic. Germans knew better, though: the real art was ignoring the fear of failure and allowing the game to take you where you needed to be. Like Paul Breitner when he grabbed the ball ahead of regular penalty taker Gerd Müller, and duly scored the equaliser from the spot in the 1974 World Cup final against the Netherlands. (Müller would go on to net the decisive second in Munich's Olympic Stadium twenty minutes later.) 'I have absolutely no recollection of this moment, it's a blank,' Breitner admitted to me twenty-seven years later. 'The entire two minutes from the referee's whistle to kick-off after the 1-1 are missing. I must have been so focused that nothing else existed. At moments like that you mustn't think about what you're doing, otherwise you'll become so afraid you'll fall over your own feet.'

Breitner suffered an out-of-body experience when he watched the game back on television at home the next day. 'I was shouting at this guy, saying, "You're crazy, why are you shooting? What are you doing? You must be mad!"'

The capacity to block out everything probably remains one of a German professional's greatest strengths but playing with blinkers on for decade after decade of trophies – or at the least, very near misses – had its drawbacks. No one stopped to look left and right at what was happening elsewhere. That kind of curiosity was the prerogative of the weak, of losers and low-level never-will-bes. People like Ralf Rangnick.

Rangnick had been released by SSV Ulm after their promotion to the second division in 1982. The following season he was a player-manager for sixth division small-town team FC Viktoria Backnang when Dynamo Kiev turned up for a friendly in February 1983. The team of legendary coach Valeriy Lobanovskyi were staying at nearby Sportschule Ruit for a mid-season training camp. Backnang's amateur side made for convenient sparring partners for the best club team in the Soviet Union, with star players like Oleg Blokhin and a young Oleksiy Mykhaylychenko.

The Ukrainians were winning the game on the frozen pitch as easily as expected. Defensive midfielder Rangnick, then twenty-four, found the experience extremely unnerving. He picks up the story, the moment of his 'football epiphany', as he calls it, sitting in the lobby of Stuttgart's Hotel Graf Zeppelin opposite the railway station with a cup of Darjeeling tea.

'A few minutes in, when the ball had gone out for a throw, I had to stop and count the opposition players. I thought there was something wrong – did they have thirteen or fourteen men on the pitch? That was the first time I felt what it was like to come up against a team who systematically pressed the ball. I had played against big professional teams before – and of course we lost those games as well – but they at least gave you a bit of breathing space, the chance to "put a foot on the ball", as we used to say, a moment's breather to calm things down once in a while. I remember people were still demanding that of central midfielders as late as the late nineties. Try that against Borussia Dortmund now. That would be fun! Three or four of them would be on you in seconds. In that match against Kiev I felt constantly under pressure for the entire ninety minutes. And my teammates did as well.

I always felt that there had to be more to this game than following your opponent around all over the pitch and if necessary all the way to the loo. As a holding midfielder, I would often get good marks in the paper if I had taken out the opposition playmaker, having had perhaps five touches myself. That never felt quite right. But against Kiev it was the first time that I sensed: this is football of a very different kind.'

Rangnick had first harboured doubts about German football's methodology while studying English and the newly created subject of sports science at Stuttgart University in the late seventies. (He spent a year at Sussex University in Brighton as part of the course and has remained an avowed anglophile ever since.) 'We were a class of twenty boys and twenty girls and everyone had a background in performance sports. One of my classmates was a member of Feuerbach, the best women's volleyball team at the time. I taught her football, she taught me volleyball. I was amazed to find that they were training ten hours a day, including two in the gym and two for tactical moves. It was fascinating; the dead-ball situations were highly choreographed. I realised that other sports were light years ahead of us in terms of professionalism and intensity. We were doing almost nothing in comparison. Training was two hours and little more than a bit of physical exercise. People thought more than one session per day was physically impossible.'

Lobanovskyi's team returned to train in Ruit every season over the next few years, and Rangnick was there, watching on the sidelines with a notepad every single day, trying to figure out what exactly it was they were doing and how. He was studying for his Pro coaching badges in Cologne at the time, the youngest on his course, eventually graduating as best in class. The German FA's tactical syllabus was stuck in the seventies, he says. 'Basically things had not moved on since 1974. Bundesliga teams, like the national side, lined up with a sweeper, and man-marking was the preferred system. There was no need to change – we were successful. The only innovation came courtesy of foreign coaches like Pál Csernai, under whom Bayern

Munich were playing a version of possession football, and Happel, who had brought in zonal marking from his time as coach of the Netherlands [1977–8]. Happel used to say [he puts on an Austrian accent]: "If you have man-marking, you have eleven donkeys on the pitch." But his HSV didn't really press the ball either. They mostly moved sideways.'

Rangnick was appointed coach of VfB Stuttgart amateurs in 1985. That year, he met a trained structural engineer who had taught himself football tactics and become the first coach to introduce '*Ballorientierte Raumdeckung*', a system that combined zonal marking with aggressive pressing of the ball, to Germany: his name was Helmut Groß.

Looking at Happel's *Oranje*, Groß had understood that zonal marking meant a much more efficient use of energy by the defending team. But then why not use that spare energy to defend on the front foot, to force mistakes and win the ball back early, deep inside the opposition half?

As manager of sixth division SC Geislingen, a club situated in provincial Baden-Württemberg, Groß had employed this radical new method with great success. A few years later he was appointed to the regional football association's staff for teaching coaches, a kind of think-tank for managers. Rangnick became a member and his favourite protégé. 'It was a laboratory for ideas and experiments. We would discuss tactics for hours and hours, sometimes throughout the night. I found a thousand reasons why his football wouldn't work and Groß would reply that one could only control the game with a clear plan of working "against the ball". He said, "I can understand your worries and fears, because it's the way you've been educated as a player. But you have to overcome them and trust in the system." After a while, he had convinced me that zonal marking all over the pitch and high pressing was not only possible, but the way forward.'

Groß even managed to put his ideas successfully into practice against the master himself. During another one of those Ruit training camps, Lobanovskyi's Kiev could only draw 1-1 against fifth division VfL Kirchheim, who also twice won the Baden-Württemberg championship under Groß's guidance.

In September 1984, Groß's successor at SC Geislingen, Jakob Baumann, pulled off one of the biggest upsets in the history of the DFB Cup. His amateurs beat the superstars of Hamburger SV, coached by Ernst Happel, 2-0 with high pressing in the second round. 'They came over us like a swarm of bees,' former HSV midfielder Felix Magath told *Stuttgarter Zeitung*, 'we were irritated.'

Groß and Rangnick began writing coaching manuals and developing their own practice sessions 'There were no books, no exercises we could call upon,' Rangnick says, 'the vocabulary didn't exist, either.' They studied videos of Arrigo Sacchi's AC Milan that friends were sending over from Italy. It took ages to pause, rewind, fast-forward, rewind the action on Groß's clunky recorder. The equipment frequently broke down from over-use.

Sacchi's double European Cup winners with the Dutch trio of Marco van Basten, Frank Rijkaard and Ruud Gullit set a new benchmark in terms of collective brilliance. But Sacchi, the former shoe salesman, was also a role model in a more personal sense. Rangnick: 'He wasn't a big name, he hadn't had a glittering career as a player. He also looked like [French comedian] Luis de Funès. It was inconceivable at the time that a German club would have appointed such a man as their senior manager. Sacchi broke the mould.'

VfB Stuttgart hired Groß to oversee all youth development in 1989. He put in place a directive: *Ballorientierte Raumdeckung* was to be mandatory at all junior levels. Soon after, Rangnick followed him to manage the Swabian club's 'A' youth team, the German equivalent of the reserves. He, too, had become certain that neither Dutch superstars nor the collective genius of the Dynamo team were necessary to make that type of football work. 'I had changed to a back four and zonal marking at [seventh division] SC Korb and we hardly lost a game after the winter break,' he says. 'If it was possible with amateurs, it was possible with any team.'

But they had to run. A lot. On holiday in South Tyrol in 1991, Rangnick found out that Zdeněk Zeman's Foggia Calcio were having a training camp in Terenten, a mountain village an hour and a half away. 'Zeman had taken Foggia from the third division to Serie A in the space of two seasons with complete unknowns in the squad – all thanks to aggressive pressing and zonal marking all over the pitch. "Zenlandia" they called that miracle in Italy. I thought, this guy is spiritual brother to me. My wife was not happy but I drove up there every afternoon to watch his training sessions.' Zeman had his squad running for ten kilometres at pace. He told Rangnick that he needed the fittest team in the league to play his kind of football. Otherwise, the Czech-Italian coach said, his side had no chance whatsoever. 'I realised that a bit of pressing isn't enough. It is like being a bit pregnant – it's nothing,' Rangnick says.

His Stuttgart youngsters won the German youth championship, having eliminated a Bayern Munich side that were considered unbeatable (with prodigies like Dietmar Hamann and Christian Nerlinger) in the last sixteen. Rangnick was promoted to the post of director of youth and amateur football by the Swabians but he resigned in 1994 when the club overlooked him as assistant to senior coach Jürgen Röber. It would take another eighteen months with decent but unspectacular results at the reins of third division SSV Reutlingen and and a difficult start at his next stop, SSV Ulm, at the same level of the football pyramid, before Rangnick's methods gained greater attention.

Meanwhile, elsewhere zonal marking, pressing and defending with four at the back had quietly found its way into professional football for the first time in Germany, thanks to manager Wolfgang Frank, at perennial Bundesliga 2 underdogs Mainz 05. Frank, a former Bundesliga striker (fifty-two goals for Eintracht Braunschweig) in the late 1970s, was nicknamed '*Floh*' (flea), because of his slender frame and great prowess in the air. His tactical ideas were strictly heavyweight division, however; borrowed from Sacchi's copy book and an essay by former Swiss national coach Daniel Jeandupeux entitled 'The Philosophy of the Back Four'. The paper, published in the professional coaching magazine *Fußball Training* in 1995, called for the creation of numerical superiority around the ball, a sophisticated version of 'children's football', as Frank explained to *Süddeutsche Zeitung* in 1999: 'Everyone needs to chase the ball.' Driving the opponents' game into dead ends in wide areas, Jeandupeux wrote, was a key part of the strategy. Once the ball was won, your own players were supposed to swarm out and flood into the opposition half at speed. 'It's like opening your fist,' said Frank.

Mainz were bottom of the table with one point and no goals from the first eight games when Frank was brought in in September 1995 to save them from the threat of relegation. 'We had a pretty decent group of players but we were basically dead as team,' remembered 05's solid, unremarkable centre-back, who would eventually take over from Frank as player-manager. His name was Jürgen Klopp.

Frank won the team's trust by telling them they'd be able to beat any opposition with his strategy, a certain lack of individual quality notwithstanding. 'He had us, instantly,' said Klopp. 'We were so desperate to get out of the drop zone that we would have also climbed a tree a hundred and fifty times if that brought us some points.' That wasn't necessary. But switching from man-marking to an effective zonal system took 150 dedicated practice sessions, Frank estimated. More established professionals might have bristled at a training regime that had the Mainz players standing out in the cold, for hours on end, walking around slowly in unison in intricate patterns between poles stuck in the ground. Klopp: 'In Germany, training was supposed to be fun, all-action: shooting, crosses, piggy in the middle.' By contrast, the amount of effort that had to go into Frank's system was enormous. 'But we thought: if Gullit and van Basten had to learn that at Milan, we could put up with it as well.'

With the new strategy in place, Mainz picked up thirty-two points in the second half of the season, more than any other team in the top two divisions, to finish in mid-table. In the confines of the modestly talented, financially limited second division, these avant-garde tactics had made all the difference. 'Until Frank's arrival, we had basically been in the jungle – chasing after everything with a shirt on,' Klopp said. 'He made our results independent of our talent, to an extent. Up until then, we thought that, as the worse team, we would lose.' Some sense of parity could be achieved by better organisation.

Slowly, silently, the novel concept took hold at that level, as a means to distinguish yourself from the mediocrity of the rest of the pack and find an edge that didn't cost lots of money. Volker Finke's SC Freiburg yo-yoed between leagues one and two with a more basic version of a back four, Benno Möhlmann experimented with it at Fürth, Wattenscheid and Uerdingen followed suit.

The poster child and unofficial spokesperson of this 'exotic little group' (Klopp's words) was Rangnick. He took SSV Ulm 1846, a ragtag team of capable but willing nobodies from Regionalliga Süd (third division) to Bundesliga 2 in 1997–8. But appreciation of his footballing ideology was slow to come. That summer a local paper had a dig at Rangnick for showing his players videos of World Cup winners France's games. Who did he think he was?

But when '*die Spatzen*' (the sparrows), widely tipped as relegation contenders before the start of the next campaign, continued to fly high, unbeaten in the first sixteen games of the season, the establishment couldn't help but sit up and take notice. Something extraordinary was happening in the Donaustadion. More than that: something new.

Frankfurter Allgemeine Zeitung praised Ulm as 'an island of modern football'. Former Real Madrid sweeper and Euro 1980 winner Uli Stielike, who had recently been installed as assistant manager of the German national team alongside Erich Ribbeck, told big, serious *Der Spiegel* magazine that Rangnick's side represented 'the future of German football' no less. 'Ulm's U14s can play zonal marking, in contrast to the national team,' *TAZ* newspaper wryly noted in September 1998.

A quarter-final exit against Croatia at the France 98 World Cup with Berti Vogts at the helm had brought up – for the first time in living memory – all sorts of strange, uncomfortable questions. Was German football, with its slavish adherence to the sweeper system, falling behind the times? And why were all the top foreign teams playing with four at the back? The bespectacled, quietly spoken Rangnick, who looked a bit like your typical dentist, appeared to have the answers as well as a panacea.

In December 1998, *ZDF Sportstudio*, Germany's late-night, slightly more highbrow Bundesliga highlights show (in comparison with tea-time highlights programme *Ran*, broadcast by commercial channel Sat 1), invited Rangnick to preach to the uninitiated in front of a magnetic tactics board. The slightly arch introduction from anchorman Michael Steinbrecher made it obvious just how left-field and unusual this in-depth look at football theory was for a programme that was first broadcast in 1963. 'We have been talking about four at the back and zonal marking for a few years now, there is almost a kind of awe when people talk about this system,' Steinbrecher said. 'Many viewers at home tell us they still don't quite understand what this all is about. Can you, Mr Rangnick, show us what's going on?'

Of course he could. Rangnick, all in black in a loose fitting suit, would have looked more at home in a trendy architects' office, but his patient, coherent ninety-second lecture drew spontaneous applause from the studio audience. 'They have taken notice,' said Steinbrecher, before he proceeded to repeat Rangnick's deliberations 'in my own words', omitting some of the more technical terminology.

It was a memorable appearance, but not quite for the right reasons. Rangnick's lecture embarrassed his more prominent, established peers, and it was not long before he felt the backlash. 'In Italy, Spain, England, even in Switzerland, the *Sportstudio* show would only have provoked a bored yawn, as those countries were so far ahead of us at the time,' he says. 'But the Bundesliga old guard, the traditionalists who feared the new, they didn't like it. As a young coach, I underestimated how sensitive those in football were.'

Off the record, rival coaches derided Rangnick as a 'professor', a know-it-all armchair coach who was out of touch with the real world. The belittling tag was soon adopted by the media. Rangnick was dogged by its negative connotations throughout his next few years in the top flight. 'Going on *Sportstudio* was a mistake. It was stupid to tell others about my tactics. These things were never discussed. I was considered a theorist – that was meant as an insult. A theorist, so went the view at the time, was the opposite of a practitioner.'

His great run with Ulm won him a contract to return to Stuttgart as head coach the following season. He became the fifth coach in charge of the Swabians in the space of a year, after VfB president Gerhard Mayer-Vorfelder fired Joachim Löw (May 1998) and his successors Winfried Schäfer, Wolfgang Rolf and (the future German U21 coach) Rainer Adrion, who had also been part of Helmut Groß's fringe movement. Ulm ended up winning promotion for a second year running despite Rangnick's resignation in March 1999. The professor had arrived. But what should have been a breakthrough for tactical progress turned out to be a set-back. The revolution wilted in the harsh floodlights of the first division.

At Stuttgart, resistance to change at board level and inside the dressing room proved far greater than anticipated. Coaches were supposed to stick to coaching. Rangnick's attempts to influence the decision-making process beyond the training pitch and the dugout were rebuffed by those who had a vested interest in things being done the way they had always been done. His tactical vision also proved an uneasy fit for a team which chiefly relied on the genius of Bulgarian playmaker Krassimir Balakov for goals and assists. Balakov was the sole survivor of the '*Magische Dreieck*', the magic triangle that also included Brazilian striker Giovane Élber and Germany centre-forward Fredi Bobic. The trio had won the DFB Cup in 1997 and reached the European Cup Winners' Cup final against Chelsea a year later under Löw. Balakov, the darling of club president Mayer-Vorfelder, was a classic number ten who bestrode the pitch with a natural swagger and the expectation of having every pass played to his feet.

It was one thing to play collective, relentless pressing football with amateurs and second division players who understood that hard work could compensate for a lack of individual talent, but Balakov and other seasoned pros were far less inclined to sign up to blue-collar football. 'Professor' Ralf found himself in charge of an unruly class, undermined by sniping from his superiors and by his unfavourable public image as a nerdy '*Kopfmensch*' (literally: a head person), a nobody as a player who wanted to tell stars – World Cup players and title winners, no less – that they were playing the game in an old-fashioned way.

And why the sudden need to reinvent the wheel anyway? The short burst of soul-searching after the disgraceful (by German standards) quarter-final exit at the World Cup hadn't lasted long. Vogts had blamed a FIFA conspiracy ('there are people who didn't want us to win'), everybody else had blamed him. The case for big structural change looked a lot less pressing due to the clubs' continued success in Europe. Bundesliga sides were regularly doing well in the Champions League. They made it to at least the semi-finals in every single season from 1997 to 2002, contested four finals (1997, 1999, 2001, 2002) and won the trophy twice (Dortmund 1997, Bayern 2001). Consequently, there was little demand for a self-appointed prophet to lead German football out of the tactical wilderness and towards some promised land of foreign sophistication.

Paradoxically, the disastrous reign of Ribbeck and Stielike, who oversaw the historic embarrassment of Euro 2000 – one draw and three defeats in the group stage, including one against Kevin Keegan's

England – didn't help the case for stylistic realignment either. The duo had been installed as a strange, unhappy couple after a comically inept hunt for Vogt's successor in autumn 1998.

Stielike, the first man employed for the job by the German FA before they put in the mild-mannered 'Sir Erich' above him, favoured a back four for the national team. Ribbeck, plucked from semi-retirement in Spain, was unsure if he wanted to drop the sweeper system. 'Concepts are nonsense,' he said, 'only the next game matters.' Asked about the 'biggest disappointment' of his first 100 days in charge, Ribbeck mentioned Rangnick's TV lecture. 'I'm disappointed about the overblown discussion about tactical systems, like a colleague of mine peddling banalities on *ZDF Sportstudio* as if the coaches in the Bundesliga were all total idiots,' he said. Franz Beckenbauer broadly agreed. 'All this talk about the system – nonsense,' the Kaiser told *Kicker*, 'others can do more with the ball. Our players cannot. Four at the back with zonal marking or a sweeper, it doesn't matter. Four at the back can be fatal.'

After a poor run of results in friendlies, the national coaching duo's conflicting views came out in the open, with Stielike admitting that there wasn't always 'synchronicity' between him and his boss. Ribbeck replaced his unwanted assistant with Horst Hrubesch a few weeks before the tournament.

Tactically, the former Bayern Munich and Leverkusen coach came up with a compromise between the old and the new. Veteran Lothar Matthäus, still the side's captain at thirty-nine, was tasked to play as 'sweeper in front of the defence'. Turkey were the only other side to line up with 'a last man' at the tournament. That was the extent of tactical direction, however. Ribbeck's team had little idea what they were supposed to do beyond reproducing 'the German virtues' of hard running and fighting.

'The team is in desperately poor shape,' Bayern midfielder Jens Jeremies warned publicly in April 2000. Two months before, Ribbeck had played the young attacking midfielder Zoltán Sebescen as a right-back in a friendly defeat against the Netherlands. The Wolfsburg player had never played there before. He was overrun by Boudewijn Zenden and substituted at half-time, never to be selected again. Ribbeck, it was rumoured, had told Sebescen to watch out for the 'Real Madrid' man 'going past on the outside'. Zenden was at Barcelona at the time, and he loved cutting inside.

The Bayern Munich quartet of Jeremies, Markus Babbel, Dietmar Hamann and Christian Ziege could see that Euro 2000 would be a disaster. On the eve of the tournament, they plotted a coup that would solve two problems at once. Matthäus, who no longer had the engine to play in midfield, the conspirators proposed, should take over from the hapless Ribbeck as team coach. The most capped German player (150 internationals) refused to support the putsch, however.

Three horrifically inept matches at the Euros later, *Bild* put eleven *Bratwürste* in national team kits on its cover. (To be called a *Bratwurst*, a grilled sausage, is a huge insult to anyone, never mind a German footballer.) The tabloid also printed a detailed report of Bayern players drowning their sorrows in late-night beers after the final game, a 3-0 defeat by Portugal's B team. Who had briefed the paper? Matthäus later told a glossy magazine that he should have gone public about the abortive regicide: 'Then I wouldn't have been the idiot after the event but those *Stinkstiefel* [literally: stinky boots] who had wanted me out of the national team.' Ribbeck resigned in June 2000. Matthäus' international career was finally over, too.

The sweeper system was harder to kill off. Franz Beckenbauer hadn't invented the role but he had made it his own so successfully that it had become an article of faith for German football. Deploying your playmaker so deep that he couldn't be tracked was West Germany's ingenious answer to man-marking. It had worked so well for so long that few found reason to pause and think about the relevance of a 'free man' now that man-marking itself had almost universally gone out of fashion. The national team remained shackled to their *libero*, a tactical concept that also betrayed the country's disconcerting longing for an omnipotent *Fußballgott* who'd organise the defence, lead the midfield and score the odd decisive goal as well.

Playing with a sweeper was so ingrained at national team level that Ribbeck's successor Rudi Völler took two more years to consign the role to the tactical dustbin. His Germany first played with a true back four in the 2-0 win over Cameroon at the World Cup in Japan/South Korea.

That improvement was only superficial, however. Real change was still not afoot. The unprecedented awfulness of the Ribbeck era and the increasingly obvious lack of individual talent deflected from deeper tactical deficits, a subject that was also much more difficult to grasp.

A few broadsheet articles continued to make the connection between the lack of cohesive ideas and the team regressing into the caricature of German football, defending deep in numbers, intent on destroying the opposition's game and maybe stealing a goal from a dead-ball situation. But that debate could hardly make itself heard over all the noise football was making. These were the 'new economy' fuelled boom years at the end of the nineties, a decade that had made football the number one entertainment product in the country. Commercial station Sat 1 had driven that process by turning their cameras to drama taking place off the field. Their match reports frequently featured long shots of the clubs' bosses' reactions in the stands, and the camera loved to zoom in on a coach's sweaty armpits. Immediately after the final whistle, players and officials were egged on by the interviewers to say something controversial about a rival or team-mate. Sat 1 staged the Bundesliga as a circus, replete with heroes, clowns and wild animals. Football on television was about the broadcasting of high emotion (love, hate, anger), not boring craftsmanship.

At first the clubs relished that development. At Bayern, reporters were handed a list with the players' mobile numbers at the beginning of the season. They wanted their personnel in the news, all the time.

It worked. The club hogged the limelight so much it became known as 'FC Hollywood'.

Bayern were less happy that the attention soon broadened to take in the players' private lives. Salacious reports on extra-curricular activities – drink driving, fisticuffs in a pizzeria – made for ever more sensational storylines. The public found this new direction compelling. Stadiums were packed, TV ratings went through the roof and football became a twenty-four-hour soap, clogging the airwaves and column inches with 'he said, he said' arguments, alpha-male conflict and crazy guys doing crazy things. 'Good God,' exclaimed *Der Tagesspiegel*, 'is German football nothing more than a soap opera?'

Post-match 'analysis' focused almost entirely on the psychological, on vague ideas about team dynamics, hierarchy and authority. I sat in TV talk shows (*Doppelpass*, on DSF) where one former coach blamed a defeat on 'too much harmony' in the dressing room while another ex-pro was equally convinced that 'not enough togetherness' was the issue. 'Lack of character' or 'a lack of characters' were other popular explanations. There was a widely held suspicion that many players were, in their heart of hearts, spoilt and lazy. They had to be made to run by coaches whose expertise could be measured in decibels. Only the strongest motivators were able to get their team to play well. If they didn't, if they could no longer 'reach' their charges, the club needed someone new. No need to overcomplicate things. Four at the back? Michael Schulz, a former Werder Bremen and Germany international, told me live on air in the summer of 2002 that it was a waste of resources. 'When you're three at the back, most of the time, you have nothing do anyway,' he said. 'Four would only make it worse.'

ZDF Sportstudio, a post-war institution, became increasingly marginalised as audiences switched to live games on pay TV platform Premiere and Sat 1's high-concept, lowbrow madness at tea-time.

Rangnick and his ilk had little chance in such an environment. Clarity of thought was not enough to to cut through the miasma of testosterone. He was neither brash nor flash enough. And he wasn't a big enough name either. His relationship with local hero Balakov broke down irretrievably in autumn 2000. The Bulgarian swore at the coach after his substitution in a league game against 1860 Munich, and Rangnick banned him from the squad for a UEFA Cup game in Rotterdam. Four months later, he was fired.

Rangnick went down a division to lead Hannover 96 back to the Bundesliga after the Lower Saxons had spent more than a decade in Bundesliga 2 and the third division. Hannover 96 survived the drop the following season but Ragnick fell out with club bosses and was sent packing in March 2004. A spell at Schalke 04 took him close to winning the championship in 2004–5 but differences with general manager Rudi Assauer made his position untenable six months later. Rangnick's uncompromising attention to detail had caused too much friction: 'At Backnang, me and my dad were publishing the stadium magazine, I was putting tape straps on players because I had some medical know-how from my studies. I made sure that there was no crate of beer in the dressing room after the game, introduced warm-downs and banned smoking within two hours of the end of a game. In Reutlingen and Ulm, they were happy that I did these things because there was no one else. At Stuttgart and Schalke, however, they employed people in those roles and it was hard for me accept how that work was being done.'

Overcome by emotion, Rangnick embarked on a lap of honour in the Veltins-Arena, Schalke's stadium, after a game against Rostock in December, cheered on by the home crowd. The board and some players felt provoked; Rangnick was fired two days later. Many experts agreed: he was finished at this level.

Other Swabians were making waves. The new national team manager Jürgen Klinsmann, who'd been appointed by former VfB president Gerhard Mayer-Vorfelder, was putting noses out of joint by comparing the playing style and pace in the league unfavourably with the English

Premier League and the Spanish La Liga. His assistant was Joachim Löw, a man who had worked with Helmut Groß during his spell on the Stuttgart bench. (Rangnick had been mooted for the post by the German FA but ruled out that possibility. 'I have no interest in becoming an assistant,' he said at the time.) Klinsmann was also regularly exchanging ideas with Bernhard Peters, the former manager of the German men's national hockey team who had won the 2002 World Cup and was about to secure a second title four years later. Peters was a firm believer in tactical cross-pollination. 'Hockey is very similar to football in tactical terms, from playing eleven v eleven to the defensive movement,' he said. 'I can pick up inspiration from football, and also provide an impulse for football, too.' German hockey had been a hotbed of innovation for a long time. The sport was an early adopter of video analysis, and they were coaching goalkeepers with a specially invented ball machine.

In spring 2005 Peters had spent a few weeks studying Rangnick's training sessions at Schalke to learn about the principles of zonal marking, a system he successfully transferred to his hockey team. Peters had also visited Jürgen Klopp at Mainz. Stuttgart-born Klopp had built upon the tactical foundations laid by his mentor Wolfgang Frank (also a Swabian) and won promotion to the first division in 2003–4 with the self-styled 'carnival club' after two attempts that had failed in dramatic fashion.

Bild feted 'Kloppo' as the 'Harry Potter' of German football. He wore metal-rimmed glasses and the same youthful haircut as the wizard's apprentice, not to mention that him getting little Mainz into the Bundesliga reeked of magic. 'There's no Harry Potter flying on his fucking stick – just football,' Klopp said years later, discussing his wife Ulla's children's books. But it was true of his time at Mainz as well. Klopp's success was not sorcery but the combination of cutting-edge match plans ('with better tactics, you can beat a better team') and his ability to get players to run. He and Rangnick frequently crossed swords when the latter was a rival for promotion in Bundesliga 2 with Hannover. 'They were fighting each other at the top of the table and were closely watching each other,' Helmut Groß told *Frankfurter Allgemeine Zeitung* in 2013.

Mainz finished eleventh in Klopp's first season in the Bundesliga. The young coach had gained a reputation for bringing his infectious brand of unshaven, slightly unkempt enthusiasm to the top flight but he wasn't yet being widely noticed as a managerial prodigy. His breakthrough, ironically enough, came in the same place where Rangnick's career had suffered so much damage: the ZDF TV studio.

The state broadcaster had the rights to show the 2005 Confederations Cup, the test run for Jürgen Klinsmann's new Germany. Spurred on by the Swabian's reformist agenda, ZDF's head of sport Dieter Grauschwitz wanted to try out new ideas, too. He employed Swiss referee Urs Meier, of 'Swiss Banker' (the *Sun*) fame after England's disallowed goal against hosts Portugal at Euro 2004 to appear as a pundit. Klopp, whose rhetorical talent was well known to Mainz-based ZDF – they had watched him at close quarters for a number of years – was added to the team as a youthful sidekick to Franz Beckenbauer. 'We had seen him do speeches on the *Marktplatz* that brought tears to everyone's eyes and had mothers holding up their babies, yelling that they would name them after him,' says Jan Doehling, an editor in the ZDF sports office, with only slight exaggeration.

Picking Klopp was seen as a huge risk. He hadn't won any serious trophy, neither as coach nor player; he was still a nobody. 'He was reluctant to do it at first but he agreed because he wanted to be able to see the World Cup games a year later, up close and get tickets,' says Doehling. Klopp proved an immediate, huge success, cutting his teeth on a new video tool that allowed him to draw circles and arrows on to the screen. 'It was his idea,' says Doehling. 'He basically developed the tool in cooperation with the software company we employed because he wanted to use it for his team talks at Mainz after the World Cup.'

Klopp was able to illuminate tactical details on screen 'in an entertaining, funny, sexy manner', Doehling says. Crucially, he employed self-deprecating humour to avoid patronising the audience. He spoke to them as a friend in a pub might, without airs and graces; not down to them, in headmasterly fashion. He was a revelation. 'We realised that this guy knew how to put his point across and to mesmerise people,' says Doehling. 'If he had started a political party, they would have voted him into government immediately.'

The Mainz coach resumed his pundit's role at the 2006 World Cup, where he'd occasionally be flanked by Pelé as well as Beckenbauer. The latter frequently nodded in agreement with Klopp's snippets of insights, such as identifying the problem with a full-back's position or a defender reacting too slowly to a goal-kick from the opposition. Doehling: 'Beckenbauer's approval was like getting knighted for Klopp. If the Kaiser thought he knew his stuff – he really knew his stuff.'

ZDF's coverage of the tournament in front of a partying crowd at Berlin's Sony Centre was a huge success. Doehling modestly says Germany's performances, five weeks of sunshine and the festive mood in the whole country created a wave of goodwill that swept the show along but the award-winning programme genuinely broke new ground, thanks to Klopp's input.

'He contributed something that didn't exist before his debut at the Confederations Cup: he simply talked about what was happening on the pitch,' wrote Christoph Biermann, one of the first German football journalists to cover tactics extensively, in *Süddeutsche Zeitung*. Gone was the armchair psychology, the obsession with character, the will to fight and other invisible factors that were impossible to prove one way or the other. In came attention to the little, easily fixable things that cumulatively made all the difference.

Other Bundesliga coaches should thank Klopp 'for introducing a bit more objectivity into the way football is being talked about', Biermann noted, 'but he is perhaps also lucky that he can continue to explain football relatively unhindered these days while his colleague Ralf Rangnick took years to atone for the impudence of explaining the back four.' Times had changed, at last. By enabling average audiences of twenty-five million people to view football differently, Klopp had a hand in football being viewed differently as well.

Doehling is reluctant to ascribe too much influence to the ZDF World Cup coverage and the matey, good-natured moments of enlightenment offered by Klopp. 'The first, big, heavy stone that was thrown at the glass window came from Klinsmann. He kicked open the doors and decreed that there shouldn't be any more doors in that place from now on, to let some air in. He was the locomotive, the trailblazer. Everyone else just followed in his slipstream.' But, Doehling says, giving Klopp the platform to become something like the 'Fernseh-Bundestrainer', the TV national manager, invariably gave legitimacy to Klopp's idiosyncratic footballing blueprint, too. The coach also used his time at the big tournaments to watch other teams and learn the machinations of television. 'At first he was shy,' recalls Doehling, 'but after a short time he was effectively coaching our whole team.'

Klopp continued his work at the channel until the end of Euro 2008. By that time (2006–7), Mainz had been relegated back down to Bundesliga 2 and Klopp had resigned on the last day of the next season, after 05 had narrowly missed out on promotion. Twenty thousand supporters turned out at his farewell party in the city centre that night. Klopp, overcome with emotion, told them: 'You have made me everything I am, everything I can do.'

Doehling remembers working with Klopp at the DFB Cup final between Bayern and Dortmund in April of that year. 'He said to me, "Jan, I want to be down there on the touchline one day."' Back at their Berlin hotel, Dortmund fans were serenading him with 'Jürgen Klopp, you are the best man' in the lobby. They wanted him to take over their club the next season. Leverkusen and Hamburg put feelers out, too. The latter turned him down after a scouting report had highlighted his penchant for jeans with holes and an alleged habit of turning up late for training. Even Bayern's general manager Uli Hoeness had taken a shine to Klopp, but the Bavarian giants employed Jürgen Klinsmann to bring modernity to Säbener Strasse instead. The former Germany manager was considered a safer pair of hands, probably because of his extensive experience of playing at the top level.

Klinsmann was the most prominent member of the new wave of 'Konzepttrainer' (concept coaches) who were suddenly all the rage at the start of the 2008–9 season. The term implied – not always justifiably, as it turned out – that these men believed in methodology and in the creation of a strong footballing identity for their teams. It also suggested that club coaching in Germany hadn't really bothered with concepts that much before.

Having witnessed the excellent work of technocratic managers like José Mourinho (who was now at Inter, having left Chelsea) and Rafael Benítez (then still at Liverpool) as well as the progress made by the national team under Klinsmann and Löw, Bundesliga clubs had begun to ditch their traditional player-centric model in favour of one where the coach was king. 'One of the many failures of German football in the nineties was never defining the role of the manager as the decisive figure,' said German FA sporting director Matthias Sammer. 'The manager is the most important man, he has to be the most powerful one as well.'

The clubs' willingness to hand the reins over to a new breed of coaches was also reflected in their hiring of outsiders. A third of the league benches were occupied by foreigners from smaller countries. They included Dutchmen like Martin Jol (HSV), Jos Luhukay (Gladbach) and the Swiss coach Lucien Favre (Hertha). 'Opening up to these countries is progress,' said Sammer. 'These are countries with fewer footballers [than in Germany], that's why they value the development of their players. You can only do that via the work of coaches, and that's why the figure of the coach has always been very important in these countries.'

The idea that players could be developed, along with a team, into something that was bigger than the constituent parts was music to the ears of Bayern Munich bosses. The perennial Bundesliga champions had fallen back into the second tier of European clubs since their 2001 Champions League win. They couldn't compete with La Liga and the Premier League in terms of players' wages either after their move to the new Allianz Arena in 2005. The qualitative push had to come from the coaching zone. Klinsmann hit the right notes. 'The goal is to make every player better, every day,' he said at his unveiling.

His revolution got off to an inauspicious start. He had the club build a new 'performance centre' that doubled up as the senior team's clubhouse at Säbener Strasse. The interior designer tasked with the project put a couple of Buddha figurines in the roof-top lounge. Supporters in staunchly Catholic Bavaria took great offence.

A bigger concern was Bayern's poor results. After eight games they were eleventh in the table, with only twelve points. The forces of conservatism, in steady retreat since the successful 2006 World Cup, merrily took aim from behind tabloid desks and TV talk-show sofas. The notoriously headstrong Klinsmann was an easy target. He had appointed the Mexican-American Martín Vásquez, a man with no practical experience of European league football, as his assistant. 'He was overawed by the size of the stadiums,' one club insider revealed. Klinsmann's big ideas – the introduction of state-of-the-art training methods and performance analysis – left little impression on the pitch.

Fortunately, German football modernists quickly found a new champion, with a familiar name: Rangnick. Bruised by his run-ins with Assauer at Schalke, he had dropped back down to the third division to take over the most unusual club. TSG Hoffenheim 1899 were literally a village team, a nonentity ninety kilometres north of Stuttgart, playing in the eighth division, when a former youth player decided to invest in them in 2000. Billionaire Dietmar Hopp, one of the founders of the SAP software company, took over and had led the club to the third division by 2006. That's when Rangnick was brought in to make the final push into the elite. 'As a club, they were a blank sheet of paper. There were no TV screens, no scouting, nothing. When I told them I wanted a sports psychologist, they hired a sports psychologist. At Schalke, they had told me that there was no need because they had never had one before. End of conversation.'

He installed Bernhard Peters, the former hockey coach, as head of performance, hired the psychologist Hans-Dieter Hermann who'd been part of Klinsmann's 2006 World Cup staff and brought in Helmut Groß as an adviser. 'Rangnick and Peters in Hoffenheim – it's like [celebrity chef Paul] Bocuse seasoning the stadium sausage,' wrote *Der Spiegel*.

Rangnick also advised on the construction of a youth academy modelled on Arsenal's, a training centre and a new stadium to make the club's growth sustainable. The team were a curious mix of fairly expensive Brazilians and undervalued, unfashionable locals. The common denominators were pace and youth. 'We don't buy anyone over twenty-three,' Rangnick said. 'Our player selection process is subordinate to our style of football,' said general manager Jan Schindelmeiser. 'We don't take on thirty-year-old players who can't handle our pace.'

Hoffenheim were promoted twice and made it into the Bundesliga in 2008 as a much-derided 'test tube club', a nouveau riche outfit bereft of history and tradition. But their high-tempo football was a revelation. At the end of September, they beat Klopp's Dortmund 4-1 and climbed into second place in the table. 'That's the kind of football we want to play one day,' the BVB coach gushed in Dortmund's official stadium programme for the next match. A month later, TSG destroyed Hannover 96 5-2 away in Lower Saxony. 'Please don't talk as quickly as Hoffenheim have played today,' the 96 press officer pleaded with reporters at the post-match press conference. The following week Hamburger SV were humbled 3-0. 'It was 3-0 after thirty-six minutes,' lamented HSV defender Joris Mathijsen. 'That simply can't happen.

I don't know what these guys ate before [the match], they were so much better than us.'

Hoffenheim were league leaders by now. Rangnick made a triumphant return to *ZDF Sportstudio*. This time he was no longer the upstart from Ulm but an established Bundesliga coach whose work had so obviously been validated. 'The last couple of seasons were the biggest success of my career,' he beamed. Once again, his star turn was a bit embarrassing for the rest of the league. Hoffenheim's great run amounted to an indictment of the bigger club's scouting networks and coaching methods. It was also a slap in the face for mid-level sides such as Frankfurt, or Hannover, who had become very comfortable with their inoffensive irrelevance over the years. Hoffenheim 'show that mediocrity is not decreed by law', wrote *FAZ*. Lastly, their football was all about collective movement, with a flat hierarchy where responsibility for organisation and creativity was shared. They made the antiquated debate about the need for 'leaders' on German pitches look utterly absurd. As *Frankfurter Allgemeine Zeitung* noted, 'their system is the star'. You didn't need Effenberg-type figures barking orders at subordinates. 'The Bundesliga has never seen such cool, collected novices before,' wrote *Berliner Zeitung*. Even the *New York Times* sought out this village team with a difference and reported on the 'miracle of Hoffenheim'.

Rangnick's training had evolved, to reflect wider developments in the league. 'At Ulm, we practised playing without possession in 70 per cent of the tactical exercises,' he says. 'At Hoffenheim, only 20 per cent was about winning the ball back. Defensive organisation had much improved in the Bundesliga, so the key was improving your own attacking play with specific measures.' Peters had a huge hand in that. The repetitive practice of choreographed offensive moves had been a staple fare for hockey for many years.

One of Hoffenheim's exercises forced players to pass the ball through a narrow gap in the middle of the pitch; sideways or back passes were forbidden. 'It teaches you to adopt an extremely vertical approach through channels and zones,' he says. He recalls midfielder Sejad Salihović complaining that the task was getting on his nerves. 'That was exactly what it was meant to do,' Peters says, 'but in a different sense, of course. It's about enhancing your cognitive abilities by forcing your brain to concentrate really hard.' A similar exercise, nicknamed 'banana', created a 'dead zone' in the middle of the park in order to direct play to the wide areas.

'The mini-version of Klinsmann's World Cup project,' as *Der Spiegel* referred to Hoffenheim, was heading for a big, symbolic showdown with its originator just before Christmas. Bayern and Klinsmann had recovered sufficiently to almost catch up with the leaders ahead of Hoffenheim's visit to the Allianz Arena.

The Bavarians edged a superlative match 2-1, courtesy of a late goal from Luca Toni, but, for once, (German) football was the real winner. National manager Joachim Löw applauded 'perhaps the fastest Bundesliga match ever, [with] pure quality football, an advertisement for the league'. 'All expectations were exceeded,' was Bayern vice-president Karl-Heinz Rummenigge's verdict, and *FAZ* proposed the inclusion of a match DVD 'in the curriculum for the German FA's manager course: this much pace, this much intensity, this much of all the things that have unfortunately only been characteristic of football elsewhere, has not been seen in Germany over ninety minutes'. It really was '*Autobahn-Fussball*' without a speed limit, especially from Hoffenheim, whose organisation and movement were a joy.

For Klinsmann it proved a pyrrhic victory, though. Four months later, the Bayern bosses called time on his version of modernity. His Bayern team had been humiliated 4-0 by Pep Guardiola's Barcelona in the Champions League and crashed to a 5-1 defeat away to eventual champions Wolfsburg. 'We didn't come to this decision easily,' said Rummenigge, with genuine regret. General manager Uli Hoeness was less diplomatic. 'His concept convinced us – on paper,' he remarked pointedly.

Bayern had explicitly wanted change, but change on their own terms and without an annoying let-up in wins. Klinsmann's personnel decisions were resisted because they didn't fully trust his judgement; bringing in the American Landon Donovan in January had not exactly strengthened his case.

From within the dressing room there had been complaints about a lack of tactical instructions.

Klinsmann insisted that he had 'laid the foundations for the future', before flying back to California. He was right, too. The performance centre as well as some of the fitness staff he had left behind soon helped Bayern to regain their place among the European elite under Louis van Gaal and Jupp Heynckes over the next few years.

'Clubs like AC Milan envy us for the facilities [that Klinsmann built],' Franz Beckenbauer wrote in his *Bild* column shortly before Klinsmann's dismissal. Another one of Klinsmann's predictions did not come to pass, however. 'They will go far with that team, that meticulousness and strategic work in the background,' he had said of Rangnick and his assistants at Hoffenheim. 'They will be among the top five at the end of the season, and based on their recent performances genuine title contenders, too.'

The anti-establishment, billionaire-sponsored underdogs had finished 2008 top of the table as the so-called '*Herbstmeister*' (autumn champions). But keeping up their breakneck tempo of progress was beyond them. Some players had their heads turned by offers from the Premier League over the winter break; others flew to New York and partied like rock stars. Believing that they had arrived, they eased up just a little bit, ran a few metres less and at a slower pace. The competition gained ground, and by the end of the season Hoffenheim had dropped to seventh. By no means a bad return from their first ever season at the top level, but a disappointment in relation to their early promise.

In 2009–10, Hoffenheim came eleventh. Rangnick's contract was extended but six months later he resigned in the wake of differences of opinion with club benefactor Hopp. The SAP boss wanted 1899 to be more self-sufficient and to concentrate on local talent, whereas Rangnick argued that they should push forward. He tried his hand at Schalke for a second time, beating Inter Milan in the Champions League to advance to the semi-final – where they were eliminated by Manchester United – and won his first trophy: the DFB Cup.

Schalke's exploits were overshadowed by the sensational triumph of Klopp at Dortmund, however. In the space of three years, he had taken the Black and Yellows from mid-table mediocrity to the seventh championship in the club's history. Propelled by limitless energy and a desire to work for each other, Klopp's Borussia were by far the best and perhaps even the only true club team of the 2010–11 season: a band of brothers, comprised of humble, super-fit, players well-versed in the theory of the game, prepared to leave their egos outside the dressing room.

'This team is emblematic of the kind of paradigm shift in German football that the national team stands for,' wrote *Der Spiegel*. 'Young professionals, technically and tactically well-educated, aware of their own strengths but never arrogant – Dortmund is like a miniature of the national side.' The comparison was apt in another sense, too. Rarely was a squad so well liked by the whole of the country. The unusually generous and genuine congratulatory messages from various dignitaries proved that. Perhaps the biggest compliment of all had already been paid back in February, three months before the title had been secured. Italy's national team, coached by Cesare Prandelli, had been in town for a friendly. The *Azzurri* technical staff came to look at Dortmund's training; the team's movement reminded them of Sacchi's Milan, they told a beaming Klopp afterwards.

Compared to Dortmund's rapid-transition game, the possession football that Dutchman Louis van Gaal had introduced at Bayern looked ponderous and predictable. Klopp's team were less interested in passing the ball than in winning it high up the pitch. In order to achieve this strategic aim, they would not only press the ball to stop opposition attacks but also continue pressing after their own had broken down. '*Gegenpressing*', counter-pressing, Klopp called this Pep

Guardiola-inspired method, and its successful application made Dortmund a side that overran and chewed up opponents like a colony of army ants. '*Gegenpressing* is the best playmaker in the world,' Klopp said. 'Hunting football', *Süddeutsche Zeitung* called it.

This was the 'heavy metal' (Klopp) edition of the beautiful game, where the other side were killed by a thousand cuts and where the creation of goalscoring opportunities was not the result of isolated moments of genius by one or two outstanding players but the logical, mathematically calculated consequence of relentless, frenetic work. 'When three players chase in a swarm after a ball that's just been lost, it can sometimes look chaotic. But this is chaos of a controlled and highly creative kind,' Helmut Groß explained of Dortmund's innovation in *FAZ*.

'He had the courage of his convictions, that was key,' says Rangnick of Klopp. 'One of the first things he did after arriving at Dortmund in 2008 was to remove Alexander Frei and Mladen Petrić from the line-up. They were the two star players, and if you had asked 100,000 BVB fans which two players had to play all the time, they would have named them. But Kloppo knew that they weren't able to deliver the aggressive pressing he wanted.'

In May 2012, Klopp found himself on the pitch of Berlin's Olympic Stadium, cradling the DFB Cup in his arms, just as he had predicted to Doehling in 2008. Bayern Munich had been taken apart, outclassed even, to secure Borussia's first ever double with an emphatic 5-2 scoreline. 'And that was it for him,' says Doehling. 'Now he was the supercoach, an international star – no longer the funny Harry Potter from Mainz with the floppy hair.' Klopp had changed the idea of what a coach should look like, how he should talk and, most importantly of all, where he should come from. Doehling: 'His success opened up people's eyes to the fact that football management was a vocation that could be learned, that it wasn't a God-given skill possessed exclusively by former greats on the pitch.'

*

Through Klopp, the Stuttgart school's outlandish football science – the renegade tactics of provincial lab boffins – has become recognised as best practice in Germany. The industry leaders were believers, too, by now. Bayern Munich's treble in 2013 under Heynckes, which included the first Champions League win by a Bundesliga side since 2001, owed much to their adoption of *Gegenpressing*. 'They have done it like the Chinese, they've copied us,' Klopp lamented, not without justification. Two seasons without silverware had forced the Bavarians to take a deep look at their tactical shortcomings. The arrival of Pep Guardiola as manager in 2013 has since upped the ante even further. 'They have taken up more elements of Dortmund's game than Dortmund themselves,' says Rangnick, admiringly. Statistical analysis from 2013–14 revealed that Bayern's *Gegenpressing* was, in a real sense, off the charts. No other team in the top European leagues attacked the ball so far away from their own goal (at an average distance of 46.7 metres) and so quickly (within seven passes of the opposition, on average).

Throughout the league, the systematic pressing first advanced by the Groß gang of forward thinkers has acquired the status of '*Leitkultur*' (lead culture). It's the new orthodoxy. According to the sports data company Opta, Bundesliga teams enjoy less time on the ball after winning it back than their counterparts in England, France, Italy and Spain. There are also more changes in possession and more shots on goal after quick moves relative to the those other leagues.

Rangnick: 'Football has become a completely different sport over the last ten years. The change has been brutal. The two basic elements – having the ball, not having the ball – are the same but the transitions between those two states are nothing like they used to be. The highest probability of scoring a goal is within ten seconds of taking possession. The highest probability of winning the ball back is within eight seconds of losing possession. Think about these two numbers and what they mean. Everything else just follows.'

Groß's fringe movement of modernists provided many services to German football but the greatest was to make it self-aware, to force it to realise it was stuck in the slow lane. Knowing and understanding the importance of the concept of time on the football pitch then automatically accelerated the game.

Klinsmann, and Löw after him, publicly defined 'having time on the ball' as a negative value by which Germany's poor quality in relation to the world's elite could be measured. 'Our game has become much faster,' Löw said after the World Cup in 2010. 'In 2005, there was 2.8 seconds on average between controlling and passing the ball. The game was designed to go sideways, it was slow. At Euro 2008 we improved to 1.8 seconds, and at the [2010] World Cup it was down to 1.1 seconds. In the games against England [4-1] and Argentina [4-0] we were even below one second. Only Spain were a shade better on average.'

'Players run more and they run at high speed a lot more,' says Rangnick, with a hint of pride. 'If you don't have the willingness or fitness to do that, you can't succeed. You'll fall through the cracks, the system will spew you out.' Every player, he says, has to decide whether he wants to get on board this bullet train or to get off, so the earlier they learn to play that way, the better. 'The German team at the World Cup were made up of children from the academy system,' he notes. 'They were the fittest team in Brazil and they ran significantly more than anybody else. The tournament has shown that we've not only caught up with the best in the world but overtaken them – at least some of them.'

Rangnick's influence on the game is arguably stronger than ever. As sporting director of the Red Bull family of football clubs, he controls a turbo-charged version of Hoffenheim with five professional teams in Germany, Austria, Brazil, Ghana and the US. RB Leipzig, the German franchise, will be promoted to the Bundesliga before too long. Rangnick may never have won the championship, but he has won the argument. The German top flight teems with disciples of his and Groß, who's still his trusted adviser after all these years. They all play his football.

Roger Schmidt, the Leverkusen manager, learned his trade under both of them at RB Salzburg. Tayfun Korkut, at Hannover 96 until April 2014, worked as youth coach when Rangnick and Groß were in charge at Hoffenheim. Thomas Tuchel, the former Mainz 05 coach who's widely regarded as the best young German manager of his generation and has succeeded Klopp at Dortmund, was a player at Ulm during the Rangnick years and later a youth coach while Groß was in charge of Stuttgart's player development and Rangnick a head coach there. 'I'm infected and inspired by him,' Tuchel has said. Markus Gisdol, the current Hoffenheim 1899 coach, and Groß go back even further. Gisdol played as a youngster for SC Geislingen when Groß taught the club to play zonal marking and pressing in the eighties. 'He used to mix energy drinks for the first team at half-time,' Groß recalls. Klinsmann, too, played for Geislingen before his teens, as it happens, albeit a couple of years before Groß's pioneering feat began.

Increasingly, Bundesliga clubs prefer to appoint managers with experience as academy coaches because they're in a better position to evaluate – and relate to – the young players coming through the system, Rangnick notes. The age of the former pro who walks into a job has come to an end. 'The introduction of academies has led to more positions for qualified coaches, and thus we have seen more talented people rising to the top. I read that there are ten times as many qualified coaches here than in England. That's bound to make a difference. The next logical step, in my view, is the licensing of sporting directors. It's the most powerful job at the club but you don't need any qualifications whatsoever for it as things stand. That can't be right. I'm sure that in a few years the German FA will offer courses. The precedent of coaching has shown that better candidates emerge once there are fixed criteria for a job and a process in place.'

But is it a mere coincidence of geography and managerial networks that so much of German football's innovation has come from Swabia, Swabians and neighbouring Baden? Stereotypically, they're seen as a hard-working, conscientious and financially literate tribe who don't lose sight of the bigger picture. Their high-pitched, susurrant accent routinely ranks as one of the least popular in national polls. 'We can do everything – apart from [speaking] proper German,' the regional state of Baden-Württemberg admitted, tongue in cheek, in an advertising campaign.

Löw's father was a stove setter, Klinsmann's a baker, Klopp's a master saddler and sports nut who constantly challenged his son to beat him at football, tennis and skiing. Christian Streich, the Freiburg coach (and son of a butcher), has dismissed the theory that the middle-class artisanal background of many of these mavericks from the south-west has made them predestined to embark on new paths in football management, however. Many people were artisans in that region, so you'd expect football to recruit its players and coaches from that demographic, too, Streich said.

Money might also be a factor. The south-west is a wealthy region but clubs like Stuttgart and Freiburg used to have relatively few financial resources at their disposal. 'Money had to be superseded by hard work, special ideas, the development of talents,' said Groß. 'And it wasn't just the clubs and players who benefitted. Managers were able to further their careers, too.'

It's fitting that the need for speed was first truly understood by men from Stuttgart, the home of Mercedes and Porsche. But perhaps it goes a little deeper than that. I ask both Klinsmann and Rangnick whether there is a specifically Swabian factor at play, and they both agree, after a short pause, using the same word to characterise a trait that combines diligence, professional curiosity and hard-headedness. Swabians are '*Tüftler*', they say: obsessive tinkerers and puzzle freaks. 'We like to try out things and we don't readily take no for an answer,' Rangnick says.

He adds that there's often a direct relationship between tactics and a coach's character, citing Löw as an example. 'You can say he has been influenced by the Stuttgart school, through his time at VfB, especially when it comes to vertical play and pace in attack. But he's not one of those hardliners from the church of aggressive pressing who gets on his players' nerves a lot, because that's not who he is. That doesn't make him a lesser coach, obviously.'

Löw name-checked Helmut Groß as a '*Vorreiter*' (outrider) in an interview with *Stuttgarter Zeitung* in 2010. 'The idea not to defend in constant duels against your man but in a spatial defensive arrangement has been pursued most markedly in Stuttgart,' the national manager said.

The teachings of the '*Spätzle-Connection*' have, in the meantime, become both institutionalised and internalised. (*Spätzle* are Swabian noodles.) Players who have grown up with the teachings turn into missionaries by passing on the ideas. They are also much more demanding of their managers. Lazy, old-fashioned or plain incompetent coaches are less likely to get away with it in dressing rooms full of players who are used to receiving detailed tactical instructions from their pre-teens onwards. 'Young players from Hoffenheim, Stuttgart, Munich or Mainz know what's going on, tactically,' Löw's former assistant Hansi Flick said a few years ago. 'And the national team benefits from these players being continuously educated in their clubs.'

Today's German teenagers are more or less fully formed professionals in terms of their fitness levels and theoretical background, according to Rangnick. 'Finding new ways to improve a team has become more difficult. But it is possible.' Future increases in the playing tempo are more likely to come from quicker minds than quicker feet, he says. At his clubs, the emphasis has thus shifted yet again, to cognitive training and the optimisation of thought process through video analysis and special video games. 'The biggest untapped potential lies within the footballer's brain,' says Rangnick. 'To get better in the modern game translates into taking in things more quickly, analysing them more quickly, deciding more quickly, acting more quickly. We need to increase the memory space and the processing pace.'

One day, he may take his innovative zeal to England, where Red Bull are rumoured to be looking for a suitable takeover target, or complete his long journey from ridiculed tactical geek to universally admired luminary by becoming a successor to Löw. He dismisses both notions, pointing to a 'high job satisfaction' in his current role. His point has been proved, in any case. The formula works.

The day after our meeting, the phone rings. It's Rangnick again, in his car, on the hands-free. He forgot to share a story, a moment of immense professional happiness, as it turns out. On the eve of Schalke's quarter-final away match against Inter in 2011, AC Milan's CEO Adriano Galliani paid Rangnick a visit in the team hotel. The conversation soon turned towards Sacchi. Galliani whipped out his mobile, called up Rangnick's idol and handed the phone over. 'We talked at length about tactics and Sacchi told me that the key is to get the team to move in synchronicity,' Rangnick remembers, with a smile so wide you can almost hear it through the crackling of the line.

VORSPRUNG DURCH TECHNIK

'Hallo, Joachim!'

SAP are the biggest business software providers in the world. Big enough to have their own dedicated autobahn exit. You get on the eight-lane A5 near Frankfurt, drive south for a bit until you cross into the regional state of Baden-Württemberg, then drive south a little more and turn right just past the city of Walldorf.

SAP's campus is on Dietmar-Hopp-Allee, named after the company's founder and TSG Hoffenheim 1899 benefactor. Google Maps shows four buildings in an 'H' shape. There are also three five-pointed stars slightly further out but my appointment is in the main building. Three joined-up quadrants in sober greys and off-whites, the secret national colours of pre-unification Germany.

In the understated reception area you can peek into a dark, green courtyard that houses an 'inspiration pavilion'. Into the lift, no questions asked, sixth floor, another, slightly nicer reception area, an airy meeting room. Coffee? *Bitte.*

The story, says development manager Andrew McCormick-Smith, begins in Palo Alto. 'That's where all the cool SAP people are,' he chuckles. In January 2014, German FA sporting director Hansi Flick and scout Christopher Clemens visited the company's 'Co-Innovation

Lab' in Silicon Valley for a brainstorming session. How could German FA sponsors SAP, the specialists in big data management, help the national team at the World Cup?

McCormick-Smith: 'The time frame was too short to construct a platform with a complicated architecture. It was decided to create a smartphone communication tool. Research among the players had shown that most of them were using the instant messaging system WhatsApp to chat. SAP were given the task of developing a secure, closed version that could be used by the coaching staff to keep in touch with the players in the months leading up to the tournament, and for the players to keep in touch with each other.'

A select group of players were chosen as early adopters. They were regularly sent personal performance data as well as organisational details. Clemens' scouts also 'pushed' ten-second clips of video analysis, replete with annotations, that players could watch and comment on. 'Before that, the German FA's video analysts had to make an appointment with a player if they wanted to show them something,' explains SAP project manager Jens Wittkopf. 'That was very time-consuming and also complicated to organise, because you don't get to spend much time with the national team in between big tournaments.'

Bierhoff credits the app with making the briefing of players a more enjoyable and immersive process during the World Cup: 'Every player got a couple of examples showing him doing things both well and badly straight after each game. They could watch it in their own time and also check their performance data. That was much more useful than showing a ninety-minute video tape, as they used to in my day. The players appreciated that sort of feedback.'

For the semi-final against Brazil, Clemens and his staff started sifting through four years of Brazil's games without Neymar, who had got injured in the last game, and the defender Thiago Silva, who was suspended. Key performances from their likely replacements were edited into clips that were then sent out to the phones of the relevant players. *Nationalmannschaft* defenders looked at the movement of Neymar's replacement in the Brazilian attack; forwards at the performance of the man who'd fill in for captain Thiago Silva. 'We found that this tool worked really well because it is visual and intuitive,' says Bierhoff.

The real surprise for the coaches, says Wittkopf, was the extent to which the app was a conduit for collective learning: 'The players didn't just receive and comment on clips, they also sent lots of clips on to each other and discussed them in groups. Analysis and match preparation became a social effort.' In a few instances, players looked at their opponents' style on their phones right up to kick-off.

A more powerful analysis tool was available on the black Mac Pro tube with a twenty-seven-inch screen that's in front of us on the meeting-room table but used to be installed in the Campo Bahia players' lounge. It's called 'Match Insights', and, for once, it owed its development not to solid German long-term planning but to SAP's ad hoc attempt to impress David Cameron and Angela Merkel.

The British prime minister was a guest of honour at the computer fair CEBIT in March 2014 in Hannover. SAP wanted to showcase its technology in a football context during his and Chancellor Merkel's short visit to their stand. They took full-pitch video footage of Germany's 1-0 win in November 2013 against Roy Hodgson's England at Wembley (Arsenal's Mertesacker had scored the winner with a header), synced it with positional data provided by the German FA's analytics partner Amisco and created a touch-screen user interface that allowed real-time reading of performance data and easy navigation to find significant events.

You could click on any player and his stats would come up, or you could pick out any number of players – the four defenders, for example – and follow the shape of their movement. 'It didn't have to be very deep but it had to look cool,' says McCormick-Smith. 'It had a small number of KPIs [key performance indicators] that might be fun for the chancellor to look at but was also supposed to bear some resemblance to a what a coach might want to do.'

The presentation was a big success. Merkel liked it. Cameron jokingly asked, rather lamely, whether the tool allowed a team to retake penalties. And Bierhoff, who had said a few words in his role as SAP brand ambassador, told the Hannover audience that Germany wanted to use the technology for the World Cup.

McCormick-Smith: 'That hadn't been checked with SAP beforehand. It came as a shock to everyone. It was three months before the World Cup. What were we going to do? But Bernd Leukert, who is on the board, decided that we were going to make it work.' Leukert told an audience at the CEBIT that analysis should 'move away from intuition and gut-feeling, towards facts-based support [of coaches]'.

A quick investigation into the feasibility of extending the Hannover showcase into a real tool found that it was a non-starter. The system relied on data that tracked player information, and FIFA, unfortunately, were not going to release it for World Cup games. They wanted to keep the stats for themselves.

There were hasty discussions between SAP's project manager Christoph Jungkind, Bierhoff and the scouts – what would be a sensible alternative for Brazil? They settled on a video tool that would allow players and coaches to very quickly find relevant scenarios for analysis and preparation – without the help of analysts. There were a lot more intricate, expansive systems out there but none of them were easy enough for athletes and coaches to use independently. As with the app, the idea was to enable players to use 'Match Insights' when they wanted, how they wanted, by themselves.

The same project team, five men, was assigned to put a dummy in place that could be tested within a month. The feedback was positive. Jungkind took a workable but very much unfinished version to the training camp in South Tyrol to see how it would fare in the field. Staff and players liked it. The SAP team flew to Campo Bahia to install the machine and worked a couple of days non-stop to iron out the last few glitches. The only serious bug in the system came to light ahead of the Brazil game, when only one player from Luiz Felipe Scolari's squad showed up in the system: right-back Maicon. 'The computer had a problem accounting for the Brazilians' lack of full names,' says McCormick-Smith. It was easily fixed. 'It was disappointing but we were also happy to hear that the team were really engaging with it.'

'I worked with it, every single day,' says Philipp Lahm. 'That thing was amazing. It showed you everything you wanted to know about the other teams and your own team.' As soon as you start playing around a bit on the touchscreen, it's not hard to see why Lahm got hooked.

You can navigate to games, teams or players. Important events – free-kicks, corners, goals – are synced with video footage. A couple of clicks, and you can see all of the chances Ghana created against the USA, all of Brazil's free-kicks going back a couple of years, all key moments or any given position or any given player. 'It's not particularly clever,' says McCormick, 'but its ease of use made it an effective tool. We didn't want to bombard coaches or players with numbers. We wanted them to be able to see, literally, whether the data supported their gut feelings and intuition. It was designed to add value for a coach or athlete who isn't that interested in analytics otherwise. Big data needed to be turned into KPIs that made sense to non-analysts.'

Clemens illustrated the point by sending back a slide with numbers from a World Cup knock-out game to Walldorf:

Opposition	Germany
Goal Attempts: 18	Goal Attempts: 14
On Target: 13	On Target: 12

A closely contested game, then. The 2-1 over Algeria? France? It was actually the semi-final against Brazil. The 7-1 win. 'That just goes to show that a lot of football numbers don't mean anything,' says McCormick-Smith. 'We concentrated on qualitative analysis instead. How do certain teams play? How do they defend corners, etc.'

Jérôme Boateng watched so many 'Match Insights' clips of Cristiano Ronaldo ahead of the game against Portugal that he noticed the Real Madrid superstar had a particular habit of turning away from a defender, depending on how he looked at the ball. In poker, you'd call that a 'tell'.

That probably wasn't the reason the winger underperformed so dramatically in Germany's 4-0 win in Salvador but the players at Campo Bahia were quickly won over by the tool's capabilities. 'The coaches told us that the screen was 'a social point' in the camp,' says McCormick-Smith. 'The defenders went in as a group to look back at their own defending, for example.' 'It wasn't conceived as a team-building tool, but it became one,' adds Wittkopf.

In its user-friendliness, the technology reversed the traditional top-down flow of tactical information in a football team. Players would pass on their findings to Flick and Löw. Lahm and Mertesacker were also allowed to have some input into Siegenthaler's and Clemens' official pre-match briefing, bringing the players' perspective – and a sense of what was truly relevant on the pitch – to the table. Lahm: 'A lot of things at the World Cup came from the team itself. I knew it would be my last tournament with Germany and I didn't want to regret not having done everything possible for success afterwards. I looked at every game and tried to find out where we could improve for the next one.'

'Football has so many variables. The world's fifteen best scientists wouldn't be able to work out the winning formula together,' says Thomas Müller. 'All you can do is to prepare as much as you can.' The moment you acknowledge that you're playing a game of indeterminable vagaries, you can only rage against them.

*

Christian Güttler, a Berlin-based inventor, came to the very same conclusion after he had pondered for years why football was so different from other elite sporting and cultural activities. 'I was mad about sports. I played pool, golf, football and tennis,' he says. 'I was also a music PhD student and had to practice playing guitar, cello and piano every day as a child. I asked myself a series of questions. Why were athletes in individual sports training many more hours every day, and much more intensely, than footballers? Why, unlike musicians and tennis players, did footballers not improve technically in their twenties? And why was the Philharmonic Orchestra of Helsinki, where my brother is the conductor, able to play for two hours without a single mistake while the world's best footballers couldn't do the same over ninety minutes?'

The answer to the third question, he came to realise, lay in football's complex playing patterns. 'The guy who misplaces a simple pass on the right flank to the attacking midfielder a few metres away from him would love to undo his mistake immediately, and play the same pass well, but he cannot stop the game and tell everyone to assume the same positions. So he runs around the next few minutes thinking about that misplaced pass.' What was it that Arsenal coach Arsène Wenger once said? 'They asked him "What makes a good footballer?",' recalls Güttler. 'His reply was "A good footballer is somebody who can offer the perfect solution in an unpredictable situation."'

Now Güttler had it: you had to design a machine that could 're-create randomness', evaluate how well a player dealt with unforeseeable challenges and make him better, quicker as a result.

On the day of Liverpool's miraculous Champions League final comeback from 3-0 down to beat AC Milan on penalties in Istanbul in 2005, Güttler drew up his first draft design of a contraption that could do just that. He saved up money earned from editing TV commercials ('day and night') and persuaded a friend to invest. Years later, he had assembled a prototype in an old East Berlin warehouse where the

GDR's secret police, the Stasi, used to soup up their cars. He reached out to Oliver Bierhoff. Could he come and have a look? The German FA's sporting director politely replied via a press officer that he didn't have the time but asked whether Güttler could send the machine up to his hotel room. The inventor laughs at the memory.

It took until November 2012 for his idea to become a reality. Jürgen Klopp's Borussia Dortmund installed Güttler's invention at their training ground in Brackel, west of the city centre, at a cost of €1 million. Eighteen months later, TSG Hoffenheim followed suit.

Hoffenheim's training centre is at Zuzenhausen, a genteel, winding, thirty-minute drive from Walldorf through prosperous-looking villages. It wouldn't be inaccurate to describe the club's HQ as a palace. It is – or, more precisely, was – actually a baroque, eighteenth-century palace belonging to local gentry who weren't quite rich enough to keep up with the Ludwigs. 'Schloss Agnestal', as it was known, was first turned into a farm and then run as a nightclub early in the present century, before Dietmar Hopp made it the centre of 1899's new training ground when the club was promoted to the first division in 2008. Güttler's invention resides in an adjacent limestone block. It's called the *Footbonaut*.

Two boys from the U15 team are working with it. They take turns stepping into the 14 by 14 metre facility laid out with Astro Turf. One of sixty-four quadrants lights up in green with a hissing sound – that's the target. A fraction of a second later, one of eight ball machines (two each in the centre of the four sides) emits two loud beeps and shoots a ball at them. It can be low, high, soft, hard (up to 100 kmh); it can even swerve. The player has to control the ball and pass it as quickly as possible into the right opening. Ten, fifteen times. The *Footbonaut* keeps track of the total time and the score, and the session is also being filmed and analysed by the youth coach at the controls in a small room overlooking the hall. I'm relieved to see the three onlookers depart before a staff member lets me have a go.

All squares light up red for the countdown. Then the first ball comes at you, low, at a nice pace. Controlling it is easy but you lose a lot of time unless you've seen the target first. You're thus forced to look over your shoulder before you turn back towards the pass. The exercise involves minimal movement outside the centre circle but your thighs start aching and your concentration suffers after three or four attempts. It looks and feels straight out of the science fiction movie *Tron* and it is fun, but, above all, it's an experience that's stressful in its mechanical relentlessness. 'Game over' a computer voice barks. I prefer not to look at my stats. I'll try again in five minutes. I'm now better at coordinating the various phases of the moves required but in no time I'm even more tired. I miss a lot of my targets.

'The aim is to improve the technique and coordination of players but also their cognitive response,' Hoffenheim's sporting director Bernhard Peters (now at HSV) explained when the 'football robot' (as *FAZ* called it) was introduced to the press in 2013. 'Sharpness of passing and precision are being honed, as well as the recognition and the decision-making for perfect control and second touch for passing to the target.'

Hoffenheim have found that short sessions are most effective; if you spend too long inside the *Footbonaut*, it becomes a physical workout, not a technical exercise. They use it for drills involving more than one player and also for goalkeepers. 'The players get more touches in fifteen minutes than in a whole week of team training,' Güttler says. His football holo-deck teaches 'the adaptation to randomness, broken down into the three hundred, four hundred milliseconds that make a difference', a highly individualised, repetitive training session in a stable environment that feels anything but artificial. Güttler's research found that players taking a pass from seven or eight metres was as close to the way they would receive the ball during a game. 'You can measure the progress,' says Güttler. 'After a while, players become faster and more accurate.' The benchmark is two seconds – from the ball being released and the player dispatching it to the right opening.

At Dortmund, two players – Marco Reus and Mario Götze – liked the machine so much that they frequently went in late in the evening or on Sundays, in their spare time. Güttler: 'I was there when "Tele" Santana [BVB's Brazilian defender] said to Mario: "Why do you go there?" "Because I want to get better," says Götze. Santana: "But why? I don't get it. I'm already a professional footballer."'

On 13 July, Güttler received a flurry of text messages from friends and coaches, all telling him that . . . No. That anecdote will have to wait.

'MINEIRAÇO'

By the eighty-ninth minute, the German defence were no longer able to withstand the onslaught. Innumerable Brazilian forwards were bearing down on Manuel Neuer's goal; a fleet of Manhattan cabs, racing, raging through the final third.

A sharp pass from Willian cut through the gap between Philipp Lahm and Per Mertesacker to release his Chelsea team-mate Oscar, who missed the far post with an improvised toe-poke from a difficult angle. From the ensuing throw-in, Mertesacker's attempted chip was intercepted by Dante on the right-hand side. Ramires laid off the ball to Willian, Willian found Bernard behind Lahm's back. The winger drilled his shot over Neuer's bar. Germany then lost the ball again immediately from the goal-kick. Ramires' attempt from outside the box cannoned off Paulinho's lower back into the path of Julian Draxler. The substitute ran a few metres to stab the ball through to Mesut Özil but he dragged his shot wide.

The reprieve from the constant wave of attacks by the hosts only lasted a few seconds. The *Nationalmannschaft* were too slow to retreat following Özil's miss, spread too thinly over the pitch. Left-back Marcelo hit a simple, straight long ball that unhinged the German back four completely. Three-quarters of the high defence were near the halfway line, marooned in the badlands, as Oscar ran on to the pass, sent Jérôme Boateng packing with a neat drop of the shoulder and fired past Neuer, six seconds from the end of normal time.

Boateng angrily waved his arms at his team-mates who had left him isolated. Neuer stared into the middle distance with a grim face, mumbling '*Das ist doch Scheiße*,' that's shit. The goalkeeper was so distraught he couldn't even muster the strength to raise his right arm to the assistant referee to plead for offside; a reflex so ingrained it came to the fore almost every time somebody breached his goal, irrespective of the scorer's position. '*Reklamierarm*', the arm of complaint, Germans referred to it, jokingly.

'I know how important it is for Manuel not to concede a goal, to keep a clean sheet,' Bastian Schweinsteiger later said. 'It really bugged me that we lost concentration and let that goal in. I hated that.'

During the break, Mats Hummels had sternly warned the whole team about the importance of preventing the Brazilians from scoring. 'We don't want a miracle here!' the BVB centre-back had exclaimed. But he had had to go off with a knee injury before the second half in the Estádio Mineirão, and the goal for Felipe Scolari's side had been coming, inescapably, inevitably, like the fate of a Russian roulette player chancing his luck one too many times.

David Luiz tried one more shot from distance, then Draxler went on another counter-attack that came to nothing, and then it was over. The crowd in Belo Horizonte booed the losers and bade the winners, *their team*, goodbye with polite applause.

David Luiz was on his knees, thanking God with two index fingers raised to the sky. Oscar was in tears. The Germans were wandering around the pitch in a daze, turning to each other to make sense of a result that didn't make sense, embracing their opponents.

Football is a low-scoring game, the lowest-scoring of all the popular team sports. This lack of goals increases the role of luck, makes the underdog win more often and tends to become more pronounced when teams of equal standing meet in a high-pressure situation such as the latter stages of an international competition.

In five out of the six World Cup semi-finals before Germany's visit to the Mineirão, one single goal in regular time did make or would have made the difference between the sides. Löw's team themselves had conceded the first goal in three semi-finals (World Cup 2006, World Cup 2010, Euro 2012) and one final (Euro 2008). They had not recovered to win the game in any of them.

The margins are so narrow, the line between success and failure so fine, that any arbitrary event – a deflected shot, a wrong penalty call, a ball bouncing back from the inside of the post – can tilt the balance. A study by Martin Lames, a professor of training science and computer science in sport at the Technische Universität München, has shown that almost half of all goals scored come as a result of random occurrences, which in turn means that the referee might as well flip a coin to decide the winner. And that's exactly how some drawn games were settled before penalties were introduced in 1971.

The disparity between the high emotion that football invokes and the banality of most of the action on the pitch opens up a huge void that fans, journalists, pundits and some players are instantly moved to imbue with meaning. Stories are woven. Results are framed in psychological terms. Winners have character, heart and backbone. Losers have none. Football becomes a morality play.

After Germany's Euro 2012 semi-final knock-out at the hands of the Italians, *Bild* didn't dwell on tactical, qualitative or technical explanations. The tabloid went for the jugular. Löw's players had lacked passion, their headlines screamed. 'Euro losers go home in Lear Jets' was one take, implying that they were too pampered to fight on the pitch. Worse accusations – feebleness and lack of patriotism – lurked behind the populist, borderline xenophobic enquiry into the

Nationalmannschaft's low-key rendition of the national anthem. Why didn't they all sing it? (Subtext: why didn't some of the players with an immigrant background sing it?) And why hadn't those who had sung the anthem not belted it out at the tops of their voices like the victorious *Azzurri* right next to them? (The loud singing didn't help the Italians against their voiceless opponents in the final, as it happens. Spain, whose national anthem contains no words, routed them 4-0 in Warsaw.)

That sad denouement was threatening to become the defining result of the Löw era, the epitaph for a gifted team low on moral fibre and for their oddly disengaged coach. Germany's World Cup in Brazil was officially classified as a 'success' by German FA president Wolfgang Niersbach after the France win. But the Löw cover story that appeared in *Der Spiegel* the day before the semi-final spelt out the feeling of unease that was still prevalent back at home. On the front page, Löw was called 'The Gambler' whose 'bold strategies' would be revealed inside. The actual piece, however, was titled '*Der fremde Deutsche*' ('*fremd*' translates as foreign, strange or alien), and it mostly reflected on the many reasons why the manager who'd orchestrated some of the most riveting performances in living memory did not fully connect with the German public.

Unlike his predecessors Jürgen Klinsmann, Rudi Völler, Berti Vogts and Franz Beckenbauer, Löw had no gleaming past as a World Cup winner to complement his deliberately cultivated enigmatic persona. Löw was the record scorer of (then) second division SC Freiburg, a small club near the Black Forest. He had never worn the national shirt. Despite the many years they had seen him standing on the touchline talking to them, the German public still didn't know him thanks to his extremely low profile off the pitch. With his silk scarves, mod haircut and air of a successful art director, he had also long been a natural target for all those disturbed by German football's march to modernity (with its concurrent commodification into a clean, youthful, universally appealing product) and who harked back to the days when the German FA was a bastion of social conservatism, emanating a whiff of Deep Heat, supermarket shower-gel machismo and freshly cut grass. Even the more progressive members of the media elite could be overheard complaining that Löw's side were espousing a much too playful type of 'children's football' and were not being manly enough. Worse language could be heard in the pubs and beer gardens up and down the country.

Against a Brazil hell-bent on avenging their fallen messiah Neymar, who had suffered a broken back in an ill-tempered quarter-final against Colombia, and a whole nation on the war path, willing on the *Seleção*, this bunch of nice guys needed some fire in their bellies, not just feeling in their little toes.

Inside Campo Bahia, however, that Tuesday's challenge was viewed rather differently. Half the team had first-hand experience of what could happen when extreme motivation and murderous intent got the better of you. Only a few weeks earlier, the Bayern players had suffered a crushing home defeat in the second leg of the Champions League semi-final against Real Madrid. Following a very composed but ultimately fruitless outing at the Bernabéu, where Pep Guardiola's men had dominated the match with countless clinically executed passes but gone down 1-0, five out of six regulars consulted by the coach had pleaded for a more gung-ho approach in the return leg. Madrid are the one side who always get the notoriously cool crowd at the Allianz Arena truly excited, and, with 70,000 voices cheering them on, the team wanted to overpower the visitors from the first whistle. Guardiola, despite his better instincts, committed 'the biggest fuck-up of my career', as he later admitted, by listening to his players on this occasion. Bayern drove forward with reckless abandon, and right over a cliff, as Madrid waited for them deep in their own half and skilfully picked them off on the break. The game finished 4-0 to the Spaniards. It was Bayern's biggest home defeat in a European competition.

*

Passion, the Germans knew, could be their enemy on Tuesday night. And the plan was to turn the enemy's passion against them.

For Löw, Miroslav Klose, Lukas Podolski, Philipp Lahm, Bastian Schweinsteiger and Per Mertesacker, it was easy to appreciate the weight of expectation that was resting on their opponents' shoulders. 'A defeat in the semi-final, that's a disappointment for the whole nation,' said Löw. 'We experienced that ourselves in 2006 on home soil when we lost against Italy in the 119th minute. We know how that sort of pressure feels.' This time Germany were cast in the role of spoilsports. They set about ruining the host nation's dream with cold-hearted detachment. Huge effort was made to tone down the rhetoric immediately after the France game. The Brazil match was not a gargantuan tussle between two of world football's leading teams, simply a game they needed to win to avoid another, unwanted, game, the third third-place play-off in a row. 'I can do without it,' claimed Lahm. Löw, asked about inching closer to the trophy, did a convincing job at feigning disinterest. 'Trophies, trophies . . . Of course trophies are wonderful, in a way, but first we need to play in this semi-final,' he shrugged. 'Would you like to come back to the Maracanã for the final?' somebody asked Mertesacker. 'I'm open to that,' answered the centre-back, as if considering a slightly unwelcome dinner invitation.

Playing the match, not the occasion, was something the Bayern players had had to learn the hard way, too: putting themselves under huge additional pressure at the endlessly hyped 'final at home' in the Champions League had been one of the reasons they had fallen victim to Chelsea in 2012. Matthias Sammer, brought in as sporting director to change the mental attitude in Munich after that disaster, spouted a very different line when the club qualified for 2013's final against Borussia Dortmund at Wembley (which they won 2-1). 'We just need to perform to our capabilities,' he said, 'the result will take care of itself.' Löw echoed these words in team meetings, telling his players that they would go into a game against an opponent whose patriotic fervour disguised plenty of problems, and that they would win if only they maintained their awareness of their own strengths. 'We met the Brazilians' deep emotions with stamina, calmness, clarity and insistence,' the *Bundestrainer* later explained, 'and we coolly exploited their weaknesses. We knew that their defence would be disorganised if we attacked quickly. But of course nobody thought it would be as clear-cut.'

Bierhoff: 'We had seen that they hadn't really played well in the competition. They had made many mistakes.'

Lahm: 'We wanted to do well defensively, either by winning the ball or breaking through their first wave of attack because Brazil would often then split into two: attack and defence. Opportunities would arise that way.'

Bierhoff: 'They were a bit like England in 2010. It's probably easier to play against a team like that than against Algeria who fight tooth and nail for every ball.'

The starting eleven's confidence was boosted by Löw having made no changes for the first time in the tournament. Germany lined up in their usual 4-3-3 formation but without the ball Kroos dropped a bit deeper to allow Khedira to push out on the right to make it a 4-4-2, pressing Brazil on their strong left-hand side, where most of their attacking moves originated. The absence of Neymar made it easier to keep the high line at the back, and the suspension of Thiago Silva caused uncertainty at the heart of the Brazilian defence.

The opening spell was *very* open, though. Brazil flooded forward with energy and purpose, fuelled by the adrenalin in the stadium, and won their first corner after only thirty-eight seconds. There was no sustained possession for either side, only sporadic attacking moves that were immediately broken up to become counter-attacks broken up again on the other side of the pitch. Kroos, who had emerged as the most important midfielder in Löw's time during the tournament, noticed that one team was handling the momentum of the game much better than the other: 'They had a go at us but you could see straight away that huge gaps were opening up behind their forwards. We had many opportunities to hit them on the break but didn't quite get it right.'

One such break sees Müller dispossess Marcelo and storm down the right-hand side. He is joined by Khedira, at such pace that they almost get in each other's way. Khedira's attempted cut-back is eventually deflected for a corner by Marcelo, who has run back eighty metres to make up for his mistake.

Kroos steps up to take it. There are four German players in the box to Brazil's eight. But Brazil are in trouble, unsettled. Dante and Fred are frantically pointing at Mesut Özil, who is completely free on the edge of the box. No one comes to help. Oscar has mysteriously wandered off to mark space ten metres to the right. Marcelo is on the far post, Maicon and Fred are zonally defending the space in front of Júlio César's goal. David Luiz is shadowing Müller, who has taken up a position near the penalty spot. Just ahead of them, Fernandinho is with Klose. Dante is marking Hummels, Luiz Gustavo has Mertesacker. The four of them are just inside Müller, a metre away.

Kroos' corner is an outswinger, '*Bananenflanke*', banana cross, they used to call them in Germany.

Mertesacker tries to attack the ball at the near post. Klose moves in the same direction and runs straight into David Luiz, who is going the opposite way, attempting to follow Müller's angled run towards the centre of the goal. With David Luiz blocked off, Müller also arrives outside the six-yard box, just before the ball drops in front of him. He's waiting to hit it, shaping his body to make it easier to connect, waiting a bit longer. There's still no one near him. David Luiz at last scuttles over, all hair and bluster, having found a way through the bodies, just as Müller's side-footed ball hits the back of the net: 1-0. Time played: 10 minutes, 20 seconds.

The opener bore the hallmarks of a routine training ground move but Hummels later admitted it hadn't been: it was impossible to anticipate the woefulness of Brazil's defending and therefore pointless practising a ploy that relied on so much disorganisation and mindlessness in the opposition box – in a World Cup semi-final. Brazil hadn't conceded a goal from a cross or free-kick all tournament. A half-decent pub side would have been ashamed to go behind in such a fashion.

The Brazilians still believed, however. Marcelo, the Real Madrid full-back, burst through on the left but Lahm cleared the ball for a corner with a perfectly executed tackle. Marcelo half-heartedly claimed a foul and got a mouthful from Boateng for his trouble. Neither team was able to make any decisive inroads but Löw's well-organised men needed far fewer players crossing the halfway line to create semi-dangerous situations than the Brazilians, who charged forward in numbers but without much of a plan.

The prelude to the second goal was a repeat of the first: a failed German counter-attack. Marcelo was in line with the German defence, hoping for a pass from Hulk. Boateng intercepted the forward's pass and laid it off to Khedira, who sent Müller on his way. The Bayern player raced the entire length of the opposition half, crossed into the middle, and Dante got a foot in. Throw-in.

Lahm takes it. Müller lays it off to Lahm, back to Müller. Four Brazilians fail to intervene. Müller looks up and sees Kroos twenty-five metres out from the Brazilian goal, all alone. Müller's pass is a little underhit. Fernandinho comes out but he is a fraction too late. The Brazilian back line, what's left of it, push out to deny Kroos a chance to shoot or pass to Klose and Özil. Marcelo, though, is ten metres behind, still near the touchline. Müller makes a little diagonal run to pick up Kroos' straight, buttery through ball. The ball is on his weaker left foot and Marcelo has closed down the angle of the shot so Müller stops the ball and leaves it for Klose, who has moved towards him and, with a dip of the shoulder, is now free in front of Júlio César.

The striker's low finish is weak and lacks direction. Júlio César saves it but the rebound lands at Klose's feet again. The second shot finds the bottom right corner: 2-0. Time played: 22 minutes, 7 seconds.

Up in the VIP stand a man in a suit sighed. He had been beaten at this point, and there would be no comeback. Klose, the 'rust resistant' (*L'Équipe*) then thirty-six-year-old had broken his, Ronaldo's, World Cup scoring record. It was the German's second strike in the competition and his sixteenth overall in four tournaments, one more than the Brazilian had managed in three competitions. This, in a nutshell, was Germany, wasn't it? The not inelegant but decidedly unflamboyant goal poacher, stealing the crown of one of modern football's most exciting strikers, by virtue of sheer tenacity and longevity.

Klose had wanted to make it into the history books, no question. 'I am a striker – and strikers want to score goals,' he said after the final whistle. 'Naturally, I want to be top of that list as long as possible.' But his story, that of the veteran of the dark, pre-Klinsmann days who'd survived all the revolutions and tactical developments to emerge as the most effective finisher on the greatest stage of all, was but a fitting detail of the strangest, most unexpected result in World Cup history. And he much preferred it that way. Klose left it to his manager to sing his praises ('The record is incredibly important. An outstanding achievement – I couldn't be happier for Miro') and joked that he would play 'as long as I can carry that body of mine around. The moment I notice the young guys running faster than me, I'll quit.' One or two already were by now, truth be told, but Klose's unique skill set, his ability to drop deep to combine with the midfield, coupled with the natural-born finisher's touch in the box, was still as valuable as ever.

Lahm crosses in low from the right. Müller misses the ball completely. His air shot turns into a dummy as the ball goes through to Kroos, who smacks it into the near corner from the edge of the box, thumping the ball emphatically with his weaker left foot: 3-0. Time played: 23 minutes, 56 seconds.

Brazil kick off and play it back to the centre-back. Safety-first now. But Fernandinho, hounded by Kroos, loses the ball outside the box. A short ball releases Khedira. Back to Kroos: a tap-in: 4-0. Time played: 25 minutes, 6 seconds

Hummels chests down a long ball and takes it out of defence. There's a gap in the middle, so he keeps on running. Suddenly, there's David Luiz in front of him, thirty metres outside the Brazilian goal, with an overcommitted tackle that misses Hummels and the ball but takes out Luiz Gustavo instead. The Germany defender squeezes it through to Khedira who runs at three Brazilians in total disarray. A one-two with Özil is almost cruel in its simple practicality. Like somebody pushing a button to destroy a whole country, 10,000 miles away. A tap-in for Khedira: 5-0. Time played: 28 minutes, 48 seconds.

Four goals in six minutes and forty-one seconds: 5-0 to Germany, against Brazil, *in* Brazil. The remainder of the first half passes everyone by. Both sets of players appear totally bewildered: all they can do is see out the rest of the first half, unable to comprehend the total collapse of the tournament favourite, the world's greatest footballing nation. 'No words' was *Bild*'s headline the next day.

Hummels: 'It's hard to rationalise what happened. I didn't anticipate that, nobody did. At 4-0, I asked myself what was going on here. I just thought, please, don't let this be a nice dream.'

Müller: 'You look into each other's smiling faces because the goals are going in bang, bang, bang and you don't know what kind of emotional realm you're in; somewhere between delirious and "let's just carry on playing."'

Kroos: 'You could sense from the first minute that we could do it today, the Brazilians were so unsettled.'

Draxler: 'At 2-0, I believe the Brazilians were already worried about not getting humiliated. They were under enormous pressure and weren't able, mentally, to play on calmly. And we didn't stop.'

Löw: 'They just didn't know what to do any more. They panicked a little and and fell apart.'

'In days gone by, radio reporters would have called this disorientated Brazil a bunch of headless chickens but that would be unfair on the chickens,' wrote *Frankfurter Allgemeine*.

The Germans had pricked Brazil's bubble, a mere illusion of strength created by patriotism and overloaded public sympathy for the golden boy, the indisposed Neymar. It had been spine-tingling to see Scolari's men hold up Neymar's shirt during the rousing rendition of the national anthem but Kroos' spine, predictably, hadn't tingled. 'It was really loud in the stadium but I was very calm,' he later explained. And that wasn't him being boastful, just the simple truth. 'There are no sweaty patches on his [Kroos'] shirt,' *Neue Züricher Zeitung* observed.

Kroos, a player so cool that you could never guess the scoreline from his behaviour and movement on the pitch – 'he's only got one facial expression for the whole gamut of human emotions,' wrote *Süddeutsche* – never let feelings get in the way of a short, clean pass. Born in Greifswald – on the Baltic coast in the former GDR, politically rebranded as the 'new federal states' after reunification – he cultivated his reputation as a cool-headed northerner. Not everybody appreciated his unfaltering, room-temperature excellence, however. Kroos' ability to concentrate solely on his game sometimes veered into a kind of apathy bordering on footballing autism, critics felt; self-absorbed, flat performances that failed to acknowledge the wider issues at hand.

Werner Kern, Bayern's former youth director, had once described to me the Golden Ball winner at the 2007 U17 World Cup as the 'the most naturally gifted player I've seen since Karl-Heinz Rummenigge', but also expressed regret that his club had sent the teenager on an eighteen-month loan spell to develop at Bayer Leverkusen. Kern didn't go into details but the inference was that Kroos could have been an even better player. Had he been infected by the sense of lethargy and contentedness that could often be detected at Leverkusen, a club of skilful players who had never quite managed to win any titles? Bayern Munich seemed to think so. They refused to put him on the same wage level as the Lahms and Schweinsteigers; even Götze earned three times as much. In terms of his football, there was no question that he warranted an improved contract, but at Säbener Strasse they always wanted your soul, as well as your feet. Kroos, they felt, was too aloof and self-centred to buy into the idea of Bayern as one big family. He didn't identify enough with the club. And didn't he go missing in some of the bigger games? Some people hadn't forgotten that he'd refused to take a penalty in the 2012 final against Chelsea, despite being the best striker of the ball technically. (He'd missed one in the semi-final against Real Madrid, he explained.) Nevertheless, coach Pep Guardiola would have very much liked to have kept him. But he was set to join Real Madrid after the tournament.

Schweinsteiger's and Khedira's injury worries had made him indispensable for Löw but he'd never truly won over his detractors until that semi-final. A few days before, somebody had brought up his volley against Spain in the 2010 semi-final again. It was an old story, but it kept popping up, as *the* Kroos story: the scene that explained who he really was. As a twenty-year-old substitute, he had missed the only chance the *Nationalmannschaft* had created in Durban with a tame, side-footed volley straight at Iker Casillas. He could have done better but what *really* got people was the way he had shrugged indifferently after the game and told reporters that there had been no other way to hit it, sadly, as if he was recounting a stray seventy-third-minute pass in a 3-0 Bundesliga win over SC Freiburg. Kroos' technical style could make him look as if he didn't care, and that was exactly the impression many were left with when Löw blundered in putting him on as a wholly ineffective man-marker against Andrea Pirlo at Euro 2012.

Kroos made the third semi-final his own, however. He was voted man of the match, and universally praised for his maturity and incisive passing. 'It was probably one of my better games,' he said, typically modest. Countless articles in the German press tried to paint the picture of a reformed character, a player who had woken up from his slumber to take control of his country's destiny. But that narrative was unconvincing. Kroos hadn't changed at all in Brazil, only become even more like himself, a player serenely in tune with his own game, supremely assured of his craft and relaxed about his ability to deliver. His unflappability on the ball no longer made him look lethargic but gave him a zen-like aura. Germany knew the ball would be safe with him.

Playing him in the number ten role, instead of the more ethereal Özil, helped Löw achieve something that had been of no concern to a German national team before: the domination of midfield as an end in itself. Löw had been heavily influenced by the tactics employed by Louis van Gaal and Guardiola at Bayern; whoever controlled the ball and the majority of the space, he believed, controlled the game. While conditions in Brazil had made a partial retreat from high-possession football advisable, Kroos was at once the main beneficiary of and driving force behind Germany becoming a team of midfielders whose competence at the centre enabled them to switch between attack and defence at will. Brazil, by contrast, had nothing where it mattered most. Their capitulation was a worse footballing catastrophe and national tragedy than the '*Maracanazo*', the 2-1 defeat by Uruguay in the decisive game of the 1950 World Cup on home soil. The semi-final would go down as the '*Mineiraço*', the disaster of the Mineirão. *O Globo* came up with a sort of German expression, calling it the '*Mineiratzen*' the next day. An appropriately frightful word for a horrible night.

At half-time Germany's dressing room was awash with totally unfamiliar sentiments. Disbelief jostled with a genuine sense of pity for the opposition ('In hindsight, I would have preferred to win 2-0 because the Brazilians were such great hosts, the people love and live football there,' said Schweinsteiger months later) and what Germans call '*Fremdschämen*', being embarrassed on behalf of somebody else. 'We promised ourselves that we would continue playing very seriously, and that we would, under no circumstances, take the piss out of them or try to humiliate them [with tricks],' Höwedes said. The place they found themselves in was so unexpected that the team held on to one challenge that hadn't dissolved, along with Brazil's resistance, to find their bearings. They were not going to concede a goal. 'Not even 5-1,' Höwedes vowed. A small but nagging sense of fear might have played its part as well. Once you've seen the unbelievable happen, you can't help but worry a bit that it might happen again, in reverse, to you. Thus, the idea that a Brazilian goal in this semi-final would be utterly meaningless remained incomprehensible right until the end, when Oscar's non-consolation made the scoreline a fraction less humiliating and brought about Germany's (short-lived) disappointment.

Before that, substitute André Schürrle, on for Klose from the hour mark, had added two more goals in the sixty-ninth and seventy-ninth minutes, the second a superb half-volley that hit the underside of the crossbar before going in. The crowd defected to the Germans at that point. They were applauded, the Brazilians jeered. 'We noticed it,' said Lahm, unsure of what to make of it. Bierhoff had had the idea of creating an away shirt in the colours of Brazil's most popular club, Flamengo, for the competition – imitation and flattery and all that – but who could have dreamed that such a magical transformation would actually take place? 'The Germans showed us how football should be played,' said former international Juninho. 'They forced their incredible rhythm on us,' groaned Scolari. 'The Germans played like Brazilians today.'

It was almost too much; wrong even. 'Nobody would have had a problem with the national team shooting down the Italians with seven goals, nor the Austrians, certainly the Dutch,' wrote *Süddeutsche*'s Holger Gertz. 'But against the Brazilians, it felt insolent. There aren't many phenomena Germans view with admiration, they are the best at many things, or they believe themselves to be the best. But Brazilian football was always the great role model, an unachievable ideal, like British humour. This was an eerie result, by eerie Germans. Also a very German emotion, certainly: to be a little afraid of yourself, occasionally.'

The win was so preposterously good that a concerted campaign to downplay it was immediately set in motion by Löw and his men after the final whistle. 'We shouldn't overestimate it,' said the *Bundestrainer*. 'To put it bluntly, all we have done is get to the next round, just like against Algeria. After that game, they had slaughtered us. Now they want to praise us to the heavens. That's the wrong approach. We are just a pretty good team,' added Müller. The Germans weren't playing at false modesty. All Müller's 'pretty good team' had had to do was turn up, do their thing and watch Brazil self-destruct. By the fifth or sixth goal, the law of diminishing returns had well and truly kicked in, as Germany's achievement appeared that little bit less impressive, along with the perceived quality of the opposition, with every additional goal.

'What's astonished me most was the way the team could evaluate their own performance so properly afterwards,' says Bierhoff. 'They did that after the Algeria game, and they did that again after Brazil. If somebody had said "Wow, that was superb, boys" they would have told them to get lost. It was too easy. It wasn't a real game at all. There was more joy after the France game.'

The Germans were restrained in their celebrations, out of consideration for 200 million people in tears and their vanquished opponents ('I feel sorry for them, they're great guys who have put a lot into the World Cup,' said Müller) but also for themselves. 'There was no euphoria in the dressing room,' said Kroos, his own behaviour true to form. 'We know that no one's ever become world champions in a semi-final. We are all totally focused because we are aware of the chance we've got.'

Mertesacker: 'High-fives and thanking the fans was the extent of it today I'm afraid, the joy is muted. Sunday is the bigger challenge. That's when it matters.' 'Now it's about staying calm and not being too happy, in spite of this extraordinary result,' warned Neuer. 'We mustn't believe that we're favourites because of this game.' Löw didn't have to preach 'humility' and the need to 'move on'; the players were already ahead of him. They had been in similar situations often enough to know that premature celebrations did not help. 'This team were aware of their own history and how far they had come to get into that situation,' says Lahm. 'There was no chance we would get carried away.'

Löw said the same on the night, employing a tone so neutral it could have come straight from a foreign ministry press release. 'This team is very grounded,' the *Bundestrainer* stated in his finest hour, a triumph of planning and execution over the South American 'supernatural forces' he had feared. 'I think I recognise that they are unconditionally ready and willing to win the final.'

THE GALLIC VILLAGE

In mid-April 2014, Rainer Ernst put on his bathing trunks, stepped on to the sodden training pitch of Campo Bahia in the middle of a tropical downpour and let out a scream. The drainage was working.

Ernst, the German FA's lawn specialist since the 2006 World Cup, had planted the first green shoots only a few days before. Using this method of 'vegetative propagation' – planting individual sections of grass at intervals and waiting for the gaps to fill in naturally – was very risky, only two months before the national team were due to hold their first training session. But the qualified landscaping engineer had little choice. The best roll turf available in Brazil had already been laid inside the World Cup stadiums and official training bases. Germany had simply been too late. Importing rolled turf was considered but ruled out, too. The lengthy transport would have loosened the soil, which in turn would have made the surface uneven.

Non-stop rain and floods in part of the village of Santo André posed another threat to Ernst's green but, on inspection, he found that the excess water had actually helped the lawn take root. He was ecstatic. Bierhoff was relieved to receive the news in a phone call. A waterlogged, only half-finished pitch would have been impossible, one problem too many.

*

Scare stories about a national team's accommodation not being ready, dirty, or, if you want to go the extra mile like the *Daily Star* in 2006, 'haunted by the ghost of Hitler' (guests at England's Schlosshotel Bühlerhöhe were said to be terrorised by visions of the Nazi dictator, said the British tabloid) have become a staple diet before every big football tournament. The number of negative headlines about Campo Bahia was unprecedented in Germany, however. The *Nationalmannschaft* weren't really building their own resort, as many reports suggested – they had only committed to being the first-ever guests in a new complex that was being constructed by German developers on the Costa do Descobrimento – but their decision to go it alone, spurning the opportunity to stay in FIFA-approved accommodation, smacked of hubris to some. There were articles about 'killer mosquitos', 'non-stop floods', problems with the internet and the many grievances of locals, who were said to despise the extensive security arrangements and to fear an influx of prostitutes servicing the workers on the construction site.

Campo Bahia had been Bierhoff's idea. He had scouted the region a couple of times but the FIFA hotel he had initially liked most, near Salvador, had one fatal flaw. It was too big. The German FA were wary of players breaking off into cliques in the vast five-star resort and not spending enough time together. 'We didn't want the players getting lost in the hotel,' said Bierhoff, 'it wouldn't have been good for team spirit.' Campo Bahia, by contrast, a modest array of closely situated bungalows near the sleepy village of Santo André, was rather tiny. Bierhoff: 'When I saw the blueprints I thought it might be too small. But then our [team] psychologist Hans-Dieter Hermann said: it can't be small enough.'

'I'm a bit of a dreamer,' says Bierhoff. 'When I first saw that place, and the approach on the ferry through the mangroves, I had this image in my head of the players being astounded, asking themselves what was happening there. We wanted something different, a new impulse. But my head was on the block, I had full responsibility. Two weeks before the start of tournament, people within the FA were saying: "Campo Bahia, that's Bierhoff's thing." I knew that if it didn't work out for whatever reason, it would have been the end of me. But I remembered the Klinsmann days. Sometimes you have to stick with the tough decisions. We really wanted to go for it because there was a sense that this was it. Something new had to happen if the World Cup didn't come off.' Some*one* new, he means.

Local builders were working day and night to finish the job in time. Five days before the delegation's scheduled arrival, another phone call. 'They said there needed to be a plan B – they couldn't get the rooms ready in time. Fifteen people would have to stay somewhere else. I said no. Nobody is staying anywhere else. I put a gun to their heads. I told them that I would sleep on a blow-up mattress if necessary.' Bierhoff sat down with a few players in South Tyrol and prepared them for the odd complication: a toilet might not flush, maybe there'd be no hot water. 'Manuel Neuer just looked at me and said: "What's the problem? We can sleep in tents. I always wanted to go camping anyway." He was totally serious. That shows you the attitude of these guys. Of course, we didn't go public with that one week before the World Cup. But among [the coaching staff] we were discussing things and I was saying it is better if the odd thing does not work; not everything should be 100 per cent perfect. You almost want to build in some flaws. Imagine, for example, if there had been a powercut: we would have put out ten candles and all sat around the bar all evening, talking. That would have been fantastic.' Maybe that's one for the European Championship.

The team's arrival in Brazil was deliberately arranged for daytime to make the most of the unfamiliar surroundings. The players stood on the ramshackle ferry across the João da Tiba, open-mouthed. 'It was very quiet, you had to take everything in,' says Mertesacker. 'It was a kind of magical moment. You felt that you were crossing into a very special place.' He stood next to Benedikt Höwedes on the ferry; they maintained that ritual, on the same spot, throughout the tournament.

Mertesacker, Philipp Lahm, Miroslav Klose and Bastian Schweinsteiger were appointed head boys for each of the four houses. 'We sat down together and said: we are a team, we want to make something extraordinary happen,' says Mertesacker. 'How can we do that? It only works if you leave all prejudice and bias behind.' Easier said than done. 'But we really did adopt that mindset. The four of us thought about how we could arrange the houses so that everyone is happy but so that there's also some variation and a new dynamic. Otherwise, the same people would have hung out with the same people again.'

The base camp became an experiment in social engineering. The four heads carefully assigned the other nineteen players to avoid the development of factions along club or age lines. Bayern Munich midfielder Schweinsteiger's '*Wohngemeinschaft*' (commune), for example, was inhabited by the hard-core Borussia Dortmund supporter (and player) Kevin Großkreutz, two players from BVB's fierce local rivals Schalke 04 (Benedikt Höwedes, Julian Draxler), goal machine Thomas Müller and Matthias Ginter of SC Freiburg. 'There was no other way,' says Mertesacker. 'It was obvious that we had to create special relationships that didn't exist before. There was rivalry, partly due to the Bayern–Dortmund tussles in the club competitions. Rivalries are normal but they can be poison for the national team. The particular make-up of the houses suspended that. The World Cup deserved that. It needed that. Before that, it had been okay. But nobody said: "I will walk through fire for you, I will tear myself apart for you!"'

The three Arsenal players, Mertesacker, Lukas Podolski and Mesut Özil, lodged together. 'We got on well and Arsenal were neutral towards the other clubs so we didn't have to be split up,' says Mertesacker.

The television sets in the rooms only had two channels (ARD and ZDF, the two German public broadcasters). Players were encouraged to talk or to go to the main bar area near the swimming pool to watch football with others. Bierhoff: 'It was our little Gallic village. Everything happened outside, around the pool area – breakfast, lunch, dinner, treatment by the physios, players talking to Jogi. It was a different way of working together but one that was right for this team. People often talk about modern football but for me being modern also relates to the way we communicate with each other, in a way that's far less hierarchical than football used to be.'

Mertesacker: 'Usually, you sit in your little room with your laptop and hope that you don't get cabin fever. But Campo Bahia had a special effect on us, from the start. You arrive, you sleep in houses with living rooms right next to the beach, eat outside. Our house discovered the ping-pong table on the first day. Four of us played round the table barefoot, in forty degrees. After ten, fifteen minutes of bawling, fifteen guys were at the table. The result was a lot of fun and a lot of blisters on the feet. We couldn't run properly at the first training but it didn't matter. Nobody wanted to stop.' Mertesacker says it felt a bit like one of those school trips where suddenly the whole class gets along: 'Those were the eight weeks of our lives. Everybody struck up a small relationship with everybody else.'

Ahead of their departure for the final in Rio, a sense of melancholy had set in: nobody wanted to leave Campo Bahia after four blissful weeks without a hint of trouble. 'We've all agreed to come back in twenty years' time if we win,' said Lahm. 'We are incredibly happy we've had these facilities,' said Höwedes at the penultimate press conference. 'We have developed a team spirit that has been very good for us. It's been perfect.'

Apart from one or two drinks too many after the 4-0 win against Portugal, nothing remotely controversial had happened. The players were allowed a glass of wine or a beer in the evening, Bierhoff explained, but unlike at past tournaments, where sheer boredom had often led to players and coaching staff resorting to regular nightcaps, the beautiful landscape, gentle pace of life in north Brazil and early sunsets had put everybody into a supremely relaxed, easy-going mood.

'It's hard to describe but we enjoyed coming back there after every game, to recharge the batteries and go again,' says Mertesacker.

The boat trip marked the delineation between work and pleasure; the staff felt it strongly, too, says Bierhoff. 'They said, "It's so cool: you step on the ferry, you know it's serious. Then you return and can relax a bit again."' With the players, Löw in shades and the team bus on the ferry, Germany set off like a friendly army conducting amphibious raids on nearby cities. The local population turned out to welcome them back each time with songs. Even after the 7-1 win over hosts Brazil, 'samba drums and fireworks greeted us,' Müller said. 'And one day after training a group of them serenaded me with a ukulele.'

'I see how respectfully everyone is treating each other here,' Höwedes said on his last day in paradise, 'that goes for the training pitch, too. That's the most important thing. The team that plays against the first team in training always works really well. The team spirit is there, but nobody pulls out of tackles. Everyone is always totally alert.' That was another coded reference to Euro 2012. Players who didn't play in the games had agitated aggressively to get selected, upsetting the team's mental balance in the process.

Bierhoff, 'the youth hostel warden' (Mertesacker's words), makes no attempt to hide his pride about it all coming together, after all the storms he had experienced beforehand. But Campo Bahia 'shouldn't be overplayed', he says. 'Maybe we could have won the World Cup staying in a hotel as well. Who knows?' No, forget that, says Mertesacker: 'The forces that were unleashed there brought us the trophy.'

DIVING WITH THE MALDIVES

Assistant coach Hansi Flick and goalkeeping coach Andreas Köpke glanced at each other on the bench. They wouldn't do it, would they? Not now, surely? Was this really happening? *Jawohl*. It was. Bastian Schweinsteiger stepped over the ball, then turned away to his right. Thomas Müller set off at top speed behind him but stumbled over his own spindly legs before he got near the ball. The crowd in Porto Alegre cheered. A German footballer on the floor! Müller picked himself up, untangled his legs and continued his run. Toni Kroos stepped up, chipped the ball without any backlift – and tamely hit the Algerian wall. The crowd cheered again. A couple of minutes later, referee Sandro Ricci blew the whistle for the end of regular time. Extra-time beckoned.

'Most epic free-kick failure ever,' screamed the videos and vines on social media. Germany had failed, certainly, but not in the way most observers had seen it. Müller's stumble was a ploy, designed to confuse the opposition. 'It was a super trick,' the Bayern forward said later, with no apparent sense of irony, 'only Toni Kroos' ball needed to be a few centimetres higher.' Benedikt Höwedes confirmed after the final whistle that the team had indeed planned that routine: 'The final chip wasn't right.'

Not everyone wanted to believe that. As if to prove the players' version of events, the German FA included scenes depicting Müller et al. practising this 'falling down' move at the Campo Bahia training ground in their World Cup documentary. Maybe they felt a little embarrassed. The team employing novelty free-kick routines was one thing. Doing so at 0-0 in a hard-fought last sixteen game, with two minutes to go, was another. 'I was a bit surprised,' said Löw.

So was Flick, even though it was all down to him. He had shown the players videos of many unusual dead-ball variations, including one from the Maldives' penalty shoot-out in their third-place play-off win against Afghanistan in the AFC Challenge Cup that May. One 'Red Snappers' penalty taker, Ashad Ali Adubarey, threw himself to the ground, pretending to fall over his own feet in the run-up, before dusting himself off and converting coolly past the bemused keeper. (The footage also shows the Maldives' Croatian coach Drago Mamić laughing in disbelief.)

Müller deigned the move worthy of a try, in a modified free-kick version. He, Kroos and Schweinsteiger practised in training, and, before the Algeria match, Müller told everyone in the Beira-Rio dressing room that they would try it for the 'first central free-kick' they were awarded. It took until the eighty-eighth minute before they got the chance, by which time Flick half hoped that the players had changed their minds. But they hadn't. Perhaps it did work out, in the long run. If Germany had advanced to the quarter-finals thanks to Müller's stumble, Per Mertesacker wouldn't have stirred the pot with his defiant 'What do you want?' TV interview. '[The Algeria game] was a key moment, without a doubt,' said Flick. 'Everyone realised: we have enough quality to decide a difficult match in our favour, even if it's not really going well for us – if need be, through virtues such as willpower and effort. After that game, the players were totally focused on winning. But a key moment, for me, was also the tournament preparation.'

*

Dead-ball situations, '*Standardsituation*' in German, were practised more extensively than ever since Klinsmann's 2004 takeover. It made good sense to do so, in anticipation of a hot, sticky World Cup in which clear goalscoring chances from open play might be at a premium. You don't have to play good football to score from free-kicks and corners.

A third of all goals in the two previous World Cups had come from such '*Standards*' but Germany had only scored three out of their thirty-one goals in 2006 and 2010 that way. Two dead-ball goals out of twenty-two at Euros 2008 and 2012 spoke of the same inefficiency in that respect. For Löw, however, this was a deficit by design. '*Standards* are not top of my list, but not at the very bottom either,' he said in 2012. Despite the fact roughly a third of all goals, including penalties, are scored from dead-ball situations, the manager regarded the practice of in-game attacking moves as more relevant and devoted little or no time to free-kicks and corners. The justification for this garbled set of priorities was circular: 'Most goals are being scored from open play, especially by the national team,' Löw said.

Flick disagreed with his coach's views. 'We are not effective enough from "*Standards*", that's our problem,' he said at Euro 2012. 'My opinion differs from Jogi's here. We have to train more, have to become dynamic. But Jogi looks at the big picture, his emphasis is a different one.' Löw's low opinion of dead balls – 'you get the feeling he thinks they smell bad,' *Süddeutsche* wrote, was in stark evidence during tournaments, when he used to bet Flick a couple of bottles of wine or a dinner, that Germany wouldn't score a '*Standard*' goal. It was as if Löw considered these basic goals somewhat beneath him, as primitive tools employed teams who couldn't score goals any other way. Like German national teams in the not so distant past, for example.

After Euro 2012 (one headed goal from a free-kick), however, Flick got Löw to change his mind. '*Standards*' were being ignored at Germany's peril. Not only did the *Nationalmannschaft*'s haplessness from set pieces impede them in tight, closely contested games, it also hurt them at the other end. In the 2006 semi-final against Italy, Fabio Grosso scored following a corner for the *Azzurri*. In the 2010 semi-final against Spain, Carles Puyol scored from a corner for *La Roja*. In the 2012 semi-final against Italy, Mario Balotelli scored on the counter-attack following one of fourteen unproductive German corners. A month earlier that same year, six German internationals playing for Bayern Munich had lost the Champions League final in Munich to Chelsea. The home side had twenty corners, the Blues one – enough for Didier Drogba to score the equaliser that took the match into extra-time and later penalties. ('And now: goal,' Chelsea defender David Luiz had told Schweinsteiger on his way into the Bayern box.) For Löw, watching from the Allianz Arena stands, and for the German internationals involved in that traumatic defeat, this was an important lesson. Even if it didn't register straight away.

Three dead-ball goals from Real Madrid in their 4-0 destruction of Bayern in the 2014 Champions League semi-final made Flick's case more persuasive still. 'We had to value *Standards* more,' said the former Bayern player, who'd lost the 1987 European Cup final when Porto's Rabah Madjer, a member of the 1982 Algeria World Cup squad, scored the 1-1 equaliser with a famous back-heel.

Flick had noticed that SC Freiburg, Löw's club when he was a second division striker, had an above-average success rate from free-kicks and corners. He asked Lars Voßler, the assistant coach responsible for '*Standards*' at the Bundesliga team, to attend a workshop with German FA youth coaches in spring 2014. Voßler presented a few ideas; Flick adapted them for the national team.

Practice began in earnest in South Tyrol. 'We had never trained [dead balls] to such an extreme before,' says Lahm. Löw's and Flick's idea was to foster a spirit of competitiveness to prevent the exercise becoming tedious. Lahm: 'We were split into two teams. Each one was allowed three corners, three wide free-kicks and three central free-kicks, and five minutes to prepare. The defending team were able to play one counter-attack – the second goal was on the halfway line – and the attacking team could counter that counter. Each group wanted to win very badly, as you can imagine.'

'You could see the how the players took on the responsibility [to improve] themselves, how they put their minds to it and developed their own ideas,' Flick told *Süddeutsche*. 'And of course it's amazing for a group if you have somebody like Thomas Müller involved.' Müller didn't shy away from trying out wacky variations, like the Maldives' trick. (Alex Ferguson's Aberdeen had scored with a similar routine in a Cup Winners' Cup game against Bayern in 1983. Gordon Strachan and John McMaster both stepped up to take a free-kick, then stopped as if unable to agree who should take it. Strachan then quickly took the free-kick and found the head of Alex McLeish. 'We thought it would never work, it was embarrassing to try it on the training ground,' admitted the goalscorer.)

Müller was bold enough to give it a go, but he was also 'very serious and professional', explained Flick. 'He has a good sense of what's going on, he sees a lot of things. In that respect, too, he's a gift for every coach.'

Löw's 'sacrificing' of chunks of training time to the basics, as he put it, was only half the story of Germany's new-found specialist skills; having the right personnel available to make the extra tutoring count was the other. Toni Kroos' superb passing technique and his cool head provided the consistent, precise delivery – the Algeria chip aside – that made preordained patterns possible in the first place. 'It's amazing how well he crosses the ball,' says Mertesacker. The unusual number of tall players on the pitch afforded by Löw's system of four central defenders also made finding the right target in the box much easier. 'We had this basic attitude of only taking the positives from everything,' says Mertesacker. 'For example, the formation with four central defenders. What do we do with that? Do we talk about players playing in unfamiliar positions and our problems in the build-up play? No. We only thought about our advantage at dead-ball situations.'

It worked. Müller's opener against Brazil had taken Germany's dead-ball goal tally to five at the tournament; six if you included his penalty against Portugal. Four goals from thirty-two corners, one in eight, was a particularly remarkable haul. In elite competitions, the average success ratio tends to hover around the 1:50 mark. Germany had gone from dead-ball dopes to masters, at both ends. A switch from zonal marking in 2010 to a mixture of zonal and man-marking (Mertesacker: 'The two or three best headers of the ball were marked individually, the rest of the team defended in the zone') had helped them to reach the final without conceding a single goal from '*Standards*'.

Löw, who had always preferred to concentrate on more sophisticated matters, had fallen for the discreet charm of the mundane. 'Dead balls are a good weapon for any team,' he said. 'Hansi Flick has done an outstanding job looking at an incredible number of options and practising with the team.' 'Dead balls have helped us a few times already,' admitted Lahm. 'Thank God we're strong in that department,' said Müller. Germany had reconnected with the efficiency of the past, rediscovering short cuts to goal so obvious that Löw had considered them unworthy of attention before. 'If nothing works out for us in attack, we simply score from a *Standard*,' Müller half joked ahead of the final against Argentina. 'We have become the kings of that recently.'

GETTING CLOSER WITH ARNE FRIEDRICH

We were at the training camp in Sicily. Joachim Löw called a team meeting and came straight out with the bad news: Michael Ballack was injured in the FA Cup final against Portsmouth and would miss the 2010 World Cup. The news set a bomb off back in Germany. The media reaction was: panic stations. He was the captain, a really important player. How could the national team do without him in South Africa? There was a sense of shock. But the very next moment, the players and coaching staff flicked a switch. We had to do it without him now. It was huge setback, that much was obvious. But football is a tough business. One player gets injured, another comes in, life goes on. In Philipp Lahm, we had a new captain. A new chapter.

Michael Ballack was the last of the old guard, a type of player like Oliver Kahn and Torsten Frings. His injury paved the way for a transformation. The new guard took over: Lahm, Mertesacker, me, Miro Klose. The team spirit was very good, better than in 2006 and 2008. It's not as if things hadn't been harmonious with Ballack but he saw things differently. He didn't mind the friction. It's impossible to say if we would have played as well with him in the team but I personally believe that we could have done with his experience and attitude in the semi-final against Spain. And we could have done with his dead-ball skills. We lost the game after a dead-ball situation.

Oliver Bierhoff was always keen to bring in other sportsmen who would tell us about their experiences. Jonah Lomu, from the New Zealand All Blacks, came and spoke to us about his kidney condition, which wasn't known at the time. It was inspiring to hear of the passion and the incredible hard work that went into being the world's best rugby player. 'Power within', the tattoo on his back, became our slogan during the tournament. We kept talking about it, saying it out loud in team meetings. You could feel that we were steadily improving as a group in all areas, especially when it came to togetherness. I know from working for Chinese television during the World Cup in Brazil that 2014 was the pinnacle in that respect.

We did a lot of conditioning work in the training camp in Sicily. Everyone had a special wristwatch to keep track of his running; we were mostly trained individually but also had group runs, across golf courses, for players who were of the same level. Acceleration was another key area we worked on. Training was very hard.

Tactically, 2006 was about having the right shape without the ball. In 2008, we made progress playing with the ball. By 2010 we had a more attacking set-up. But it wasn't like 2014, where there was high pressing. That's a process you have to learn. But we made a step forward in South Africa, without neglecting the defence. We went into the competition as runners-up of the 2008 Euros. You could feel that opponents had more respect for us. The target was to at least reach the semi-final again. That was our ambition.

We had an entire hotel to ourselves in Centurion, outside Pretoria. All of the staff welcomed us joyfully, they were all dancing and singing. It was in the middle of nowhere but Oliver Bierhoff managed to make it a very happy place for us. I could have played the whole tournament and another eight weeks on top of that, I was that comfortable there.

There was no cabin fever whatsoever. We had snooker tables, we did some archery, everything was being taken care of. We were even given the opportunity to do a course in video editing. I took part in that.

Oliver was always keen for us to do things that took us away from football a bit at times. If it hadn't worked out, they would have said 'what a waste of money', they would have killed him. That's something he had learned from the Klinsmann days, however. You can't always take the path of least resistance. Picking Lehmann ahead of Kahn was a decision that went against all public opinion, but they were sure it was right for the team and they didn't buckle. Now, in Brazil, it was the same with Camp Bahia. Was it really necessary to go to such lengths? I'd say: absolutely. When you're together for seven weeks, men only, you can't be locked away thinking about football all the time. That wouldn't have translated into good results. Oliver did very well there.

So: Australia. The first group game in Durban. We didn't quite know where we were as a team. It's the same before a new season in the Bundesliga as well. The plan was to play attacking football from the start and make an impression. We did just that. We scored quite a few goals, winning 4-0. It went smoothly. I remember Cacau celebrating wildly after his goal. He was a Brazilian striker who had taken on German nationality, a couple of years before, going down the regular route of naturalisation. It included a test on life in Germany, and one of the questions was about Chancellor Helmut Kohl. Everyone in the dressing room called him Helmut after that.

Next was Serbia. There are some teams that Germany, for whatever reason, find it difficult to play against. Italy. Always Italy. Spain, at the time. Croatia, who we lost against at Euro 2008. And Serbia. Miroslav Klose was sent off early on, we conceded a minute later. The goal came from a cross. We dominated the game, we created good chances, Lukas Podolski even missed a penalty. We could have turned it around, even being a man down. But in the end we lost, narrowly. 'Where's Michael Ballack?' the cry went up in the media. 'They are going to get knocked out in the group stage.' Within the team we knew we had played a good game throughout. We knew we could definitely win the next game against Ghana. Well, we definitely had to win it.

The pressure was immense. A German team couldn't go out in the group stage, with or without Michael Ballack. Expectations were too high after 2008 for that to be an option.

The game was in Johannesburg. Ninety thousand people at Soccer City: you couldn't hear yourself think because of the noise from the vuvuzelas. They really got on your nerves. I believe on German TV they modified the sound because of the number of complaints from viewers. We were lucky that we played with two rows of four that had to be close together at all times. Small distances made it easier to communicate.

It was a match of patience. I was very tense, especially as a defender – concede one goal, and it can all go wrong. There was a lot at stake. You have to be careful not to think about going home, however. If you allow yourself such thoughts as a sportsman you have already lost. The pressure was immense but we were very confident, too. We felt that we would score eventually. We knew we had the quality. Luckily, Mesut Özil did score. Afterwards, it felt as if a heavy weight had been lifted. Per Mertesacker, who was playing beside me in defence, came over to celebrate after the final whistle, it was such a relief. The goal freed us.

It was Löw's first World Cup. There was more attention on him than in 2006, when he was the assistant, also more attention on him than at Euro 2008. If I compare those competitions, I'd say that he took incredibly big steps forward. He emerged from the shadow of Jürgen Klinsmann and managed to improve with every tournament, in terms of the rhetoric, his charisma, his own confidence and tactical things. The development was incredible. As far as I know, he had worked a lot with Hans-Dieter Hermann, the team psychologist. He was able to handle the pressure really well. It's really important that your manager, as well as the big players, leads the line with confidence, especially for the younger players. But you have to be genuine, you can't fake it. Players pick up on that immediately.

Confidence was very high after the Ghana game. We were young but there was a feeling that we could do something in that tournament. We didn't expect England to be our opponent in the last sixteen but they were, having failed to win their group. There was a lot of talk about penalties, naturally. Italy and maybe the Dutch are greater rivals but of course it was a special game. We had a lot of respect for England. They had great players. England is a big name. There was history between the two teams. And, yes: we practised penalties before.

In the pre-match analysis, Urs Siegenthaler and Christopher Clemens had done their usual, fantastic work, telling us how to adjust to the opposition, how to play, what to look out for, how to press and who to press, and who to leave well alone. The analysts had worked out that John Terry often left his position and could be lured into midfield. That's always very dangerous for a defence. You can win the ball quickly and pass it into those channels where that person has gone missing.

We had a great shape, as in the game before, and we got off to a very good start. Manuel Neuer's goal-kick turned into an assist for Klose; Podolski scored the second from a counter-attack. Matthew Upson got one back. It was a bit of shock, we struggled for a few minutes. Then came the goal that wasn't a goal. Frank Lampard's shot. It would have made it 2-2. Neuer did brilliantly. He picked up the ball and threw it across the entire pitch to Klose, as if nothing had happened. Clever. I didn't see the ball bounce down behind the line, I was too far away. Because Neuer played on immediately, I assumed that it wasn't in. Even if it had been allowed, we knew we would win that game, though. At half-time, they pretty quickly told us that it should have stood. Later on, somebody printed out a photo with a clearly doctored line that showed that the ball hadn't gone in – as a joke. It hung next to the massage bench.

We were playing 4-4-1-1 without the ball, 4-2-3-1 with it. The compact nature of that system made it very difficult for opponents to create chances throughout the competition. One of the two holding midfielders, Sami Khedira and Bastian Schweinsteiger, always screening the defence. It worked for us. Defensively, we were sound. Offensively, we were able to deliver fireworks at the right moment. We had the fitness and the players you needed for that, as well as a keeper who was smart enough to see openings and play it long to feet. Our game was more vertical than before. We could play through one or even two rows of the opposition and then join up quickly. In the second half, everything fell into place and we won 4-1. I swapped shirts with Frank Lampard. So did Bastian Schweinsteiger. We both got one.

We were riding a wave of confidence after the England game; we were in full flow. Once we had escaped that huge pressure of making it out of the group, we were much more relaxed. We had done our duty, everything else was a bonus. We were a young team and aware that people would probably have forgiven us if we'd been knocked out by England. We knew the next opponents, Argentina, would be very tough. But, having cleared that hurdle, we had nothing to lose any more.

We were all surprised how well the young players were doing in that tournament. Khedira, Özil, and especially Müller. Also Neuer in goal. If René Adler hadn't suffered an injury a few months before, Neuer wouldn't have played at the World Cup at all. That's how brutal and beautiful football can be. We were lucky to have such a world-class player available as a back-up. All these young guys didn't seem to feel the pressure at all. I believe the way Löw and the coaching staff led was key here: they projected an aura of belief.

It's not as if young players and older players can't get along in a dressing room. But I believe this team benefitted from having mostly

young players. They relate to each other differently. We all, even the
slightly older ones, felt and thought in a similar way. It was harmonious.
We were also role models for integration. Players with an immigrant
background were received really well, there was never a problem, it
was perfectly normal for us. We were all Germans, we were all equals,
and I can honestly say the topic never came up even though it might
have surprised many onlookers how multicultural the *Nationalmannschaft*
had become. Whether playing, partying or cheering, we were a band
of brothers.

Meeting Argentina in Cape Town brought back memories of the
quarter-final in Berlin in 2006. They wanted revenge for getting
knocked out on penalties. We also wanted revenge. Their unsporting
behaviour after the final whistle, when they kicked Per Mertesacker,
was at the back of our minds. Torsten Frings was banned for the semi-
final with Italy as a result of getting involved in the scrap. We hadn't
forgotten about their shitty behaviour.

They had an outstanding array of talent, and Diego Maradona
as coach. But, tactically, they had weaknesses, we knew that. They
were a broken team. There was attack and defence, and nothing in
the middle. And they always played through the centre going forward;
every ball went to Messi. The wingers, the incredibly quick Ángel Di
María in particular, were a bit lost on the flanks. That played into our
hands. We doubled and sometimes tripled up on Messi. There was a
situation where I came from the back, Schweini came from one side
and Sami from the other. Even Messi doesn't find it easy to play like
that. The plan was to clog up the centre.

Ahead of kick-off, I was a bit fearful of the opposition, for the
first time in South Africa. I saw all the names, I saw Maradona in
the players' tunnel, screaming at his boys to get them fired up. I was
impressed. But after kick-off and the first few minutes, that was all
gone again. We were even better than in Bloemfontein. Everything
worked brilliantly for us, because the game went exactly as planned.

We created a funnel for Argentina to play into, then switched quickly into attack after winning the ball. It finished 4-0. All the goals were beautiful, especially the third one: my first goal after seventy-eight or so caps. My family was in the stadium, it was truly amazing. Total ecstasy. We were singing in the bus on the way back to the hotel, and dancing the conga with the staff in the lobby. Unfortunately, I missed some of the party. I was drawn to do the doping test, after both the England and the Argentina games.

In football, the mind plays a much bigger role than most people anticipate. Bayern have this '*mia san mia*' (we are who we are) mantra, they don't only have the best players but always step on to the pitch with a self-assurance – they will win. We were the same. Until the game against Spain.

Müller was missing, just as Torsten Frings had been missing in the semi-final in 2006. He was one of the pillars of the team, the leading goalscorer in the competition. Spain were a team that didn't suit us at all. The Euro 2008 final defeat to them was still fresh in our minds. But we also knew, looking at media reports, that they respected us. That had changed, in comparison to the previous years.

In our subconsciousness, however, having been beaten by them before played a part. As we were driving to the game on the bus, I asked Philipp Lahm how he felt about the match. He was, like: 'Well, Spain are a good team.' Philipp is one of the most confident players, because he is the best player, and when he said that it got me thinking. I realised at that moment that we weren't quite as assured as we had been throughout the tournament. In the end, they were too good for us again.

We went into the game with the intention of playing the same way we had played in the games prior to that – to be well organised and then counter-attack with courage – but we crapped ourselves a little. The coach had told us: 'This is a new era, we don't have to show them respect.' He really talked us up. We were very well prepared, as always, but that's the beauty of football – or the cruelty, in this case. You can't always foresee what will happen.

We never found our game out there. There were almost no counter-attacks from us. Spain didn't have that many chances either but they sort of played us off the pitch with their possession. I remember sitting in the dressing room at half-time and having to take a deep breath. They sent us from A to B and back again. That sapped all our energy. We didn't get a grip on the match. There was one situation where we could have had a penalty but, on the whole, the game went in a totally different direction from what we had hoped for.

You could tell that they had respect, they were quite cautious in the beginning. But they realised that we also had respect that day. It was typical 0-0 game, but with lots more possession for Spain. It was ironic that we lost the game from a header after a corner. Spain usually played their corners short. But they swung one in, and Puyol scored from thirteen metres out. Crazy. Puyol was good in the air, but he was no Piqué. That shouldn't have happened. Some blamed the zonal marking for it, but it had nothing to do with that. We had defended corners for a while like that.

Afterwards, you sit there and don't understand what has happened to you. How can you play so well against Argentina and then have it all disappear? That just shows you how important psychology is. You could say that their game killed us a little, mentally, but, first and foremost, I think it was down to us. We just didn't get into the game at all. Okay, Müller was missing but we should have been able to compensate for that. Perhaps we didn't have enough luck. We had one shot, through Toni Kroos, and that penalty incident. But we didn't deserve it as much as before, when we were aggressive and counter-attacked with pace.

Miroslav Klose later said that we were too tired to do anything when we did win the ball back occasionally. That's exactly what it was like. We just didn't have any power. Even players like Khedira who can run all day were exhausted from the effort we had to put in just to stay in the game. When we did have the ball, there was no drive towards goal. It was abnormal, how well they passed the ball around.

Would we have had more of a chance with Michael Ballack? He was a different type of player, ready to roll his sleeves up and hurt an opponent. We didn't have that in our team. We had a super fair team, playing super football, but we didn't have a tough guy. Maybe we were a little bit too nice. A little bit was missing. In tight games, in games that don't go in your favour, you sometimes need other methods. A dead-ball, for example. We had nothing against Spain. It was a shit day.

The mood in the dressing room was catastrophic afterwards. We had shown a completely different face from before. We talked a lot, drank a beer or some wine. The disappointment was huge. The conga dancing in the hotel, the party vibes – all completely blown away. But we didn't turn on each other. You see that quite often in football after big defeats but this team was united, from the beginning to the bitter end.

Another semi-final defeat meant another third-place play-off – the game nobody wants to play. But Joachim Löw and the coaching staff were right to explain that it was an important match nevertheless. If we'd lost against Uruguay, the general impression we had made at the tournament would have been compromised, destroyed even. We had been good ambassadors for our country, we didn't want to take anything away from that by turning in a poor last performance. We took it seriously. We won 3-2.

On the pitch at Port Elizabeth, after the game was over, I went up to Löw. There was debate over whether he would continue in the job, reports that he was considering quitting, rumours that he was about to do something else. I told him that I hoped that he would continue, that we needed him, that he was the right coach for us.

Löw didn't deliver the trophy but he went home a big winner. He had proved that the team could do without Michael Ballack. We didn't quite have what it takes to go all the way; we hadn't developed as far as the 2014 team, But in terms of the tactical set-up and our football going forward, the lightness we had, it was an obvious improvement on 2008.

On the flight home: disappointment. Feeling drained. Mentally and physically I was very low after such a tournament. Two weeks later, once my holiday was over, frustration kicked in, too. 'We should have done it differently. Bloody hell! Why didn't we play to our potential?' I was glad that the club season started again soon after to take my mind off that.

You saw in Brazil that the team didn't want to ask themselves these questions again afterwards. We had never made dead-ball situations a top priority; there were always things that were more important at the time. It was very smart to get the players involved, to give them the freedom to come up with their own ideas. That was genius. It can get very boring if you're just being made to perform the way the manager wants.

You could see how important a change that was. We definitely lacked that ability in 2010. I know from my work as Germany U18 assistant coach that dead balls are being taken incredibly seriously now. It's a constant process of evaluation and optimisation, at all levels of the national teams. The evolution of tactical systems is also something that's being worked on right now. Three at the back is a system that's being talked about among the FA coaches a lot. German football is very professional like that, very good at looking at the finer points that can give you an advantage. You'll always need luck. But, first of all, you owe it to yourself to make sure you get the best odds possible.

THE LONGEST GOAL

'Prepare for bad weather. Prepare for the storm.'

'Maybe one or two players were too happy that they had made it as far as the final,' Jens Lehmann wondered a few months after his German team had lost 1-0 to Spain in Vienna, to finish as runners-up at the 2008 Euros. There aren't many worse things you can say about a German professional than accusing him of not knowing about the importance of the game he's playing in. But the Arsenal keeper probably didn't so much question his team-mates' character as their maturity and self-perception. They had still considered themselves Young Turks crashing the big boys' party, Lehmann felt, simply pleased that they weren't being kicked out before the lights went back on. But going home with the cutest girl in the room was never really going to happen, was it?

Six years later, ahead of the second final for the class of Klinsmann/ Löw, there was no suggestion that they could settle for a nice shiny silver medal again. The players' council only took a few minutes to decide that there would be no 'welcome back' party at the Brandenburg Gate unless they came home as winners.

'They didn't need any mental tuning, they were ruthless in their determination,' says Bierhoff. 'It was the first time for me as one of the people responsible [for the national team] that I could just sit back and fold my arms for the last fourteen days. I didn't have to do anything; no pushing, no pulling. The guys did all of that themselves, they were adjusting all the time. There were enough players there who knew it'd be their last chance to win a World Cup. Mertesacker, Lahm, Podolski, Klose, Schweinsteiger: "We will get it together one last time. We will do it now." You could sense that determination from the very first minute. The team were wholly unaffected by the mood swings that were happening outside, back home. There was a calmness throughout, a fortitude.'

Nevertheless, the barely believable result against Brazil could not be ignored that easily. It was disorientating, well beyond the position the team might conceivably have found itself in. Mertesacker admits that they had to 'fight really hard with themselves' not to lose their heightened sense of alertness in the days and hours after coming back from Belo Horizonte. 'The problem was that we had always imagined meeting Brazil in the final, beforehand. That had been the vision. But now we had beaten them in the semi-final, playing the best we could. There was this feeling that this should have been it. This should have been the end of it.'

Bierhoff had noticed it, too: 'The 7-1 and all the praise was humming in people's ears. You can't ignore that completely. But two, three days later, you could sense that we had collected our thoughts again, we were back to zero. The next game was the one that mattered. Everything else was unimportant.'

How do you win a World Cup final? Thomas Müller repeats the question back to me, not quite understanding the point of it. He's on the phone in his car, on his way to spend three hours playing cards and taking part in a quiz with a Bayern fan club in Sachsenkam, a village thirty minutes south of Munich. Bayern squad members and club officials are sent out to visit supporters every year.

'How do you win a World Cup final? I don't know . . . You win it by having a good team and bit of luck. If you're asking me if we did anything unusual before the game – no. I slept very soundly and the others did, too, as far as I know. I don't get very excited before big games, because you spend the whole year conditioning yourself mentally for those moments. If you play for Bayern or the German national team, winning trophies doesn't come totally out of the blue. Your ambition, your expectations of yourself, are to win these games. And then it happens the way you imagined it. You're in the thick of it, you don't have time to feel any emotions. As a supporter, you get much more excited, because you're powerless to influence the game. You get swept along.'

Like Philipp Lahm and Bastian Schweinsteiger, he'd been brought up at a club where winning wasn't just one of three possible outcomes to a game but the *only* one. 'We are not even allowed to draw a game there, that's the end of the world,' Schweinsteiger told *Focus* magazine, in response to a question about the pressure he was under before the final in Rio. 'I've grown up at Säbener Strasse with the attitude that we must win every game. Pressure is an everyday thing for me.' Bayern players are winners, by definition – they don't get to play there otherwise – and they're very much aware of it. That breeds self-belief, which in turn leads to more wins, and is underscored by a very Bavarian type of confidence that outsiders sometimes mistake for arrogance. Müller: 'The typical Bavarian in his Lederhosen is not at all ashamed to wear a piece of clothing that looks funny to the rest of the world. But he feels comfortable in it, comfortable in his own skin.'

'I got up in the morning of the final and felt happy,' says Lahm, 'thinking: today we will be world champions. I was really looking forward to it, even in the tunnel.' It's true. A glance at the TV footage sees him smiling amidst two dozen grim-faced men, like a little boy with €5 in his pocket after school, outside the corner store.

Of course there was nervous tension but nothing like before the Champions League final in 2013, he says, pointing at a picture of himself with the European Cup on the bookshelf of his agent's office. 'There, the pressure on us, on me and Bastian in particular, was inhuman. We had lost two Champions League finals already, we had never quite done it with Germany in the big competitions. We were playing against another German team at Wembley. If we had lost that game, too, we would have been *kaputt*. Dead. It was brutal, horrible, playing that game. But in Rio, it was more a case of positive anticipation for me. I was convinced that we were the better team, and that we would therefore win.'

Bierhoff felt the strength of conviction in the camp but he still had misgivings about some hidden, deeper emotions that remained unarticulated and were thus much harder to control. 'My worry was that they were subconsciously underestimating the game. We had had one more day to rest than Argentina. We had only played ninety minutes, and forty-five of that without expending much energy, whereas they had had to go a hundred and twenty minutes and to penalties against the Netherlands. Ángel Di María, one of their most important players, was injured. We had everyone available. You can tell yourself that these things don't matter, but in your heart of hearts you probably believe that they do. You might not even be aware that you're feeling that way.'

Germany's general manager spoke to Mike Horn about that dilemma. Horn, a Swiss explorer and extreme adventurer who walked to the North Pole and circumnavigated the globe around the equator, had taken the squad out on a sailing trip ahead of the first group game against Portugal and dazzled them with his tales of adventures, telling them about the time he had to cut off his own finger to survive. Bierhoff: 'I kept in touch with him and he said to me, "You have to prepare for bad weather. Prepare for the storm. You have to drum it into them how difficult it will be out there. Otherwise they won't be able to react if complications arise." So that's what we did. Again and again.'

There would be blood, sweat and tears but the outcome was not – could not – be in question. That was Löw's line in the final team meeting at the Sheraton Hotel on Ipanema Beach.

'The mantra was: that cup will come with us to our hotel,' Mertesacker said in an interview with *Der Stern* later. 'WE WILL BRING THE CUP INTO THIS HOTEL. To talk about the cup for the first time had a big effect. It's there, within reach, only one game. That was Löw's message. It was electrifying. There were a few tactical instructions on the wall. But what gets you is this: TODAY! NOT TOMORROW! NOT THE DAY AFTER TOMORROW! TODAY! TIME TO WRITE HISTORY!'

Footballers are naturally superstitious. They tend to believe in the power of routine, in repetitiveness. It's how they've lived their entire professional lives. You do the things that work and discard those that don't.

Coming to the Maracanã for the second time in ten days, the Germans found comfort in familiarity. Mertesacker: 'The stadium, the showers, the toilets, the traffic, the statue [of Christ the Redeemer], the hotel – we had discovered all that already. These rituals give you a sense of safety.' In the dressing room, he sat between Kroos and Lahm, two of the calmest players in the *Nationalmannschaft*. Mertesacker saw that they were doing nothing out of the ordinary before kick-off. 'I knew: okay, Toni will play it cool . . . and Philipp: all good, he'll do his thing, as usual. And he'll do it well.'

Back home, eighty million people were getting ready to party. A big chain of department stores was offering the Germany replica shirt at a discount, as it would soon be 'so last season'. That fourth star above the badge: it was coming. It had to be coming. Müller vowed that the team would 'bring out everything that we have in our bag, in terms of football, mentality and fighting spirit'. The optimism in Germany was built on the belief that this team, with their newly single-minded coach at the helm, would do just that.

'Everything was clear for us,' says Mertesacker. The strapline of Germany's main sponsor – a bad joke a month ago – had magically started to ring true, like the best advertising slogans always do. Germany actually were 'ready as never before'. Schweinsteiger and Khedira were in peak condition, Lahm was back on the right in defence, Kroos was pulling strings in the centre and Özil, who had suffered from being played on the right in the first games, was visibly much happier on the left, where he had played against France and Brazil.

Löw picked an unchanged side, again. But the eleven didn't make it on to the pitch before a dramatic last-minute change. Khedira had felt a twinge in his calf muscle in the warm-up. 'The moment I was certain I couldn't play was the worst in my career,' he said. He had worked hard for eight months coming back to fitness following knee surgery, and 'out of nothing, you have a calf injury and need to make the decision: are you on an ego trip and try anyway because you want to make it into the team photo? Or is the team the most important thing.' Khedira didn't have to weigh up his options for too long. He'd been playing in the Champions League final with Real Madrid against their city rivals Atlético in Lisbon seven weeks earlier, and witnessed the obviously impeded Diego Costa struggling for nine minutes before being substituted. The Spanish international had damaged his team's chances. Khedira wasn't going to risk doing the same.

The national manager called on a man who hadn't even been in the provisional World Cup squad back in May. Christoph Kramer, born in 1991, had made it to Brazil as a late replacement for Leverkusen's Lars Bender. Now he was about to make his starting debut in a competitive game at international level. In the World Cup final. 'When I was told I would start, my heart-rate was at 210, before I had taken a single step,' he said. 'I told myself that I'd be having a good game, that this would be a good day for us.'

Kramer, a holding midfielder, was tasked with disrupting Argentina's build-up play early, as Khedira had done so effectively against Brazil. Germany were able to win the ball quickly and keep it in the opposition half, as the South Americans only started pressing the ball forty metres ahead of their own goal. Löw's team dominated, and targeted Argentina's left-hand side, by overloading numbers there (Özil moved across to support Müller and Lahm) but they couldn't create any clear-cut shooting opportunities. The *Albiceleste* were set up for classic counter-attacking play. They lured the *Nationalmannschaft* into an undergrowth of black and blue legs, then aimed to bite into their exposed rear end.

Gonzalo Higuaín dragged a shot wide from a tight angle. Messi left Hummels for dead on the left, but Schweinsteiger cut out his cross. The Germans had all the possession – more than 70 per cent throughout the half – and yet Argentina looked much more like scoring a goal. They were resolute in defence, uncompromising verging on brutal in the tackle. Every time Löw's men got anywhere near the box, they were made to hurt, either by losing the ball or by suffering physical duress. Kramer was hit hardest seventeen minutes in. He ran on to a quick throw-in from Klose at the edge of box, was nudged in the back by Marcos Rojo and then caught square on the jaw by Ezequiel Garay's shoulder. He lay on the pitch clutching his face, got up and fell straight down again. The medical staff checked for broken bones and sent him back on.

Kroos, having played a flawless World Cup to come into contention for the Golden Ball award as the best individual performer, then almost knocked his own team out, heading the ball back to Neuer, and straight into the path of Higuaín, who was coming back from an offside position. The Napoli forward had time to pick his spot but inexplicably scuffed his shot to miss the goal completely from sixteen metres out. Germany were tempting fate, and fate looked inclined to take them up on the offer. The match was running away from them. Schweinsteiger was shown a yellow card by Italian referee Nicola Rizzoli for an innocuous trip on winger Ezequiel Lavezzi. He now had to make it through at least another sixty minutes of regular time without committing a second bookable offence. A few seconds later, Messi found Lavezzi in an ocean of green on Germany's left.

He controlled the ball in full flight and fired a low, curling cross into the box. This time, Higuaín made no mistake. But this time he was offside. His wild celebrations were cut short when he realised the assistant referee had, correctly, raised his flag. How many more times could Germany get lucky? Meanwhile, André Schürrle was waiting to come on near the touchline. A groggy Kramer had to be helped off the field by the team doctors. The midfielder had played on in a thick fog following his collision and asked Rizzoli whether it really was the World Cup final he was playing in right now: 'Please tell me, I need to know.' At which point Rizzoli had told Schweinsteiger that Kramer needed to be subbed straight away.

The change had a big effect on the team's line-up. Kroos had to drop deep to play next to Schweinsteiger in a defensive role that had suited neither him nor the side in previous outings. Özil moved into the number ten position; Schürrle was stationed on the left. But he was a direct player who needed to have space to pick up speed for his runs. They were truly up against it at the Maracanã, against an opponent who would not be cowed and who did to them what entire generations of German national teams had done to teams who loved to attack in numbers before: Argentina stopped them from playing their game. A timid effort from Kroos from distance, straight at goalkeeper Sergio Romero, was Germany's first shot on target. Benedikt Höwedes was booked for a high challenge on Pablo Zabeleta. Argentina kept tearing into Germany's soft left flank.

Closer to the action, things looked less gloomy, however. Khedira had watched on 'in a trance' for the first few minutes, in anguish. 'But then I remembered to give the team some encouragement from the side of the pitch. Players feel it when the bench is alive.' Did losing Khedira and Kramer in quick succession not unnerve the team? 'A good team can compensate for that,' says Bierhoff. 'You can give each other energy, especially in adversity. Hidden reserves were drawn upon. We also saw the advantage of having a strong squad. In 2006 we suffered when Frings wasn't around to face Italy, 2010 we missed Müller against Spain. Now we were able to deal with these losses much better.'

'We weren't bowled over by that difficult start, at no point,' insists Mertesacker. 'Not tactically, not mentally. It was all irrelevant on the day. We carry on and we win here – that feeling was strong. You have to be very careful not to ask yourself the wrong questions on a day like that. We didn't.'

A few seconds before half-time, Germany at last created their first real goalscoring chance. Höwedes jumped up to head a sharply whipped Kroos corner, unopposed, in the six-yard box. The Schalke defender had to score. The ball bounced out from the inside of the post, into Müller's midriff. The whistle went. The Bayern player was offside.

Sergio Agüero was on after the restart for Lavezzi. Two minutes later, Messi was onside, free in front of Neuer, after Lucas Biglia's through ball – no pressure on him from Kroos – had expertly split the centre-back pairing of Hummels and Boateng. Messi took his time, aimed for the goalkeeper's bottom left corner . . . and squeezed it wide.

Germany kept playing well between the two boxes; Argentina were much stronger in and around them. Löw's men, with their high defensive line, remained susceptible to long balls over the top. One punt from Zabaleta down the right bounced up high and into Neuer's territory, Higuaín giving chase. The German keeper fisted the ball away, smashing into the Argentinian forward on the follow-through. Somehow, Rizzoli awarded a free-kick to the Germans for obstruction.

'My opinion is still the same as it was after the game,' Neuer said about the controversial clash that was reminiscent of the Schumacher/Battiston incident in 1982. 'It was no foul and no penalty. I got to the ball and he didn't touch it at all. Of course I was aware afterwards that it was painful for him but it was not intentional, not at all. I apologised right away. I knew it was a tight situation as I had to take a big risk going into it. I had to take that decision in a split second. As a keeper you can't be afraid.'

There often comes a point late on in tied finals when fear takes over, when both teams just want to survive to go again in extra-time. Kroos' second shot from distance, another curiously mishit shot that hobbled wide eight minutes from regular time, was the last meaningful attempt to break the deadlock before Boateng stopped another counter with a strong tackle. Mario Götze came on for World Cup record scorer Klose, who'd been unable to add to his tally but was given a standing ovation by Germans, Argentinians and Brazilians alike by way of consolation. Rizzoli's whistle brought proceedings to a close. Extra-time.

Within a few seconds, Schürrle nearly scored his fourth 'Jokertor' (goal by a substitute) of the tournament, having been played in by Götze. But the then Chelsea winger couldn't get the necessary power or direction, snapping at the ball with his weaker right foot; Romero made a comfortable save.

Boateng's long legs came out like jackknife once again, this time denying Messi a run into the box. The Bayern Munich centre-back was emerging as one of the unlikelier heroes on the night. Boateng, half-brother of Ghana's Kevin-Prince Boateng, grew up in the well-to-do Berlin borough of Wilmersdorf, whereas Kevin-Prince was brought up in a much rougher part of town, Wedding. Jérôme was extremely softly spoken, to the point where reporters were sometimes worried he might drop off in the middle of the interview. On the pitch, his athleticism and deceptive pace were undermined by a tendency to lose concentration and dive into reckless challenges.

In Brazil, however, Boateng was suddenly reliability personified. He was one of a handful of players who had made use of the services of Lars Lienhard at the tournament, a former German track and field star turned 'neuro athletics coach', specialising in the 'reprogramming of the locomotor system', as his website explains. After working successfully with a few Bundesliga professionals, Hansi Flick had allowed Lienhard to showcase his methods, based on the optimisation of players' cognitive abilities and neuronal responses, at the national team's training camp in South Tyrol. Players and coaching staff were impressed enough to invite him to join them at Campo Bahia, where he was available to those who felt that they could benefit from his exercises, which were geared towards 'dissolving the traffic jam' blocking the signals the brain and body were trying to send to each other.

Götze, too, could have been seen doing the occasional workout with Lienhard. The World Cup hadn't gone at all well for him, picking up where his first, indifferent season with Bayern had left off. The €37 million the Bavarians had paid to exercise the release clause in his Borussia Dortmund contract in April 2013 seemed to weigh him down, as if he had a couple of gold bars stuck in his socks. A veritable shitstorm on social media had greeted his move south, and training under Pep Guardiola had not resulted in him reaching the next level of his development. He had, on the contrary, markedly regressed.

It was nearly forgotten that this son of an IT professor at Dortmund University had once been hailed as Germany's answer to Messi when, as an eighteen-year-old, he broke through as the most gifted member of the new generation of talents in 2010–11. Newspapers had dubbed him 'Götzinho' after he'd starred in a 3-2 friendly win over Brazil in August 2011 and Bayern president Uli Hoeness had convinced Guardiola that Götze, born in Memmingen, was a safer bet as a new addition than Brazil's Neymar. But that, too, felt as if it happened a decade ago. Far from setting the World Cup alight, Götze had been a bit-part player so far, and was last seen as an eighty-third-minute substitute in the quarter-final against France.

'It was not easy watching a World Cup final for ninety minutes on the bench,' he says with a huge smile, sitting in an interview room at the Bayern Munich HQ. 'But after a while you are able to get an objective view. So I looked at that game for ninety minutes and realised: it's only a game of football at the end of the day. It was tense, quite interesting. There were more chances than anticipated. Higuaín really should have scored. As luck might have had it I could have come on at 2-0 down. So the way things worked out . . . were pretty cool.'

'Show Messi that you're better than him,' Löw had told him on the touchline. Did the coach believe it himself? It didn't matter. 'Score the goal' had been Klose's more straightforward advice. Götze's fresh legs – and Germany playing extra-time without a regular target man – did pose problems for Argentina but it was they who were still fashioning the best opportunities. Agüero raced past Hummels, whose knee injury slowed him further with each passing minute. The Dortmund defender committed a mistake grave enough to pursue him for the rest of his professional career, jumping underneath a long Rojo cross. But to everyone's relief, Rodrigo Palacio, who'd come on for Higuaín, failed to accept the gift at point-blank range. His first touch was poor and Neuer was quick off his line. The Inter forward with the rat's tail made a rat's arse of his attempted chip, steering the ball wide of the target.

Mertesacker: 'The energy on the bench was superhuman. You saw that Argentina weren't taking their chances. They wouldn't have taken their chances playing for five hours straight. You sensed: this is all going for us.'

'You might not believe me but I knew that we would win. Because we were the better team,' says Bierhoff. 'I kept glancing over at the cup, envisaging it being with us [at the final whistle]. I believe in these things.'

Mertesacker: 'It was tremendously important that everyone kept themselves fit and ready throughout. You had to devote yourself fully to the team for those few weeks. Mario and everyone else knew that they could come on at any stage and become really important from one moment to the next. They kept their heads up.'

Bierhoff: 'You can go through the whole squad and find that almost everybody was struggling with something in Brazil. Neuer had the shoulder injury, Lahm the ankle. Khedira and Schweinsteiger arrived not quite fit. Höwedes had to play every single minute of the competition in the wrong position, on the left. Mats (Hummels) had issues with his knee. Others had to cope with not playing or playing only in some games or playing not quite as well as they could have done. Individually, there were a million reasons why we wouldn't succeed. But, collectively, we pulled together and helped each other out.'

Germany's patience was beginning to bear fruit. Argentina seemed to have tired from chasing the ball. They dropped deeper, allowing the *Nationalmannschaft* longer passages of uninterrupted possession and the ability to rest on the ball. 'We had seen ourselves in the past just how wearing it is if the opponent keeps the ball off you,' says Lahm. 'Now we were able to play that way. As a team, we had evolved from the counter-attacking days of 2010 into a side that could mix it up. Against a team like Argentina, it was vital to be patient and hurt them with a thousand cuts. We went into the extra-time break thinking that we were on top now.' Germany felt physically stronger than the South Americans as well.

Ironically, Lahm says, that was in all likelihood the result of doing less than in previous tournaments in that respect: 'We used to do very hard fitness programmes ahead of tournaments, the equivalent of a full pre-season at club level. That got us into top shape for the group stages but as the tournaments went on, we often ran out of steam a little. This time, the emphasis was much more on football, the pure fitness stuff was toned down a lot. It wasn't necessary to do so much any more because we all had the basic fitness anyway. We had played fifty, sixty matches that year; many of them in the Champions League. If you're not in shape after that, there's no point anyway.'

Löw's final team talk during the break carried short, simple messages, Mertesacker recalls. 'He said: "We will continue on our path. We're stronger now. And we won't let up now. We won't panic. We play on, calmly, but with motivation, assured of victory." You don't take in anything more complicated than that.'

Schweinsteiger spent most of the next few minutes lying on the floor receiving treatment after a variety of fouls. Just after he'd got up again, a stray arm from Agüero caught him beneath his right eye. Blood streamed down his face. For a couple of minutes you could see his legs twitching, as the medical staff were stapling up his wound. 'I was so pumped with adrenalin, I hardly felt anything,' the midfielder said. 'I didn't even mind getting knocked about a little bit. I just wanted to avoid penalties at all cost.' He had missed Bayern's penalty kick in the 2012 Champions League final against Chelsea and experienced 'an emptiness [he] never wanted to feel again'. Schweinsteiger returned, a gladiator freshly patched up, in time to see Lahm getting pulled back by Palacio in Germany's half.

Germany's captain plays the ball short to Schweinsteiger, who passes it back to Boateng. He switches play to Hummels. Kroos comes deep to pick up the pass, turns and finds Schürrle just ten metres inside Argentina's half, near the touchline. The winger's first touch is poor; Gago and Zabaleta are closing him down, so he has to give it back to Kroos. Zabaleta drops back into the full-back position. Biglia is concentrating on Kroos. Schürrle, now by himself, moves inside then comes out again to receive the pass from Kroos. There's nothing on. So he starts running.

'I had talked to Thomas Müller in the break a short while ago, and we told each other that we need a few individual moves, a few dribbles, to get chances against the Argentinians,' Schürrle explained in an interview with *FAZ*. 'It was relatively late in the game, and I had planned to try out this or that. And then I got the ball and immediately tried to sprint down the line – and I hoped that there would be someone in the middle.'

Gago can't get to him. Mascherano comes across. Schürrle shapes to turn inside but drops his shoulder and just keeps going, towards the corner flag. 'It was tight on that flank and to be honest I didn't even look any more to see who was coming towards me. I simply wanted to get that ball into the box somehow.' Götze: 'I made the run into the box blindly, when I saw that "Schü" was going out wide on my side. It was simple intuition. I didn't know what he was going to do. He could have checked or passed it back. All of a sudden, there was no defender left around me. It was strange.'

Zabaleta is drawn towards Schürrle. Martín Demichelis, the right centre-back, is marking Müller. But Müller moves away from goal. Demichelis follows him and then can't recover his position to get goalside of Götze, who's made a simple diagonal run past Zabaleta.

Schürrle: 'When you put in that kind of cross, on the turn, you don't see the ball any more. I only saw it again once it was on Mario's chest – and there was nobody around him!' Götze turned away from goal to meet the cross, chested it down and volleyed the ball, on the turn, past Romero into the far corner. 'I had a great view of it going in,' said Schürrle. 'And then there was a wave of happiness, like never before. Mario was running towards me. I think he wanted to run a bit more but we are all so knackered we had to stop him somehow.'

In Germany, the mobile phone of Christian Güttler, the inventor, lit up with text messages from people congratulating him. Götze had just scored a goal that came from *his* football machine. Control, turn, volley. Bang. One fluid, instant motion. A *Footbonaut* move. Götze agrees. 'Yes. It was a bit like that. But I only really saw what I did later, on TV, thinking, "Oh, you scored with your left". Everything was perfect at that moment. I've got a feeling that goal will stay with me for a while.' He laughs, shyly, a twenty-two-year-old who's already done it all in those few seconds but still has a good ten years of his career left. '*Verfolgen*', the verb he uses, is best translated as 'to pursue'. It can also mean 'to persecute'. Immortality is a hard thing to escape.

*

'It's the technique, stupid,' Martin Mazur of Argentine football publication *El Gráfico* wrote in his post-match piece, in recognition of the undeniable logic behind that beautiful, dream-like strike, a minor miracle of football artistry ten years in the making. Schürrle, born in Ludwigshafen, a south-western city without any nearby Bundesliga club, had enjoyed four years of elite training in two of the German FA's 366 regional centres as a youngster, before Mainz, coached by the maverick Jürgen Klopp, picked him up at sixteen. Götze had joined Dortmund as a nine-year-old and grown up in the club's academy, systematically training to play with the instinct and imagination of one of those mythical 'street footballers' older people in Germany were always fantasising about.

The game wasn't quite over yet, however. 'The coach said: Put a shirt on, you're coming on,' Mertesacker says. 'The guys on the bench went crazy. They were screaming at me: "Come on, you will do it, you will head out every ball."' The Arsenal defender was brought on at the end of extra-time, and his only touch of the ball was a header out after a long, desperate punt from Argentina. 'I've never heard so much cheering after winning a header,' he laughs. Khedira felt vindicated. 'We were able to bring on Per Mertesacker to stave off two difficult situations in front of the defence late on. That substitution could not have happened if I had played.'

On the touchline, Özil, who had come off, was 'hoping and praying' that Rizzoli would blow the final whistle. The Italian did blow it, too, but to award Argentina a free-kick in a promising position twenty-five metres from Neuer's goal. Schweinsteiger, cramping up, had stopped Messi with a last-ditch tackle. It was the third minute of additional time, man v *Mannschaft*, the showdown: the last chance the world's best footballer would have to beat the the World Cup's best team. The Maracanã fell eerily quiet.

'Please, dear God. He mustn't score,' Götze was saying to himself.

Mertesacker: 'I was thinking: Just smash it over the bar. No cross, just try to get it on target and sky it. That's the best thing you can do right now. And then he smashed it over the bar.'

And then it was done. The fulfilment of a promise, as well as a last service to the host nation, who were spared the ignominy of an Argentinian World Cup win in their own home. 'We were all hugging each other in tears at the final whistle. That's when I realised what a long way we had come as a team to get to this success,' says Bierhoff.

Schweinsteiger, the son of a sports shop owner from the village of Oberaudorf, at the foot of the Alps, had been so good at skiing that he regularly beat his childhood friend Felix Neureuther, a silver medallist in slalom at the World Cup in 2013. Going professional had been an option for the kid they called 'Schweini' but football had exerted the bigger pull. At Bayern, he broke through as a spotty teenager into the team of Stefan Effenberg and Oliver Kahn. The latter sat next to him in the changing room but only spoke to him for the first time after two years. Louis van Gaal played an important role in his transformation in the 2009–10 season from versatile attacking midfielder into a playmaker able to control games with the direction and pace of his passes, allowing Schweinsteiger to take over the mantle from Michael Ballack for Germany in South Africa.

He came through the mixed zone with his own personal trophy: a Germany shirt signed by most living members of the the previous three World Cup winning squads that Löw had put in the dressing room ahead of every game for inspiration. 'I'm empty, my legs are gone,' he admitted. Schweinsteiger had run fifteen kilometres, more than anyone else on the pitch, run until he had dragged his team over the line. 'I don't think we realise at this moment how big our achievement is,' said Thomas Müller, 'it doesn't feel real at all. Very strange. But very positive, I'd say. And we deserve it, because we have worked hard for it as a team.' Behind him, Neuer and Mertesacker were storming through, singing '*Die Nummer eins der Welt sind wir,*' we're number one in the world, to the tune of the 'When the Saints Go Marching In', like a couple of schoolkids chanting about a Sunday afternoon triumph in a kick-about.

Lahm was unable to relax and spoke earnestly about the problems Argentina had posed ('it was a World Cup final, we knew it would be hard'), ever the head boy. The 1.70-metre-tall captain had won the trophy in a new way for Germany, as a very different kind of leader for a different kind of team. 'Football's philosophy has changed,' Bayern CEO Karl-Heinz Rummenigge told *Welt* a few days later. 'There used to be *Führungsspieler* [leading players] like Beckenbauer, Fritz Walter, Lothar Matthäus, who took up the flag and the others marched behind them. Today's generation of players is more sophisticated in its thinking. It's not enough any more to kick in a door at half-time and shout your head off. That used to work in the past, today's players want to be brought on board. The work of a captain has become more sophisticated, more nuanced. Philipp is the ideal type for that.'

After preparing so hard to win the game, Germany seemed touchingly unprepared for the feeling of having won it. They didn't quite know where they were. But they could trace back their steps to understand how they got there.

Schweinsteiger's thoughts immediately turned to 'the beginning of this team', under Jürgen Klinsmann. He remembered the rapturous reception the inexperienced and incomplete side had received at the fanfest at the Brandenburg Gate after finishing third in 2006. 'They gave us so much love that day in Berlin and now they have got it all back,' he said. 'That's the best thing: that we have made all these people at home happy by making that final step.' Why did they win now, after failing in 2006, 2008, 2010 and 2012?, somebody asked. Schweinsteiger thought for a moment and then replied that 'the players on the bench' had played a special part. 'It's incredibly difficult to make sure that everybody's happy. But the manager has found some incredible words to make it happen, to bring us all together. Praise him. Praise him to the moon today. He deserves it. He got so much stick.'

'We started this project ten years ago and what has happened today is the result of many years' work, starting with Jürgen Klinsmann,' Löw said. 'We've made constant progress, we believed in the project, we worked a lot and, if any group deserves it, it's this team.' At the Maracanã, 'ten years came full cycle,' says Mertesacker, more than a little moved by the happy ending to a very German success story: a job well planned and executed. 'Their triumph leaves you with the good feeling that you can earn good fortune,' wrote *Der Spiegel*.

'It's great to hear the players say these things,' says Klinsmann six weeks later, visibly pleased. 'That shows that they have really thought about that process and taken responsibility. We told them it was their career, that they would define if they would win. Seeing these statements, I feel that they really understood what's going on. They realised that they had to make that World Cup their own.' Brazil could also be viewed as validation of the German way of life, he says. 'It's not a coincidence that Germany are strong [in football]. The players grow up in an environment, in a society that spurs them on to achieve things. It's fascinating to see how that impulse shapes them and makes them take responsibility for their profession, for the things they do. In America you'd say: there's a culture of accountability. Football has been lived that way in Germany for decades.'

In strictly footballing terms Löw's men brought home the trophy because they had been 'the most complete side, combining the individualism with a team ethos, very modern technical skills with a healthy dollop of good old German virtues', Bierhoff says. They had changed so much that reconnecting with their past was no longer a step back but the consummation of their evolution.

'What's the best thing about this Germany?' a French reporter had asked Schürrle during the tournament. 'We win,' Schürrle replied.

*

But Germany have done more than that in Brazil, Bierhoff feels. 'Something special happened there. The team played in a way that made every German happy. They made them proud, proud to be a part of that team, to belong to them. When you meet people today, they always talk about what a good impression these boys have made, the actual sporting success has almost become an afterthought. Everyone knows where they were during the Brazil game, and what stayed in people's minds was the players' humility, the way they consoled their opponents and didn't go overboard celebrating. People relate to this team, to these guys. I believe football always mirrors society. In 2006, singing the national anthem and waving the flag became normal, fun even, whereas you really did not want to be too near those who sang the national anthem in the stadiums before that. Two thousand and ten was about integration. We lived that. Two thousand and fourteen was about working as a team in the modern world. Being mobile, communicating. And we surprised ourselves with something that usually can't happen: we were being graceful in triumph. In 2006 we were good hosts, we stepped aside for others. This time we dominated, and we won. And were even likeable as well.'

'They have managed to become an eternal part of our culture and society,' says Klinsmann. 'It's unforgettable because it was an experience shared with millions of people. That is the mind-boggling thing: that a whole nation feels the same way as you on the pitch at that moment, at the final whistle. As a player, I never understood that. You couldn't think about that, you would have gone insane. It will take them a few years to appreciate what it is they have done there, how extraordinary that achievement was and how incredibly highly it is valued in German society. It's great for these boys.'

And then he's off, and the sun keeps on shining, and the palm trees keep on shaking, gently, to the rhythm of the crashing waves.

ACKNOWLEDGEMENTS

David Luxton's persistent encouragement helped me through the dark winter months, and Matthew Phillips, my editor at Yellow Jersey Press, thankfully kept faith with me all the way to the deadline – and a good few months beyond.

I've also been extremely fortunate to have had the support of many of the people at the heart of this story. Jürgen Klinsmann, Oliver Bierhoff, Philipp Lahm and Ralf Rangnick were all extremely generous with their time and provided invaluable insight. Thomas Hitzlsperger and Arne Friedrich each took a day out to share their World Cup recollections with me. Per 'BFG' Mertesacker made himself available over mineral water in his local pub in Hampstead more than once. His thoughts – always honest, always concise – light up these pages. Thomas Müller was, as you can imagine, a dream interviewee.

Toni Kroos, Mario Götze, Bastian Schweinsteiger, André Schürrle, Benedikt Höwedes, Jérôme Boateng, Lukas Podolski, Jens Lehmann, Didi Hamann, Christian Ziege, Markus Babbel, Steffen Freund, Mario Gómez, Manuel Neuer, Mesut Özil, Paul Breitner, Karl-Heinz Rummenigge, Werner Kern, Bernhard Peters and Michael Ballack all kindly contributed over the course of the last decade or so. I'm grateful for the assistance from Jens Grittner and Harald Stenger from the DFB, Markus Hörwick, Martin Hägele and Christopher Keil (FC Bayern),

Roland Eitel, Roman Grill, 'Doc' Michael Becker and VfB Stuttgart's Oliver Schraft in the same respect.

Bundesliga CEO Christian Seifert, Susanne Jahrreiss and everyone at the DFL proved supremely helpful, too.

And I'd especially like to thank Uli Hoeness for adding his authoritative voice at a difficult time for him.

Ulf Schott and his former boss Dietrich Weise at the German FA were the source of countless anecdotes and excellent data, as was Mainz 05's Volker Kersting. I'm also thankful for Oliver Höner for letting me in on his research findings, and to ZDF's Jan Doehling for his behind-the-scenes account of World Cup 2006. The great Ronald Reng was, as ever, a superb springboard for ideas. Patrick Strasser: thank you for your fantastic research help. I'm also indebted to Viola Faulhaber for allowing me to use the SZ archive. Hannes Winzer: you're the man.

Thank you Christoph Jungkind, Andrew McCormick-Smith and Jens Wittkopf for revealing SAP's role in Germany's success in Brazil. Thank you Christian Güttler for talking to me about the Footbonaut and TSG 1899 Hoffenheim for letting me try it out myself.

Thank you Klaus Höltzenbein, my editor at *Süddeutsche Zeitung*, to James H. Martin and the entire ESPNFC gang, to Robert Priest at *Eight by Eight* magazine, to Volker Martin at Sport1, everyone at Sunset & Vine/BT Sport and to the *Guardian*'s Marcus Christenson for your understanding last season.

Heartfelt thanks also go to Christian Zaschke, Ludger Schulze, Philipp Selldorf, Christof Kneer, Andreas Burkert and many more colleagues at *Die Welt, Die Zeit, Bild, Frankfurter Rundschau, FAZ*. Their magnificent reporting of the *Nationalmannschaft*'s travails and eventual triumph was the backbone of this tome.

Mama and Papa: Thanks for your love. Mani: Thanks for teaching me everything I know about football. I'd be totally lost without your expertise.

But my thanks, most of all, go to my amazing wife Elinor, without whose unwavering patience and support not a single line of this book could have been written. Mia, Ayalah and Naomi, my three wonderful daughters, were equally understanding of me hardly being there, physically and mentally, throughout most of the year. I love you all very much.

C1 Photography

RAPHAEL HONIGSTEIN is the world's top expert on German soccer. He is a columnist for the *Guardian* and ESPN, writes for *Süddeutsche Zeitung* and *Sport 1* in Germany, and appears as a pundit for BT Sport and ESPN as well as Sky Sports in Germany. He is also a regular fixture on the *Guardian*'s award-winning podcast, Football Weekly. Born in Bavaria, he lives in London.

NATION BOOKS

The Nation Institute

Founded in 2000, **Nation Books** has become a leading voice in American independent publishing. The inspiration for the imprint came from the *Nation* magazine, the oldest independent and continuously published weekly magazine of politics and culture in the United States.

The imprint's mission is to produce authoritative books that break new ground and shed light on current social and political issues. We publish established authors who are leaders in their area of expertise, and endeavor to cultivate a new generation of emerging and talented writers. With each of our books we aim to positively affect cultural and political discourse.

Nation Books is a project of The Nation Institute, a nonprofit media center dedicated to strengthening the independent press and advancing social justice and civil rights. The Nation Institute is home to a dynamic range of programs: the award-winning Investigative Fund, which supports groundbreaking investigative journalism; the widely read and syndicated website TomDispatch; the Victor S. Navasky Internship Program in conjunction with the *Nation* magazine; and Journalism Fellowships that support up to 25 high-profile reporters every year.

For more information on Nation Books, The Nation Institute, and the *Nation* magazine, please visit:

www.nationbooks.org

www.nationinstitute.org

www.thenation.com

www.facebook.com/nationbooks.ny

Twitter: @nationbooks

31901056745930